DEBATING MULTICULTURALISM

DEBATING ETHICS

General Editor

Christopher Heath Wellman

Washington University of St. Louis

Debating Ethics is a series of volumes in which leading scholars defend opposing views on timely ethical questions and core theoretical issues in contemporary moral, political, and legal philosophy.

Debating Multiculturalism

Should There Be Minority Rights?

**PETER BALINT AND
PATTI TAMARA LENARD**

OXFORD
UNIVERSITY PRESS

OXFORD
UNIVERSITY PRESS

Oxford University Press is a department of the University of Oxford. It furthers
the University's objective of excellence in research, scholarship, and education
by publishing worldwide. Oxford is a registered trade mark of Oxford University
Press in the UK and certain other countries.

Published in the United States of America by Oxford University Press
198 Madison Avenue, New York, NY 10016, United States of America.

Library of Congress Control Number: 2021950225

ISBN 978-0-19-752838-9 (pbk.)
ISBN 978-0-19-752837-2 (hbk.)

DOI: 10.1093/oso/9780197528372.001.0001

1 3 5 7 9 8 6 4 2

Paperback printed by Marquis, Canada
Hardback printed by Bridgeport National Bindery, Inc., United States of America

CONTENTS

PART II. AGAINST MULTICULTURAL MINORITY RIGHTS

Peter Balint

PART III. RESPONSES

ACKNOWLEDGMENTS

Peter Balint would like to thank an anonymous reviewer of Oxford University Press for their extensive and thoughtful feedback, as well as John Balint, Ned Dobos, Tiziana Torresi, Tariq Modood, and Umut Ozguc for comments and suggestions. He'd also like to thank Lars Moen and Samuel Nicholls for research assistance. Finally, he would like to thank Patti for suggesting this joint project and helping see it through.

Patti Tamara Lenard would like to thank the very thoughtful members of the European Consortium of Political Theory's Standing Group's virtual seminar series, whose audience offered comments on the major strands of the argument that she has developed here. She would like to thank Maliha Mollah and Madeleine Berry for research assistance. Additionally, she would like to thank Emanuela Ceva, Alice Pinheiro Walla, and Andrei Poama for their constructive comments, and Jacob J. Krich and Alasia Nuti for offering very helpful comments on the entire manuscript.

Finally, she would like to thank Peter for being a great—if tough—interlocutor!

We would both like to thank the University of Ottawa's Graduate School of Public and International Affairs for inviting Peter to visit during his sabbatical, during which we decided to embark on this project. As well, we would like to thank Christopher Heath Wellman and Lucy Randall for their encouragement and support of this project from its inception.

Introduction

Multiculturalism and Minority Rights

WHY ARE PEOPLE TALKING ABOUT MULTICULTURALISM NOW?

"Multiculturalism" has become a political touchstone in many countries around the world. While many of those on the right oppose it, and many of those on the left embrace it, as we will show in this book, things are not quite this simple. For those who defend them, multicultural policies are generally seen as key to the fair and successful integration of minorities, many of whom are immigrants, into diverse democratic societies. They ensure that minorities are able to access high-quality educational and employment opportunities without being disadvantaged by either their minority status or their specific cultural practices. For those who oppose multiculturalism, who have become part of the so-called backlash against multiculturalism, multicultural policies are charged with generating segregation rather than inclusion, undermining national cultures, reinforcing difference, and privileging minority groups.

Much of this recent backlash has been driven by the apparent challenge posed by Islamic practices, and for some, the presence of Islam in general. Immigration from

Debating Multiculturalism. Peter Balint and Patti Tamara Lenard, Oxford University Press. © Oxford University Press 2022. DOI: 10.1093/oso/9780197528372.003.0001

Muslim-majority countries to Western liberal democracies—the countries where the multiculturalism debate has been most heated—has increased over recent decades. From 2010 to 2016, for example, the number of Muslims in Europe increased from 19.5 million to 25.8 million, and estimates suggest that, at the current rate of growth, the number of Muslims in Europe by 2050 could more than double, from 5.0% to 11.2% of the continent's population (Hackett 2017).

Even in many of the Western liberal democracies that have at least partially embraced multiculturalism, some Islamic practices have been seen as very threatening to majority ways of life. Thus we see vigorous public debates over headscarves and burkas, including proposals to ban them for students and teachers or for those who offer or access publicly provided services; minarets and more generally the building of mosques or Islamic cemeteries; the supply of halal meat, for example in school or work cafeterias; the request for separate prayer rooms in work and education spaces; and the funding and regulation of Islamic schools, among other things (Klausen 2005; Joppke 2009; Miller 2016; Adrian 2009; Ceva and Zuolo 2013; Laegaard 2010; Galeotti 2015; Ercan 2017). European and other immigrant-receiving nations have responded in myriad ways, in some cases offering accommodations for practices commonly associated with Muslim culture and religion, and in others rejecting them as inconsistent with liberal democratic norms or contrary to the values and norms that are thought to define the state.

But multiculturalism is more than simply "the Islam question," even if for many this has become the core issue. Similar questions arise in all minority religions: Orthodox

Jews, for example, want to wear different clothes, including head coverings, build sites of worship, eat kosher meat, avoid contact with the opposite sex, and have their children attend religious schools. Many Buddhists want vegetarian food options provided. Many Sikhs want to wear turbans and not helmets, and to carry ceremonial knives in public places. The Amish want exemptions from the minimum age to leave school, and the Quakers an exemption from compulsory military service. There is nothing particularly unique, or even new, about the kinds of requests that Muslims have made on the basis of their religious and cultural commitments (Laborde 2017).

Nor are multicultural issues always about religion. Another common issue is language. There are questions about the languages of public and political discourse, as well as the range of language provisions offered to minorities or migrants who speak other languages (such as the Welsh and the Québécois). Questions here include whether there should be publicly funded interpreters in courts and hospitals; whether schooling should be permitted in minority languages; whether public funding should be directed to minority-language schools more generally; whether city infrastructure, including street signs, should be in minority languages; and whether the state should contribute resources to sustaining, or even growing, media in minority languages.

Beyond the accommodation of religion and language, multiculturalists also consider questions around whether to support ethnic organizations, whether to modify dress codes, whether to teach multiculturalism in schools, whether to encourage or even require public-facing institutions to hire minorities in order to secure sufficient representation of their views, and whether constitutions or other legislative instruments should formally recognize the multicultural nature of their respective communities. In very general terms, those who defend multiculturalism tend to believe that accommodations along all of these dimensions are warranted; those who reject multiculturalism do not. Most immigrant-receiving democratic states adopt some but not all of these policies.

The "backlash" against multiculturalism has been expressed in various ways (Vertovec and Wessendorf 2010), and has involved several "crises" and "retreats" (Joppke 2017, 1–2). In some countries, most famously, the UK and Germany, national leaders have publicly denounced multiculturalism. In 2010, Angela Merkel declared, in the face of increasing anti-immigrant sentiment in Germany, that multiculturalism had "failed, utterly failed," and that instead a new and better integrative approach would be required (Connolly 2010). In other countries, citizenship tests have been introduced making naturalization harder and usually demanding language competence (Michalowski 2011). Anti-immigrant political parties have been formed and have become increasingly successful, and sometimes their policies have been adopted by more mainstream political parties. There has been increased tolerance of anti-immigrant views in public spaces, as well as violence against minorities in all kinds of spaces. But if we are to ask if multiculturalism has failed, then we need to know what multiculturalism is and how we can know if it has failed. We can only then start to address the question of whether it ought to be supported or abandoned or reinterpreted. There are two broad understandings of "multicultural" that sometimes get confused in this debate.

The first, which is common in the public debate about multiculturalism, is sometimes simply about the fact of diversity. That is, some countries or cities are home to a relatively high proportion of people from different ethnic, cultural, and religious groups, often a result of immigration. These places are multicultural in a descriptive sense. They quite literally have a greater cultural (and often religious and ethnic) diversity than places that are described as more monocultural. Typically, these descriptively multicultural places are large cities in migrant-receiving countries, including New York, London, Toronto, Melbourne, Dubai, and so on (Shalit 2018). Most political theorists simply accept this fact of diversity as a given, with which political communities must engage and contend, and direct their attention to how they can do so fairly.

There is also a debate about what is the right response to this fact of diversity. That is, diversity exists, and immigration and social policies should not be explicitly racist, ethnocentric, or exclusionary, so what *should* be the response to this diversity? A second understanding of "multicultural" focuses on the appropriate normative response. Here the sort of questions that arise include these: Should those who speak minority languages have public services provided in their own language? Should exemptions be granted to those whose cultural commitments preclude the wearing of standard uniforms? Should schools be able to teach a variety of curricula in a variety of languages? And should public institutions be allowed to reflect and reinforce the values and practices of the majority? These are the kinds of questions that occupy normative political theorists of multiculturalism, and it is this normative political theory of multiculturalism that is the subject of this book. Both of us recognize the fact of diversity, but we disagree on what the appropriate policy and legislative response should be.

MULTICULTURALISM IN PRACTICE

It is important to stress that the political theory of multiculturalism is not simply "ideal" theorizing, but is focused on whether real-world multicultural policies can be justified. Countries around the world have adopted, at various levels, policies that are rightly described as multicultural. But what makes a country "multicultural"? At Queen's University in Canada, Keith Banting, Will Kymlicka, and colleagues developed a Multicultural Policy Index to assess the extent to which a country warrants the designation "multicultural." Banting, Kymlicka, and their colleagues identified eight major policy indicators that suggest whether a country is multicultural, including constitutional affirmation of the state's multicultural status, the formal adoption of multiculturalism in the school curriculum, and permitting dual citizenship. They then rank countries according to the number of such policies they have implemented, designating those who have adopted all or most of them "strongly multicultural" and those who have adopted few or none of them as "weakly multicultural" (Queen's University 2020). Of the 21 democratic states that feature in their analysis, in 2010, Australia, Canada, and Sweden rank as most multicultural and Japan, Denmark, and Switzerland as the least (Queen's University 2020). The low scores assigned to the bottom three countries indicate clearly that not all countries adopt, or embrace, multicultural policies; some explicitly rejected them from the outset, whereas others adopted multicultural policies but have withdrawn them, declaring them to have been a failure.

It is also worth noting that what happens at a national government level may be very different from what happens at other levels. Many countries are federations (e.g., Australia, Canada, and Germany), and there is a great deal of multicultural policy at the provincial/state level independent of the national level. At an even lower level of government, many local councils enact multicultural policies in order to accommodate the diversity of their constituents—for example, local swimming pools sometimes add "women only" slots to their schedules, designed to improve access for Muslim and Orthodox Jewish women. Likewise, many large institutions such as universities and corporations also have multicultural policies to accommodate the diversity of their students, customers, and employees, including reserving rooms for daily prayers, or selecting vegetarian caterers for conferences and business meetings to accommodate Jewish, Muslim, and other dietary commitments. When we look at multiculturalism in action, we need to look for policies and laws—and not simply the fact of diversity—at a number of levels and spaces, adopted for a range of principled and pragmatic reasons, within a particular state.

Multicultural policies have been adopted for at least three major reasons. First, they may be adopted as part of a commitment to welcoming and protecting diversity. On this view, diversity is good in and of itself, and for the ways in which it contributes to the vibrancy of political and social culture. It offers benefits in the form of diverse cuisine, and new ways to see and interpret the world, via "ethnic" films, literature, cultural events, and general social interaction. Among those who defend multiculturalism for its role in welcoming and protecting diversity, a connected moral claim is often made, tying this welcome to the importance of protecting and supporting the equality of all citizens, regardless of their ethnic, cultural, or religious background (Parekh 2002).

Second, multicultural policies can be adopted for more practical reasons. Service providers, for example, will often modify the way they deliver their services in order to best serve their clients. While sometimes this may be because of a principled commitment to equality, it may just be about finding the most efficacious way to achieve their aims. Health clinics, for example, may adopt policies that require cultural sensitivity training for staff members to ensure that their clients receive the medical support they need. Multicultural policies adopted in the electoral process may also be done for instrumental reasons. For example, many American states translate voting ballots and electoral information into the languages most frequently spoken by potential voters. This translation is not only to ensure that they can access their right to vote, but also to ensure that voting process proceeds smoothly.

Third, many multicultural policies are more strategically motivated, and are used a way of achieving longer-term social and economic goals. Since developed countries compete for skilled labor and have falling birth rates, a welcoming attitude toward newcomers—as manifest in the adoption of multicultural policies—is one key strategy adopted to attract the young skilled migrants that are key to economic growth. A similar strategic motivation appears to be the case for large institutions such as universities and corporations. Ultimately, there can be several reasons why jurisdictions adopt multicultural policies.

So, if these are some of the ways that multiculturalism is manifest in practice, and some of the motivations for doing so, to what extent can it be described as a "failure"? When political actors declare its failure, they often cite the persistence of ethnically segregated neighborhoods, high rates of anti-immigrant sentiment, high rates of violence and acts of hate directed at minorities, the poor integration of minorities into political, economic, and social spheres, and the (allegedly connected) existence of "home-grown terrorism." But it is never clear that these phenomena—undoubtedly true in many immigrant-receiving countries—are the result of the adoption of multicultural policies, or whether they are the result of a lack of support for newcomers to integrate into the dominant society. According to multiculturalists, the adoption of genuinely multicultural policies—attentive to the importance of creating the conditions under which integration on fair terms is possible—will eliminate these phenomena, not exacerbate them. Indeed, for multiculturalism to be declared a failure, it would need to have been implemented first, and it is not clear that there has been enough implementation of multicultural policies to support such a claim.

MULTICULTURALISM IN POLITICAL THEORY

Multiculturalism in political theory really took off with the work of Canadian Will Kymlicka, who extended John

Rawls's earlier observations that we live in a diverse society (Kymlicka 1989b; Rawls 1999). Rawls was concerned with the way that people's natural talents and their socioeconomic circumstances shaped their opportunities; people from wealthy backgrounds or with greater natural talents had a distinct advantage over others. Kymlicka applied this concern to "cultural" difference as well, and argued that without attention to the way cultural difference also affected life chances, fair equality of opportunity—Rawls's goal—could not be fully achieved.

Kymlicka focuses on individual autonomy, arguing that individuals require a robust "societal culture" to provide the basis from which they can make autonomous choices (Kymlicka 1995, 2001). Without the structure of a societal culture—which is usually territorially concentrated, based on a shared language, history, values, institutions, and practices in both public and private (Kymlicka 1995, 76–80)—individuals will be less able to make sense of the world, and therefore less able to make meaningful choices about their life plans (Kymlicka 1995, 83–84). To see why, imagine if you were suddenly dropped into a society with a totally different language and very different culture. It is not hard to see that your choices and opportunities would be very limited, especially compared to existing members of that society who would have a much greater "context of choice."

Kymlicka's theory is "choice-sensitive," and so privileges minorities who have been colonized or incorporated into larger political units over those who have immigrated into a society, largely by choice. National minorities, such as Indigenous groups and the Québécois in Canada, are accorded significantly greater minority rights—including self-government—to protect their societal culture than immigrant groups whose "polyethnic" rights are intended to ease the transition into the host nation's societal culture (Kymlicka 1995, 85–86, 94, 95–98). The defense of both self-government and polyethnic rights takes seriously the fact that culture matters to people, and that cultural affiliation can affect how well one does in the dominant society. At around the same time as Kymlicka, another Canadian, Charles Taylor, articulated a different argument for minority rights, highlighting the importance of recognition (Taylor 1994). Taylor argues that, following Hegel, people's identities need to be recognized both as what they really are (that is, "authentically") *and* as worthwhile. If someone's identity is misrecognized (perhaps as Mexican when they are Puerto Rican), or if their identity is viewed as being of lesser social status (such as has been the case with Indo-Fijians in relation to the iTaukei) they can suffer serious harm. Our identity matters, and failure of it to be seen correctly or as worthy wrongs us. In a multicultural sense, the institutions of modern states already recognize majority identities correctly and as worthwhile, but commonly fail to do the same for minorities. On the identity recognition argument, minority rights are a corrective that allow the proper recognition of all citizens' identities.

Since the publication of these foundational views, there have been many different cases made in favor of minority rights in political theory, as well as variations on these two core arguments. Here we highlight the main schools of multicultural thought.

A dialogic understanding of culture responds to the worry that the account of culture in "multiculturalism" can be essentializing in problematic ways. That is, it treats members of a cultural group as though they all share the same set of views and to the same degree. This understanding can manifest in assigning dominant members of the minority group a kind of veto over what the culture is and what demands it places on members. The result is that this kind of view often permits the violation of the rights of women, curtailing them in the name of preserving and protecting their culture. While one response is to abandon multiculturalism, an alternative is to interpret "culture" as a matter of constant dispute and subject to dialogue, among members, and between members and outsiders (Benhabib 2002). One key benefit of adopting a dialogic understanding of culture is that it recognizes that even those who are disadvantaged—again, often women—inside of a culture find belonging to be valuable, and so aim not at dismantling the culture but at changing it from within (Deveaux 2006; Song 2007).

A contextualist approach to multiculturalism begins with attention to the details of the ways in which cultural claims are made and responded to in specific political spaces (Carens 2000; Parekh 2002). It is an approach that takes seriously abstract normative principles, but recognizes that their implications cannot be understood until attempts are made to implement them in practice. *How* they are treated and interpreted, in other words, will be highly context dependent. Context will tell us what kinds of accommodations are important and how they can be implemented in a specific political and social environment. It can also encourage us to develop a richer understanding of what justice or equality requires. That is, a contextualist approach will guide us to move "between, and mutual correction of, theory and practice" (Carens 2000, 4).

On the view of scholars who are sometimes described as liberal nationalists, states are right to focus on sustaining shared norms and values, since they serve to motivate widespread support for redistributive policies and democratic participation (Kymlicka 2001; Gustavsson and Miller 2020; Miller 1995; Lenard 2012; Soutphommasane 2012). On this view, minority rights should operate in tandem with a nation's attempt to build and sustain a shared national culture. Multicultural policies, and the cultural rights they protect, operate to secure fair terms of integration into shared institutions. Without certain accommodations, integration will prove difficult or impossible for the minorities that ought to be welcomed on equal terms into the public space. This model of multiculturalism treats both newcomers and the societies that welcome them as required to make modifications to accommodate each other: as Kymlicka describes it, integration on this view is a "two-way" street (Kymlicka 1998).

There has also been a quite different sociological approach—what Geoffrey Brahm Levey (2019) has called "The Bristol School of Multiculturalism"—which has studiously avoided starting from liberal principles, and has rather adopted a "bottom up," sociological approach to the political theory of multiculturalism (Levey 2019; Uberoi and Modood 2015). Like other multicultural theorists, they too have seen minority rights as essential for inclusion and generating a wide sense of belonging among diverse citizens. Their starting point is "negative difference," which is the lived experience of minorities. That is, many minority's differences are not viewed by others in their society in a positive light. This school of thought wants more than simply the erasure of this negative view of minorities and their identity, it recommends policies that encourage a positive view of difference. They argue that such a change will serve to generate social solidarity in a diverse society, and will foster a sense of belonging among its members.

There are many other arguments for multiculturalism, beyond those we list above. There are those, for example, who argue that diversity itself has an intrinsic value and should be protected (Margalit and Raz 1990). There are value pluralists who argue for minority rights because they want to take diversity seriously (Crowder 2013; Galston 2002), and there are theorists who argue that multiculturalism provides all of us with richer lives (Goodin 2006).

FIVE MAJOR OBJECTIONS TO MULTICULTURALISM IN POLITICAL THEORY

The view in political theory that multicultural accommodation should be endorsed as a guiding principle across multiple levels of government, and in society more generally, is not universally shared. There are five major objections.

The first objection to multiculturalism resists the thrust of the entire project, suggesting that in fact there is nothing wrong about demanding that immigrants assimilate to a national culture. This can be for several reasons: a shared national culture can operate as a source of unity among citizens in a diverse state, generating trust which supports democratic institutions, redistributive social policies, and other forms of social sacrifice such as military service. It can also simply be the right of a state to possess a national culture, which it imposes on citizens, as part of its exercise in self-definition. Or it can be a democratic right of a people as part of their self-determination to uphold their own national culture and resist its dilution.

On this first objection, states are justified in adopting and implementing public policies to ensure that the national culture is and remains robust. Such policies include assimilation policies that target newcomers and strongly encourage them to take on a majority culture's language, customs, norms, and values. Newcomers must often be prepared to adopt the national culture to gain citizenship. Switzerland, for example, requires people to show that they are familiar with the Swiss way of life and that they are successfully integrated in order to gain citizenship. Sometimes this cultural adoption is even a condition of admission. The Netherlands, for example, produced a video for potential migrants outlining Dutch values, which included images of gay men kissing and topless women, suggesting that migrants who found these images offensive need not apply for admission in the first place (Embury-Dennis 2020; Crouch 2006). Some citizenship tests aim to support the assimilative process, with many requiring a high degree of competency in the national language/s, and knowledge of culture and history. Some citizenship tests even try to test for values, requiring applicants to express views on gender equality and same-sex affection. For the liberal political theorists who support this position, as long as a state also protects citizens from blatant discrimination in public spaces, it is permitted to impose its majority culture on all citizens, including immigrants.

The second objection to multiculturalism in political theory expresses skepticism at the notion that there are distinct "cultural" claims in need of accommodation. There may be important claims being made for or by minorities, but they are not usually "cultural" in nature. Rather, so-called cultural claims are in fact either claims about the importance of religious accommodation, or about securing protections against discrimination, or about supporting reparations for historical injustice. Describing any of these three things as "cultural" can be confusing, and it can obscure other—perhaps less controversial—reasons that liberal democracies may have for responding to these particular claims (Song 2009). This confusion is perhaps most clear when examining many of the recent "multicultural" controversies in liberal democracies, which, as we noted above, are centered around Islamic religious practice.

Consider the request to accommodate Muslim women's religious dress requirements, via permitting head or face coverings, in spaces where people are ordinarily expected to show their heads or faces. These requests are being made in multiple public spaces: in schools, by teachers and students; in universities; in courtrooms; and in institutions that delivery public services of various kinds (Laborde 2008). Muslim women are demanding that their *religious* rights be respected. These public institutions must either make exceptions to rules and regulations that deny the right to cover heads and faces, or they must abandon such rules and regulations altogether. The same might be said in cases where the right of Muslims to add minarets to mosques is considered. But, says this objection, these changes to rules and regulations, if they are justified, are not justified because "culture" matters but rather because liberal democratic states have a long tradition of respecting matters of *conscience*, that is, "beliefs and convictions, not cultural identities" (Song 2009, 182). This respect must extend to Muslim religious beliefs and convictions just as it does to the Christian beliefs and convictions that are more familiar in liberal democratic states.

Historical and/or continuing patterns of discrimination are, according to this objection, another cluster of claims that are co-opted by multiculturalism. Here, for example, affirmative action policies (which are among the policies that multiculturalists also defend) are not justified because they are attentive to the "cultural" specificities of a particular group, but rather because they are concerted attempts to remedy historical patterns of discrimination, patterns which continue to disadvantage certain groups in what ought to be open competitions for scarce but valuable goods, including educational and employment opportunities. These policies render equality of opportunity *fair*, to borrow Rawls's terminology.

The same sort of response is issued to policies that are intended to remedy historical injustices that are more severe than discrimination. For example, calls to respect Indigenous self-determination, and to provide the resources needed in order to make real this commitment (that is, to rebuild communities suffering from the ongoing effects of colonialism), do not require anyone to be committed to the larger multicultural project, even though such calls are often found within it. One can simply be persuaded that remedies for historical injustices are owed to Indigenous communities, and that these debts are appropriately repaid in the form of rigorous support for their self-determination. On this second objection to multiculturalism in political theory, one can defend the rights of religious minorities, antidiscrimination policies, and the self-determination of Indigenous and other minority groups, without accepting the view that there is something special about culture itself, and without agreeing that multiculturalism is the proper way forward in diverse democratic states.

A third objection to multiculturalism worries that there is a trade-off to be made between recognizing and respecting diversity and sustaining support for redistributive welfare state policies. One variation of this view adopts a dismissive tone toward multicultural accommodation policies in general, suggesting instead that distributive equality is the central objective at which a democratic society should aim (Barry 2001). Another variation on this view acknowledges the importance of recognizing minority groups of all kinds, but worries that political recognition policies are insufficient to remedy the challenges faced by minority groups and that well-meaning political actors could believe that by adopting recognition policies they have done "enough" to resolve the challenges that minorities face (Fraser 1995). Moreover, since the adoption of recognition and accommodation policies is literally less costly than the redistribution of resources, well-meaning political actors may opt for developing and promoting recognition policies as a way to avoid confronting the more systemic challenges that some minorities face in liberal democracies.

A variation of this third objection argues that multicultural policies serve to divide rather than unite a population; they highlight differences and in so doing undermine the solidarity that is required in order to support robust welfare policies. This view does not suggest that a state has the right to impose the majority's national culture on minorities (the first objection). Instead, it highlights cases where ethnic, cultural, and religious minorities self-segregate in ways that, facilitated by multicultural policies, render more difficult the development of a wider solidarity among a population which, they argue, is required to support universally accessible redistribution policies. Essentially, multiculturalism leads to segregation, which in turn undermines solidarity. All three variants of this objection worry that directing political attention to the adoption of multicultural policies undermines a state's commitment to doing the work required to achieve genuine equality, either by distracting us from the larger project of dismantling systemic injustice or from the project of developing robust solidarity, the former or latter project (depending on the view) being the key condition for sustaining socioeconomic equality among a diverse population.

A fourth objection to multiculturalism in political theory comes from feminist scholarship, and argues that granting multicultural accommodation can be bad for women. This view highlights the multiple ways in which demands for cultural protection focus on the bodies and lived experiences of women, especially in the context of family life (Okin 1999). So, for example, some cultural groups demand the right to regulate the laws of marriage and divorce for their cultural group members, including the custody of children. There have been several cases where Orthodox Jews and Muslims have tried to get some state-level legitimacy ascribed to their separate religious courts, and similar issues have arisen in Indigenous contexts. According to some feminist critics, this type of cultural protection often translates into the domination and marginalization of women by giving power to minority group men to dictate the terms and conditions of women's membership in the group (Shachar 2001, 2008). The granting of cultural accommodations tends, say these critics, to lead to the continued marginalization of minority women in ways that result in violations of the rights to which they are entitled in liberal democratic states.

Feminist critics point out additionally that the cultural sensitivity that is demanded by commitments to multiculturalism—especially in courts of law—often manifests in accepting the so-called cultural defense offered by minority men who are accused of violence against women (Phillips 2007). Feminist scholars point out the frequency with which male minority-status defendants claim that certain forms of violence are understood in their culture as acceptable and even required, and that legal punishments should be curtailed to account for their cultural context. Accepting the cultural defense as a mitigating factor in determining punishment, in effect, reduces the expressed value of cultural minority women's lives; it refuses to treat them as equal citizens entitled to protection from violence and abuse and compensation for the harm they have suffered. The comfort that legal systems have displayed in accepting the cultural defense for those who have harmed women, some scholars suggest, stems from the systemic sexism that continues to pervade legal and political institutions in general, legal systems which more generally devalue the harm that women experience at the hands of men (Song 2005).

Typically, feminist scholars do not call for abandoning multiculturalism as a whole, but rather for a contextual and nuanced evaluation of demands for cultural protections and the ways they may harm women or reflect the preferences held by powerful men inside of minority cultural groups (Deveaux 2006; Song 2007). Many women, such scholars note, do not wish to exit their cultural groups, but rather to reform them from the inside in directions that are more compatible with protecting their rights (Shachar 1998).

The fifth and final objection to multiculturalism in political theory comes from liberal neutralists who argue that the state should be neutral in matters of culture and identity. Traditional neutralists hold that the state should stay out of matters of culture and identity, either because they are not issues of justice, or because neutral states should be "difference-blind" (Barry 2001).[1] On this view, if institutions make some life choices harder than others, then as long as they do not explicitly prevent certain citizens from doing something, there is no issue of justice to address. On this view, culture is simply another choice. In contrast, some neutralists actually argue that neutrality justifies multiculturalism and minority rights (Galeotti 1998; Patten 2014) because the advantages given to majorities can only be neutralized by giving equal weight to the claims of minorities. Finally, other neutralists have argued that the state should be neutral in matters of identity of culture, but that the force of neutrality needs to be turned back onto majority privilege, rather than used to either ignore minority claims altogether or add minority rights (Balint 2017). Here, neutrality justifies the removal of majority privilege, and so leaves no need for minority rights at all.

1. Barry (2001) accepted the moniker "difference-blind," but it is used to describe most procedurally neutral theorists of justice.

OUR TWO POSITIONS

In this book, we debate the role of minority rights and multiculturalism, with Lenard broadly in favor of minority rights, and Balint broadly opposed. As we have shown, there have been many important arguments both for and against minority rights, and in this book we offer an original approach to each side of this ongoing debate. Lenard focuses on the importance of political inclusion as her justification for minority rights, while Balint defends a radical form of neutrality to show why minority rights are not necessary for multicultural accommodation.

While both of us agree that some form of minority accommodation must be secured, we disagree with respect to the appropriate scope of multicultural policies. Whereas Lenard treats questions arising in the context of cultural and religious minorities, national minorities, and Indigenous peoples as all within the broad scope of "multiculturalism," Balint treats the questions that arise with respect to cultural and religious minorities as fundamentally distinct from those that arise with respect to national minorities and Indigenous peoples. For Balint, these latter groups are to be treated as importantly external to multiculturalism and raise quite distinct normative worries and responses. Not only do we disagree with respect to the scope of multiculturalism in general, we disagree with respect to how best to achieve the protection of minority rights.

Multicultural questions arise around the world. In this book, however, we are focused on the accommodation debates as they transpire in liberal democratic states; the reason for our constrained geographic focus is that we are focused on examining when and how a range of accommodations support or undermine the traditional values of liberal democracy. Our arguments are as follows:

In Part I, Lenard defends a robust multiculturalism. In chapter 2, she defends the view that a wide range of claims made by cultural minorities are defensible and ought to be accommodated in multicultural states. Here she outlines multiple clusters of claims that have been demanded by minority groups and the justifications that have been offered in their defense. In chapter 3, she proposes that there is one underlying justificatory principle on which these claims rely, namely, *political inclusion*. She argues in defense of the widest range of multicultural policies, on the grounds that these policies work together to ensure that minorities are included in all political, economic, and social spheres on equal terms. Her focus is on the importance of *inclusion*, and the ways in which multicultural accommodative practices serve to give voice to minorities across the spheres of democratic society.

In chapter 4, Lenard focuses on three cases to elaborate how her view operates in practice: the case of public resources directed toward ethnically exclusive civil society organizations; the case of religious and culturally segregated schools (which she largely defends); and the case of Indigenous self-determination. In her fifth chapter, Lenard tackles cases in which minority groups request state support to preserve their culture, even as they remain largely isolated from the larger community. In this chapter, the focus is on how a commitment to political inclusion guides policymaking with respect to communities who ultimately wish to remain politically (as well as socially and economically) excluded from the majority community. Lenard argues political inclusion directs us to focus on the conditions under which trust between these minority groups and the larger community can be sustained. To those who worry that accommodating such rights will erode a "shared public culture," she argues instead that a carefully constructed public culture—focused on norms and values that can be adopted by minorities without their being forced to give up cultural practices and values—can and, indeed, should be adopted. She outlines the content of this shared public culture in chapter 6.

In Part II, Balint argues against minority rights, in particular multicultural minority rights. He accepts that the challenges faced by minorities are valid and significant, and that there is a problem when it is harder for minorities to follow their ways of life than it is for majorities. He approaches the problems of minority accommodation through the lens of the oft-maligned concept of neutrality. If neutrality means showing no relative favor or disfavor, then neutral institutions should favor no particular way of life, neither majority nor minority. In chapter 8, he argues that supporters of multicultural minority rights are actually supporters of neutrality, even if they don't say so. The introduction of multicultural minority rights to address relative minority disadvantage is precisely about countering the favor many institutions show to the majority ways of life.

But, as he argues in chapter 9, multicultural minority rights are not the only way to help neutralize minority disadvantage. Balint introduces the concept of *active indifference* to show how neutrality can accommodate minority ways of life *without* granting minority rights. Put simply, the idea is that if majority privilege is the problem, then that privilege should be removed rather than adding new balancing forms of privilege in the form of multicultural minority rights. If institutions are willing to offer accommodations for certain minorities (as is the case with minority rights), then they should be able to open up these accommodations to everyone. He argues that if an institution can still serve its purpose with multicultural minority rights, then it will likely still be able to serve it if these accommodations are generalized. This form of neutrality not only avoids the much-discussed problems of recognition (such as the political construction of identity and increasing the vulnerability of minorities within minorities), but offers more freedom to all of us while still meeting particular minority needs.

In his final two chapters, Balint addresses two issues raised by this argument. Chapter 10 examines the question of Indigenous peoples and other national minorities. Here he argues that the justifications for minority rights in these cases are very different (usually grounded in questions of sovereignty, legitimacy, and/or a desire for political autonomy) from multicultural contexts which are centered on questions of inclusion, and that minority rights in one context do not justify them in the other. Chapter 11 looks at minority accommodation beyond institutions, and at what sort of multicultural virtue might need to be cultivated among all of us if minorities are to be fully accommodated. Here he argues that despite its initial appeal, respect and appreciation of difference is not as accommodating as tolerance of difference. Tolerance, by focusing on behavior and not attitude, will accommodate a much broader range of ways of life than respect and appreciation of difference. It is also, Balint argues, much more neutral.

Part III of the book contains our responses to each other. These responses help to further illuminate our points of disagreement.

Part I

PRO MULTICULTURALISM

1

Introduction to Part I

NEARLY 30 YEARS AFTER POLITICAL theory demonstrated
the importance of being attentive to the rights of cultural
minorities, they continue to struggle to have their rights
respected in democratic states. Rather than easily accepting the importance of accommodating the cultural practices, norms, and values that travel with the immigration
they claim to welcome and depend on, many states continue
to erect and defend roadblocks to their integration, including, for example, in the form of newly adopted citizenship
tests and more robust language competency requirements.
Cultural minorities must still fight to be included on equal
terms in all of the dominant structures of liberal democratic societies: they remain underrepresented in the political sphere; they remain underpaid for equivalent work in
the economic sphere; and willful segregation of minority
communities persists.

In some ways, the status of cultural minorities is worse
now than it was when political actors and academics first
posed questions about how best to tackle the ways in which
the supposedly neutral state imposed its norms and values
on newcomers, demanding that they assimilate in order to
gain access to its coveted goods. Today's climate is one in
which political leaders across democratic countries have

Debating Multiculturalism. Peter Balint and Patti Tamara Lenard, Oxford University Press. © Oxford
University Press 2022. DOI: 10.1093/oso/9780197528372.003.0002

recognized the value in courting an anti-immigrant vote and in publicly challenging the view that cultural diversity is among the strengths of liberal democratic states. Instead, many political actors use their positions of power to issue dire warnings about the dangers posed by immigrants flooding borders, bent on undermining liberal democratic values (Brock 2020). The impacts on the lives of cultural minorities are damaging and, in some cases, devastating: not only have democratic countries made it harder than ever for immigrants to gain entry to their states, but many have created discursive space for the expression of violent and hateful views. As a result, rates of discrimination and racism against cultural minorities remain high across liberal democratic states (Quillian et al. 2019) and are rising in many (Moreau 2020; Hassan 2019), and far-right nationalist networks are endorsing and celebrating violence against them (Weinberg and Assoudeh 2018).

Although anti-immigrant voices remain loud across democratic countries, at least for now these same countries persist in retaining at least some protections for minorities and commitments to welcoming them. Now, more than ever, it is important for liberal democratic states to reiterate and substantiate their commitment to the cultural minorities that call them home. This commitment can be demonstrated in many ways, and in my view one important way is by defending a robust multiculturalism, the view that cultural minorities, as individuals and as groups, are entitled to a wide range of differentiated rights in liberal democratic states. Differentiated rights are rights granted to some individuals, and sometimes groups, but not to all of them. They are granted on the basis of a range of characteristics, and in what follows I will defend the granting of differentiated rights to individuals and groups based on their cultural identities. I argue that a defense of multiculturalism, that is, a defense of differentiated rights based on minority cultural identities, is best founded on a commitment to *political inclusion*.

In what follows, I offer a full-throated defense of multiculturalism in liberal democratic states. In my view, nearly all multicultural claims warrant recognition by the state, by which I mean that nearly all of them are entitled to protection by the state. The claims that cultural minority groups raise have multiple defenses—sometimes they are defended for the ways in which they protect fair equality of opportunity and other times for the ways in which they support historical reparation. I use the lens of "political inclusion," with a focus on *voice*, to defend multicultural claims. Where a particular claim supports the capacity of minority cultural groups—whether immigrant or long-standing—to have their voice heard in public spaces, I argue it must be respected.

My argument proceeds as follows: in chapter 2, I give an account of culture, followed by a voice-centric account of political inclusion. Here, I emphasize the importance of trust in sustaining collaborative democratic politics. In chapter 3, I show how a range of cultural claims can be effectively defended by the role they play in securing political inclusion. In chapter 4, I tackle the trickiest of multicultural claims—those that demand state resources to preserve cultures. I focus on three cases—public support for ethnically exclusive organizations, culturally separate schools, and Indigenous self-determination—to argue that cultural preservation claims are generally defensible from within a political inclusion framework.

In chapter 5, however, I consider claims made by cultural groups that aim to separate rather than integrate, which demand noninterference rather than state support. Here, I suggest that although the groups in question are focused on segregation and isolation from the larger community, a focus on the spirit of political inclusion can guide us in responding to their claims. In particular, I suggest that the exemption rights they demand, to support cultural preservation, must be subject to limits set by a commitment to political inclusion. Even in these cases, political inclusion has specific recommendations which I outline. Finally, in chapter 6, I respond to the worry that, if all of these varied multicultural claims are accommodated, then there will be no room for the production and support of a shared public culture. I argue, instead, that there is much rich content on which an inclusive public culture can draw and outline it in some detail. A well-constructed and supported shared public culture can underpin the solidarity in multicultural democratic states.

2

What Is Culture? Why
Political Inclusion?

IN THE INTRODUCTION TO THE book as a whole, we noted
an observation that Sarah Song made, that many apparently cultural claims are not cultural claims as such.
Instead, they are often claims made in terms of some other
widely shared value, for example, the importance of remedying historical injustices, or securing an equal playing
field among citizens as they compete for valuable opportunities. One of her motivations for making this observation
was to point out that there does not seem to be anything
special about cultural claims per se; in many cases, she
says, culture simply "signifies the different rituals, food,
dress, family roles and interactions, musical and artistic
preferences, and other such aspects that constitute *a way
of life* for some people" (Song 2009, 185; emphasis added).
So, in cases where cultural claims are made, suggests Song,
they are often at base a claim about a specific harm that
requires remedy, and often that harm is one that is widely
agreed to be in need of remedy or protection in liberal
democratic states, for example, in the form of protecting
religious freedom and prohibiting racial discrimination.
On this view, it is not the cultural nature of a claim that

Debating Multiculturalism. Peter Balint and Patti Tamara Lenard, Oxford University Press. © Oxford
University Press 2022. DOI: 10.1093/oso/9780197528372.003.0003

matters; rather what matters is the underlying justification for the specific demand that is being made, alongside the recognition that the basis of the claim is often already one that commands wide adherence.

In what follows, I argue that it is not sufficient to conclude that because racial discrimination is not permitted, or that religious freedom is protected, the specific cultural manifestations of these commitments are thereby protected. On the contrary, a distinct set of arguments is essential to defending the importance of accommodating the *cultural* expression of religious, ethnic, and racial commitments, and that is what cultural rights understood as a group are aimed at doing, as I will argue.

So, in what follows, I defend cultural claims in part because culture, and the cultural expression of religious, racial, ethnic commitments, matters to people. People hold dear the practices, values, and experiences that stem from membership in particular cultures—and so it matters how these are treated in the political sphere. It matters as well whether the political sphere can be structured in such a way that individuals with minority cultural backgrounds are not forced to choose between their culture and political engagement. I suggest, even as the justifications for specific cultural claims may not be homogeneous, and even though the claims may be made in terms consistent with a wide range of shared democratic values, they ought to be evaluated with respect to a common framework. As I said in the introduction to my defense of cultural rights protection, this common framework is focused on protecting substantive political inclusion in democratic states; I distinguish political inclusion from a broader social integration, suggesting that the former can be achieved without the latter, and furthermore that it is the former, political inclusion, at which we must aim first and foremost. I begin with an account of how political theorists have approached culture and cultural rights, before offering an in-depth account of the voice-centric political inclusion framework that guides my analysis in later chapters.

WHAT IS CULTURE? WHAT ARE CULTURAL RIGHTS?

In order to assess demands that states respect cultural rights, whether individuals or groups are claiming them, it may seem important to first know what *culture* is. But nailing down a definition of culture is no easy task. The term "culture" is deployed in multiple contexts. We refer to the culture of workspaces, or the culture of sports fans, or the culture of "hipsters" or "bros." We also refer to national or political culture, and the culture of cities, religious groups, and the deaf. In each of these cases, the use of the term "culture" conjures something real—even if we might disagree about what the culture of bros or hipsters *is*, it is meaningful to speak of it as an entity. It describes, in all of these cases, a set of norms, practices, behaviors, and interests that are in some cases adopted by, and in other cases attributed to, members of a particular group. In some cases, ascribing culture to a group is harmless, and in others the ascription is the manifestation of racist or discriminatory stereotypes. White settler colonialists have often described Indigenous culture in ways that Indigenous peoples do not recognize as their own and that perpetuate harmful and degrading stereotypes that ought to be abandoned.

Can we say more specifically what culture is, especially when it applies to groups that may be demanding its accommodation in public spaces? One well-known early account is Clifford Geertz's, who describes culture as "a system of inherited conceptions expressed in symbolic forms by means of which men communicate, perpetuate, and develop their knowledge about and attitudes toward life" (1973, 89). This account, which emphasizes the ways in which cultures offer an interpretative framework for understanding the world and what is valuable within it, persists. It emphasizes that members of a particular culture are members of a group defined by shared practices, norms, and values, which operate to shape their lives both individually and collectively, as well as to make them meaningful. Individuals often describe their identity as deeply connected to their membership in a particular cultural group, acknowledging that the norms and values they hold dear are culturally inflected.

More recent accounts of culture similarly observe the meaningfulness of culture to its members and the ways in which its central values shape how members interact in the world. They add to this observation that a group's "culture" is often a product of negotiation and deliberation among members, or that it ought to be treated as such (Tully 1995). This modification to the original account highlights that cultures are not static, but rather that their defining characteristics change over time in response to a variety of internal and external factors (Benhabib 2002). It also highlights that no single member or group of members has the capacity, or the right, to identify the central characteristics of a culture. This interpretation of culture—as constantly in flux and resulting from conversations by and about members in a range of forums—serves to protect it from many objections.

First, a dynamic account of culture responds to the worry that, too often, its core features are defined by men in situations of power, in ways that operate to undermine the rights and voice of less powerful members of the culture, including, in particular, women (Okin 1999). Indeed, it is often precisely through the activism of women in minority cultures that change within such groups transpires (Deveaux 2006; Bassel 2017, chapter 2). Second, acknowledging the dynamism of culture, and indeed accepting this dynamism as central *to* culture, responds to the worry that a culture is somehow unable to change in response to the needs of its members, or other external factors that press it toward change. Third, it responds to the worry that members of a culture will be required or expected to hold exactly the same values, to exactly the same degree of importance. The degree to which members value their culture varies; some are fully immersed in the norms and values—the ways of life—of a culture, and others dip in and out, making choices about which aspects they value and carry with them, and which they abandon. Acknowledging that members of cultural groups have varied attachments to their cultures, and the practices and norms that define them, does not require me to deny the reality that there will be cases in which some members of a culture are coerced to sustain connections to a culture that they do not value, and to participate in practices that they might prefer to reject. Liberal democratic states must find ways to support individuals who would prefer, if they could, to abandon their connections in these kinds of cases (I return to this topic in chapter 5).

This account of culture treats members themselves as key players in defining a culture's contours and recognizes individual members as able to make their own choices about whether to identify with that culture or not, and to what degree (Moore 2006; Boran 2001). In describing culture, and cultural identity, in this way, I do not mean to deny that politics, and in particular the choices that the majority makes with respect to recognizing and accommodating cultures, can shape a culture. On the contrary, the ways in which states make choices about which cultural practices to accommodate, and which cultural communities to recognize, have a profound and lasting effect on cultural minority groups and the identity of their members (Minow 1991). When a government makes a choice to protect a cultural right, in other words, it inevitably inserts itself into the question of defining the group itself. As Maria Paolo Ferretti says, in getting involved with the business of evaluating cultural rights, the "government defines those practices that are necessary (or at least crucial) for identification" (2009, 271). I recognize that governments that take on the job of evaluating the place for specific cultural minority rights play a role in defining communities and their practices, however, without thereby concluding that "in this way, artificial groups replace 'spontaneous' ones, or groups as they would form, prosper and modify in the absence of state intervention" (Ferretti 2009, 271). Governmental intervention changes groups—think of the ways in which colonial governments interfered with traditional Indigenous practices, and the devastating impacts this continues to have on Indigenous communities (Joseph

2018)—and so does its absence. I believe it is sufficient to note going forward that, to the extent possible, cultures should be treated as self-defining, and individual members should correspondingly be treated as in charge of the extent to which they are defined by, and identify with, the culture's central norms and practices.

This treatment of culture— as dynamic, with varying strength of connections among members, and which survives so long as members hold it to be valuable—is generally recognized across political theories of multiculturalism. The source of ongoing and vigorous debate among political theorists of multiculturalism is located elsewhere, namely with respect to what rights cultural groups are thereby entitled. Minimalist views believe that cultural groups never or rarely have group-specific rights that require protection and respect. Maximalist views, like mine, believe that cultural groups often have group-specific rights that require protection and respect.

Speaking very generally, a cultural right is a right that individuals or groups have to ensure that specific aspects of their cultural values and practices are accommodated, protected, and recognized, in a wide range of public spaces. Theorists disagree about whether cultural minority rights are only or mainly group rights or individual rights (Casals 2006; Vitikainen 2015). Going forward, I accept that cultural rights can be claimed both by groups, for example, when minority cultural groups demand resources to protect their language, and by individuals, for example, when individuals claim the right to cover their heads and faces in legal spaces that otherwise demand that hats be removed and faces remain uncovered (Levy 1997). Individual and group claims are often connected. For example, many individuals who request accommodations in their work-space are doing so on the basis of their membership in a group; when a practicing Muslim requests midday breaks for prayers, she is doing so on the basis of the obligations she possesses as a member of a group. In this sort of case, it matters that the group she belongs to is *recognized* as a cultural group entitled to some forms of accommodation. Usually, the result is that cultural rights are claimed at the political level only where the group is sufficiently large to lobby for the respect of certain rights as a group; until then, individuals with specific cultural practices hope for accommodation in public spaces and negotiate these on an individual basis with their employers, schools, and so on.

The rights that minority cultures claim against a state are many and varied. For example, minority cultures demand changes to uniform regulations; access to state-provided translation when accessing public services; non-interference in the education of their children; exemptions from legal requirements in the domain of family law, and correspondingly the space to regulate their family lives according to their own traditions. So, it will not do to say simply that minorities are entitled to have their claims recognized or that they are not. Many liberal democratic states are welcoming and respectful of diversity, and willing in principle to accommodate certain cultural rights, but that does not mean that they are obligated to respect every cultural right that is demanded. It is my view that liberal democratic states must take each claim seriously, that they must err on the side of accepting the responsibility to respect a particular rights claim, but that they must carefully evaluate the claims and the justifications offered in favor of them. There will be cases, inevitably, where claims for cultural accommodation ought to be denied rather than accepted. In the next chapter, I examine how this adjudication can transpire fairly, given in particular the assumption that the majority in a liberal democratic state is more powerful than the minority groups that make claims against it. But first, let me turn to the account of political inclusion that motivates the analysis to come.

INCLUSION AND VOICE IN THE PUBLIC SPHERE

At its core, democracy is about *inclusion* on an equal basis in collective decision-making procedures; this inclusion, I shall argue at various stages over the course of the book is key to the trust that supports effective democratic politics. But what counts as inclusion, and how it can be secured equally, is complicated. Indeed, the question of what counts as "equality," in the sense of equal inclusion, is an especially thorny question: some democratic theorists understand it in minimalist terms, to include mainly the right to vote and run for political office, and the set of basic liberties that must thereby be protected, and others understand it in more robust terms, to include representational and material equality.

A voice-centric account of inclusion is founded on a robust rather than minimalist understanding of democratic equality (Anderson 1999). By focusing on political inclusion, my objective is not only to ensure that the basic political rights of all citizens are respected, but that citizens can expect a genuinely equal say in the laws that govern their lives, and that they can expect that these laws treat them as equals, rather than prioritizing the interests of some over others without good reason to do so. A focus on having an "equal say" recognizes that having a voice, or a say, is not simply about voting. It is also about the conditions in which people raise their voices and that shape how they are heard, if at all. Where citizens do not have an equal say in the collective decision-making procedures that produce the laws and policies that govern their lives, they are not treated equally in a meaningful way (Christiano 2004, 276).

To achieve democratic equality, we must be respectful of the voices that do, and aim to, gain space in the political conversation (Williams 1998). A voice-centric account of democratic equality has, therefore, these four distinct objectives: to ensure that all citizens have (a) formal access to the political sphere, (b) effective representation, (c) substantive access to the political sphere, and (d) recognition as legitimate interlocutors or, if one prefers political theoretic jargon, recognition as "self-authenticating sources of valid claims" (Rawls 2001, 23). Where all four of these dimensions of voice are adequately respected, it is a sign that "democratic equality" in the way that I am using it in this book has been achieved; that is, to "stand as an equal before others in discussion means that one is entitled to participate, that others recognize an obligation to listen respectfully and respond to one's arguments, that no one need bow and scrape before others or represent themselves as inferior to others as a condition of having their claim heard" (Anderson 1999, 313). Each of these four dimensions of voice requires some elaboration before I can show the deep connection between cultural claims and securing voice-centric inclusion.

First, a minimalist account of democracy emphasizes the formal political rights to which citizens are entitled, alongside a commitment to the rule of law and free elections. In other words, democracies must protect at a minimum something like "one person, one vote," to ensure that formally each citizen can have a say. Although many states do not even protect democracy in this minimalist form—for example, by refusing to hold elections or by excluding some citizens from the right to vote—most democratic states are committed to more than this simple, formal story about the nature of the equality that underpins them.

Second, modern democracies are dependent on some form of representation, according to which individuals are elected to represent the interests of their constituents. Modern democracies are far too large to permit each and every citizen to vote on all major political issues, and moreover, most citizens do not wish to spend their time deliberating public policies, and so instead they select representatives whose job it is to represent their views in collective decision-making bodies. At least in principle, competing representatives run on platforms that outline their major preferred policy directions, and voters can choose among them. Of course, much of what representatives do once elected is respond to unexpected political circumstances, so in addition to attempting to press specific issues forward, the ideal is that representatives have enough understanding of their constituents' preferences and interests, and their underlying values, that they are able to respond, even in these unexpected circumstances, in ways that are adequately representative (Hayward 2009; Garsten 2009; Dovi 2018). To meet the minimalist conditions of democratic rule, all citizens of a state must have the right to vote for representatives, on a regular basis.

The voice-centric account of democracy to which I am committed emphasizes more than these formal elements of democratic rule, however. Third, a voice-centric democracy must be focused not only on formal inclusion, but also on ensuring that citizens' access to the political sphere is substantive. Substantive access to the political sphere has two distinct dimensions. To begin, substantive access means not only that citizens can vote for representatives, and that they can run for office themselves, but also that formal political spaces—political parties, most significantly, but also all major political bodies across a state— are genuinely open to all citizens, not only those who share ethnic, gender, cultural, or religious characteristics with the majority. When John Rawls acknowledged that mere "formal" equality of opportunity was insufficient to produce justice in a democratic state, what he meant was that ensuring that, legally, all valuable opportunities were available to all members of society was insufficient to meet the requirements of justice.

Contemporary democracies continue to struggle with sexism, racism, and other forms of structural discrimination, both explicit and implicit, that render certain categories of individuals—though equally meritorious, in the sense of having the same educational and experiential credentials—less likely to gain valuable educational, political, and other opportunities, for which competition is supposed to be fair (Young 1989). So, said Rawls, focus must be given to what makes the competition for valuable opportunities genuinely fair, and doing so means paying attention to the barriers that minorities continue to face through no fault of their own. This analysis applies to many domains, including the political domain, in which ensuring fairness in access to political opportunities may require, for example, that political parties take proactive measures to ensure that those selected to run for election or sit in legislative bodies are selected from outside of the majority group. In many democratic states, these kinds of measures are key to ensuring more than formal representation in the main political spaces of a democratic state.

The second meaning of substantive access highlights that an inclusive political process requires that citizens actively engage with it to ensure that their needs are met and their preferences are counted. Political engagement is demanding—it can be both expensive and time consuming—and it is a key factor in ensuring that interests are given consideration by political decision-makers. As a result, citizens with resources are more likely to be able to invest the time and energy needed to make sure that their voices are heard. This key insight emerged from an extensive study of American political engagement, which showed that those whose voices are *heard* are those whose have the resources, understood broadly, to make themselves heard (Verba, Schlozman, and Brady 1995). Citizens whose livelihoods are precarious, and who must direct their energy toward ensuring that there is food on the table and that rent is paid, struggle to find the time necessary to do the work to make political decision-makers listen to them and their concerns. Correspondingly, to the extent that citizens with fewer resources are less likely to participate in politics, their needs and interests are less likely to be considered by political decision-makers. A voice-centric account of democratic inclusion needs to take seriously the material differences in the lives of citizens. Ensuring an equal voice certainly requires the adoption of redistribution policies—and I support these—but in this context it demands a focus on adopting mechanisms to ensure that even those with fewer resources can be assured that they, too, have an equal say.

Finally, the fourth dimension of a voice-centric account of inclusion focuses on whether citizens who make claims in political spaces are *being listened to*, that is, whether they are treated as having the authority to speak and make claims (Appleby and Synot 2020). Where majority political leaders fail to recognize leaders as legitimate and authoritative spokespeople, in particular where they are speaking with authority with respect to the views and preferences of this minority group, inclusion is substantively denied, even if it is formally available. All of the criteria I have described work together to generate the trust that is central to effective democratic politics, but it is perhaps this final criterion—the willingness to listen—that is most connected to supporting wide trust relations, among citizens, and between citizens and political leaders (Lenard 2012).

It is important to distinguish this criterion from the question of whether any specific individual or group of individuals (majority or minority) gets its way; that is to say, it is possible and indeed ought to be the case that people can be genuinely listened to, even if, in the end, their particular policy preference is rejected. In principle, the "duty to consult" that is acknowledged to operate in Canadian law, for example, requires that the Government of Canada engage meaningfully and respectfully with Indigenous communities where specific policy choices will have an impact on their territories—for example, with

respect to major infrastructure projects including especially the building of gas pipelines (Eisenberg 2020b). In
many cases, minority groups feel that their voices are rarely
listened to because, too often, their preferences or interests
are ignored or, worse, mocked—as, for example, where cartoons of revered religious figures are printed in newspapers and satirical magazines, knowing that this will cause
offense (Carens 2006; Moran 2017; Modood 2006)—even
where according to the rules of the game, they have been
permitted to express them in the relevant formal political
spaces (Bassel 2017, 9). There have been ample empirical
investigations to show that women's voices, or the voices of
minority groups, while *expressed* in political or legal spaces,
are not correspondingly heard or acted upon (Sanders
1997). But when minority voices are listened to, "new possibilities for political equality" can emerge; "listening can
be a source of recognition and a challenge to existing [and
unequal] distributions" of resources in the political community (Bassel 2017, 9 and chapter 5; Tully 1995).

Earlier I described political inclusion in individualist
terms, and that is largely how I shall treat it. But there are
important group dimensions to political inclusion as well.
To give a few examples, there are cases where minority
groups may systematically vote in fewer numbers, leading
to their underrepresentation in political spaces; elected
representatives who are members of minority groups
may be treated as though they represent the entire group;
often, minority groups members en masse lack substantive access to political spaces as a result of material conditions that their communities face in general; or majority
political spaces may implicitly or explicitly act in ways
that undermine the political voice of minorities, reducing

the likelihood that their interests or needs are heard and responded to. Any assessment of how best to adjudicate minority rights claims needs to be attentive to both the individual and group dimensions of political inclusion, in ways that I articulate in what follows.

An important caveat: political inclusion is related to integration, though it is not the same thing. When social scientists evaluate whether immigrants are well integrated, or whether they are in the process of integration, they typically consider whether immigrants are employed or attending educational institutions, whether they live in mixed neighborhoods, whether their social interactions include individuals from a wide range of backgrounds, as well as whether they participate in associational, and political, life (Carens 2005; Favell 1998; Goodman 2010). In what follows, I focus on political inclusion, which often tracks these other measures of integration, including especially employment and education, as I noted earlier in my consideration of the substantive access to the multiple dimensions of political life. However, it is my contention that political inclusion does not require, as a condition, social integration; and as I suggest in what follows, cultural communities that live separate lives can often be meaningfully politically included.

CONCLUSION

To summarize: I have articulated the four dimensions of "voice" that must be met in order to ensure that all members of a political community are substantively included in the political process. When any of these dimensions are not met, some members of a political community suffer from a "deprivation of voice," that is, their "say" is not treated equally in the political space, and that space's claim to inclusivity is undermined (Norval 2009, 298). In what follows, I suggest that cultural claims almost always target a barrier to achieving an equal say, and that to the extent that they focus on removing that barrier—to reducing an individual or group's deprivation of voice—they should be respected in multicultural democracies.

3

Cultural Claims and Political Inclusion

IN THIS CHAPTER, I ARGUE that in the vast majority of cases minority cultural claims support the political inclusion I defended in chapter 2. In chapter 2, I suggested that political inclusion has four key dimensions, focused on ensuring the formal protection of equal political rights; representation; substantive access; and recognition. Now I examine several clusters of cultural claims, for each cluster asking whether it produces more and better political inclusion. When the answer is yes, I argue that the cultural group must be treated as having a cultural right that the majority community has the political duty to respect. I present each of the main clusters of cultural claims, for exemption, assistance, affirmative action, special representation, self-determination, and recognition. I suggest that although there are many possible ways to defend each of them, each of them is best justified with respect to its role in protecting political inclusion.

In very general terms, cultural protection claims aim at two objectives: the *inclusion* of minority cultural groups in political and social spaces or the *preservation* of cultural groups as distinct, and often self-determining,

Debating Multiculturalism. Peter Balint and Patti Tamara Lenard, Oxford University Press. © Oxford University Press 2022. DOI: 10.1093/oso/9780197528372.003.0004

communities. In practice, these may overlap, as they do in one of the case studies in chapter 4, where the demands for public support to enable minority groups to preserve aspects of their culture are justified with respect to their future success in the economic and political spheres of the dominant society. That is to say, the preservation of culture is not inherently connected to separation or a failure of integration, as critics of multiculturalism often suggest. Rather many, if not most, cultural claims are demands to preserve important elements of cultural practices in the name of inclusion. In what follows I proceed by sorting cultural claims into groups according to the type of accommodation, or other demand, they make of the larger society. This chapter focuses on claims that are straightforwardly directed toward inclusion; chapters 4 and 5 focus on claims that are directed toward separation.

EXEMPTION CLAIMS

Perhaps the most well-known of cultural claims are *exemption claims*, that is, claims to be exempt from laws or practices that conflict with some aspect of a minority culture; common examples include the Sikh request to be exempt from helmet requirements and Jewish and Muslim requests to be exempt from Sunday closing laws (before they were abolished). Exemption requests respond to existing laws and practices that make it hard for a member of a minority to simultaneously uphold their cultural commitments and access a good that is widely valued and *supposed* to be accessible on an equal basis to all citizens—a job or education, for example. Exemption claims are perhaps the easiest to assess using a voice-centric analytic lens. In most cases, exemption from a particular law or policy enables members of cultural minorities to access goods and opportunities on fair terms, including access to political opportunities, government services, and legal rights.

Among Canadians, the most commonly cited example of a demand for exemption is the one made by Sikh applicants to join the Royal Canadian Mounted Police (RCMP). The RCMPh had traditionally demanded that officers wear a Stetson hat on certain key occasions, which is not possible for turban-wearers. Sikhs requested an exemption—that is, a modification to the standard-issue RCMP uniform. The request was controversial because the RCMP, and its complete uniform, was said to be a major Canadian symbol, such that any modification to its uniform might undermine its capacity to act as such a symbol (CBC 2017). This objection was ultimately overcome after many years of contested disagreement (politically, in 1990, and legally in 1996), and not only was the exemption itself permitted, but it was ultimately embraced as a symbol of a welcoming and multicultural Canada. In 2016, the RCMP modified its uniform requirements again, to permit hijab-wearing.

A variation on this exemption, which has proved more controversial, is the Sikh demand to carry a kirpan, a ceremonial dagger, in public spaces. As a symbol of their faith, observant Sikhs carry a sheathed dagger, underneath their clothing, as a reminder to stand up against injustice. But, according to many critics, the kirpan poses a threat to security and thus, when carried in public, violates a range of generally recognized safety laws—it is, after all, a dagger. In this case, multicultural states are asked to

consider whether Sikhs should be permitted to carry kirpans in public spaces—official government buildings or
on airplane flights—where they may pose a danger to others (Dhamoon 2013). At first glance, it appears that there
are two valuable goods in tension with each other, public
safety and the right to follow faith-based practices. Here,
however, an easy resolution is available: the Sikh obligation can be met even by relatively small daggers that do
not pose a threat to public safety. For example, global aviation standards explicitly exempt daggers shorter than six
centimeters from the list of banned weapons, permitting
Sikhs to carry them on flights (CBC Radio 2017). While
many traditional kirpans may be longer than six centimeters, in this case the accommodation can be made by the
minority without a threat to minority inclusion or public
safety.

Questions of the appropriate mechanisms for inclusion are also central to whether and how to accommodate
Muslim women who cover their heads, and sometimes
their faces, as a symbol of their faith. If accessing goods
and services, including employment, education, and public transportation, or entering government buildings,
require that head coverings, or face coverings, be removed,
then those goods and services are available only to those
Muslim women who are willing to forgo an important cultural practice in order to access it. This requirement therefore poses a burden on Muslim women that is not placed
on other similarly situated citizens (Laborde 2008; Bakht
2009; Joppke 2009).

Among the justifications offered in defense of the view
that Muslim women must remove head or face coverings

to access certain goods and services are these: face and head coverings symbolize the rejection of gender equality; women are forced by male partners to cover, and so banning coverings serves to protect women from this coercion; religious symbols ought not to be present in a secular public space in the first place; or basic, civil interactions among citizens require that faces in particular be visible to others. In some cases, defenders of policies that would ban face coverings also cite a range of security reasons, having to do with difficulties in identifying who is behind a face covering, and the possibility that nefarious actors will dress up as women who cover their faces to carry out wrongdoing. It may well be that there is some truth to each of these claims; some women may be coerced into covering their heads and faces, others may reject gender equality norms, identification may prove marginally more challenging, and so on. Yet, even if there is some truth to these claims, the case for banning coverings in public spaces remains weak in light of the importance of protecting the *inclusion* of all citizens in public spaces. Where Muslim women are required to remove head and face coverings, those who are unwilling to do so will be denied access to a valuable goods and services. Prioritizing the importance of securing inclusion at a basic level— with respect to access to the sets of goods and opportunities that are intended to be available to all citizens on an equal basis—means permitting exemptions in this case. Moreover, the global donning of face masks to protect against the transmission of Covid-19 suggests societies can function well—identification is possible and public safety does not appear to be at risk—even where we cannot see people's faces when we interact with them.

ASSISTANCE CLAIMS

Assistance rights are just what they sound like: demands for assistance—usually material—from cultural minority groups who, without this assistance, will struggle to access the goods and services to which all citizens are entitled equally. Assistance demands are wide-ranging, including for public support for translating a range of materials into minority languages (for e.g., driver instruction manuals or election materials), for sustaining cultural community organizations and artistic endeavors, for providing culturally sensitive healthcare options, and so on. While exemption claims are sometimes thought to be costless, assistance rights typically do impose some costs on the majority community.

As with exemption claims, assistance requests are aimed at supporting equality of access to the set of goods that are supposed to be available to all citizens on equal terms. Proactive support in the form of assistance can enable minority cultural groups to participate on equal terms with members of a majority community in a range of political and economic spheres. The assistance is intended to "help in overcoming obstacles to engaging in common practices," including basic political acts like voting or engaging with courts of law (Levy 1997, 133). Assistance can also serve to overcome obstacles that stem from systemic, structural racism that interferes with minority groups' capacity to compete on fair terms for jobs or coveted educational spaces.

One common form of assistance claim asks for the translation of key information into minority languages. Immigrants sometimes arrive to new countries having no or little capacity in the dominant language; most immigrants gain this capacity over time, although many, especially those who arrive later in life, do not gain proficiency. So, new immigrant minorities may request that materials related to the provision of basic goods and services be translated, including healthcare information (side effects for medication, for example, or the importance of physical distancing to reduce Covid-19 transmission), legal information (for example, having to do with the rights of tenants and landlords), legal proceedings (for example, where newcomers are accused of, or are witnesses to, wrongdoing).

Consider a specific example, translating election materials, including in particular voting ballots, into languages spoken by relatively newly naturalized immigrants. The translation of ballots or other political material is intimately connected to protecting basic rights of those who are not yet confident speakers of the majority language.[1] The assistance provided by this translation is a direct contribution to political inclusion on equal terms (Song 2009). In the United States, the Voting Rights Act specifically stipulates the conditions under which substate jurisdictions are required to provide standard election material—ballots, for example, and voter registration information—in minority languages. In jurisdictions where 10,000 people or 5% of the population (whichever is smaller) speak a minority language, election materials must be prepared in those languages. Some critics—usually connected to the so-called English-only movements—say that integration into the United States requires competence in English,

---

1. Some minority communities may demand translation into minority languages, as a sign of recognition of their equal status in society, which I consider later.

and translating materials into minority languages delays and even discourages English language learning and, correspondingly, integration; moreover, doing so is costly and difficult. Yet evidence fairly consistently suggests that this translation does have an overall positive impact on voter turnout among those who use minority languages, suggesting that they serve to promote the inclusion that is central to democratic politics (Tucker and Espino 2006; Hopkins 2011; Fraga and Merseth 2016). What if the evidence had suggested that integration more generally was slowed by the provision of this form of translation? Even here, the importance of protecting access to basic rights for all citizens suggests that translation ought to be provided, to enable voting, and also beyond. In particular, political inclusion justifies the translation of materials that are connected to the wide range of publicly provided goods to which all citizens are entitled access on an equal basis, including medical information, educational information, and legal information.

AFFIRMATIVE ACTION CLAIMS

One form of assistance claims deserves special mention: affirmative action claims. These are policies that preferentially reserve certain opportunities for members of groups that have suffered disadvantage historically, in particular with respect to employment and educational opportunities—including, for example African Canadians and Americans, Indigenous peoples around the world, and the Dalit in India. The objective of affirmative action policies is to combat past or present discrimination faced by cultural and religious minorities in their attempts to secure high -quality employment and educational opportunities (Song 2009). In some cases, they operate by instructing those selecting candidates for admission and hiring to be attentive to, and favor, candidates with certain ethnic or cultural backgrounds; in others, some spots are simply reserved for specific minority groups. Justifications for such policies typically focus on the importance of equality of opportunity: all the various goods, including employment, education, or political office, that are valued in democratic society must be, to the extent possible, distributed fairly. One way that their unfairness is manifest is when certain categories of people—where they have credentials that are equivalent to, or better than others—nevertheless do not "win" the opportunities for which they compete (Patten 2014). To borrow from John Rawls, while there may be formal equality of opportunity, it is not *fair* equality of opportunity, the latter of which requires that the personal characteristics (religion, culture, sex) do not play into whether a candidate is successful in competing for a particular good (Rawls 1999).

Affirmative action policies are often controversial for the ways that they are claimed to disrupt the distribution of opportunities on the basis of merit. However, their justification emphasizes the ways in which such opportunities have not been based on merit alone, historically and presently (Anderson 2010, chapter 7). Unlike language rights, affirmative action policies do not obviously impose costs on the majority community; however, their detractors sometimes argue that those from the dominant community who do not thereby gain admission to university or access to high-quality employment, pay the price of affirmative action. This way of responding to affirmative action is only legitimate if there was no harm that caused adoption of affirmative action policies in the first place—however, such policies are typically adopted as a way of compensating for myriad f obstacles (some historical, but many of which persist in contemporary democracies) that are placed in the way of qualified minority candidates as they try to access valuable spots in education, politics, employment, and so on, on fair terms, and evidenced with empirical research delineating the underrepresentation of such candidates across these sectors.

How specifically does an emphasis on political inclusion support the adoption of affirmative action policies? First, affirmative action policies that are directed toward cultural minority groups are justified with respect to the importance of providing a level playing field with respect to the valuable opportunities that are meant to be widely available to all citizens on equal terms, including especially higher-education opportunities and high-quality job opportunities. Where people secure these opportunities, and correspondingly the benefits that attach to them, they are better positioned to engage politically: the availability of these opportunities on fair and equal terms is key to securing citizens' right to an equal say, via this indirect route.

Second, having cultural minority groups well represented in socially valuable sectors can have the additional benefit of helping to ensure that the services they offer are themselves culturally appropriate. Consider the choice to reserve medical school spaces for Indigenous students. The stated affirmative action plan at one Canadian university, Dalhousie, explains that the process for evaluating Indigenous candidates will focus on whether a particular applicant is qualified to study medicine, full stop, rather than on how she compares to other applicants more generally (Dalhousie University n.d.). Here the objective is at least in part to ensure that Indigenous patients can have culturally appropriate medical care, by having access to qualified, competent, and culturally sensitive doctors. This culturally specific justification for affirmative action has been made also in the context of supporting victims of domestic abuse, where cultural minority domestic abuse victims are more likely to seek support from women doctors who share their background and cultural context. The capacity of a state to provide culturally sensitive care to all citizens *depends* on an educational system being willing to support minorities in gaining the appropriate education. As these examples illustrate, treating educational and employment opportunities like prizes to be awarded to the meritorious frequently misunderstands their roles in producing a just society; allocating scarce educational positions and jobs at least in part to enable an inclusive democracy requires a broader understanding of the role and importance of doctors, educators, and lawyers, in providing basic services and protecting basic rights.

SPECIAL REPRESENTATION CLAIMS

Special representation claims are demands to open democratic spaces so that more than the dominant views are represented therein. Special representation policies focus on securing representation, usually in political forums, of minority groups whose views have been historically under-represented, often because of discrimination and racism. They attempt to secure the political inclusion of distinct *perspectives* or *identities*, and rest on the view that group membership—usually, but not always, in minority groups with a history of marginalization or dispossession—shapes political preferences in a range of ways that require representation.

The voice-centric account of political inclusion thus supports representation rights, and "requires that these different voices be heard and responded to, that they have an opportunity to affect legislative decisions" (Williams 1998, 138). The most basic way in which political inclusion is secured is via the vote, but as noted already, in modern democracies electors select *representatives*, whose job it is to speak on behalf of constituents (Dovi 2018). It is a common complaint in democratic states that representatives do a poor job at representing the wide range of views and perspectives held by their citizens, however. In most democratic states, it continues to be the case that representatives are dominantly well-off white men, who may be unwilling, or simply unable, to represent the views of those whose identities or demographic circumstances they do not share. The result is that nondominant views, identities, and perspectives are not well represented, even in proportion to their numbers in democratic spaces, and correspondingly that policies and laws adopted therein do not necessarily well represent their preferences. So, the justification for special representation rights is broadly democratic: to the extent that minorities are not able easily to run for election, or are not elected when they do run, their voices are not heard in the central governing institutions of the state in which they are equal members. Special representation rights can ensure that their voices are heard.

For some, the benefits of special representation rights are primarily in the *visible* recognition that the democratic community is diverse; for others, it stems from the belief that minority representatives have access to the experiences of minority members, which will then be better represented in political debates (Williams 1998; Phillips 1995, 1998). When Carol Mosely-Braun offered a passionate speech in the US Senate opposing a motion that the patent for the insignia for the United Daughters of Confederacy be renewed—an insignia that features the US Confederate flag, which represents, for Black Americans, the history of slavery—many suggested her ability to do so (and her persuasiveness) stemmed from her experiences as a Black woman (Dewar 1993). In opposing the motion, she said:

> The issue is whether Americans such as myself who believe in the promise of this country, who feel strongly and who are patriots in this country, will have to suffer the indignity of being reminded time and time again that at one time in this country's history we were human chattel. We were property. We could be traded, bought, and sold. (Oh 2015)

In making this statement, on behalf of Black Americans, Mosely-Brawn was said to offer a form of "surrogate" representation, where members of a cultural minority group sometimes feel represented by group members (Mansbridge 2003), even if they were elected in jurisdictions that are not their own. Minority representatives often report that they are contacted by group members outside of their jurisdiction for exactly this reason (Sinno and Tatari 2009). That said, it is important to be attentive to the fact that the mere presence of minorities in political spaces is not sufficient to guarantee the substantive representation of their interests, and both presence and substantive representation are crucial in multicultural states.

Special representation comes in a range of formats. In places where elections use party lists, one strategy encourages parties to place individuals who are able to represent a wide range of perspectives, including those who are traditionally underrepresented, at the top of the list (Levy 1997, 151; Mansbridge 2003). Another option is to reserve seats for minorities that have historically been shut out of legislative spaces. Reserving seats is the choice that New Zealand made to secure the representation of Māori voices in its legislative assembly. The Māori are frequently raised as an example in political theory to signal one way in which special representation rights were implemented, and it is useful to pay more attention to the way in which the arguments were made in this case. The choice to reserve seats for Māori representatives was made in 1867 as a kind of concession to the them, understood as temporary, to ensure peace between the Māori and white New Zealanders. It was motivated by an assimilationist impulse that speculated that political inclusion would result in a merge of identities and ultimately the erasure of Māori as a distinct political community in New Zealand (Fleras 1985). Moreover, initial expectations were that the Māori representatives would be present to speak on behalf of their own specific interests rather than on issues facing the country as a whole. Consonant with that general view, a 1985 report of the New Zealand Royal Commission on the Electoral System recommended abolishing the seats in favor of a party-list system. That recommendation was widely resisted on the grounds that the reserved seats represented ongoing respect for the Māori as a key political player in the state of New Zealand (New Zealand Parliament 2009).

The demand for special representation encounters opposition from those who believe that minority views can be part of the conversation without necessarily being raised by members of those groups; representatives, after all, have the job of representing all of their constituents and not simply the views of those with whom they share personal and demographic characteristics. There are further objections from those who believe that granting them may disrupt what they believe is the fair procedure for selecting political representatives. However, empirical evidence suggests that minority representatives do a better job at raising group-specific perspectives and securing the adoption of policies that are favorable to minorities (Pande 2003; Banducci, Donovan, and Karp 2004; Phillips 1995); on the basis of this evidence, it is reasonable to believe that constructing political procedures, including via protecting special representation rights, that do a good job at ensuring minority perspectives are represented, will effectively serve the goal of political inclusion.

SELF-DETERMINATION CLAIMS

Territorially concentrated national minorities frequently demand the right to self-determination (Young 2004), that is, the right to regulate the institutional structures that govern the lives of those living in the relevant substate jurisdiction—think Tibet, Québec, or Catalonia. Typically, the point of granting self-determination is to ensure that a national minority, a territorially concentrated, culturally distinct minority group bounded by a "national" identity that is distinct from the majority community, is able to ensure that its central institutions are attentive to the specific cultural differences that characterize the jurisdiction. In the case of Québec and Catalonia, a key cultural difference is with respect to the languages in which key institutions operate, for example, French rather than English and Catalan rather than Castilian.

As these national minorities negotiate their space in, usually, federal multinational states, they often demand control of, or input into, policy areas that would, without their input or control, result in the dilution of their cultural characteristics (Norman 2006). Without control of these policies areas, national minorities will not be able to provide high-quality options, in consonance with their cultural values and norms—in employment, education, and so on. Their members will thereby be pressed to seek opportunities elsewhere, in cultural contexts outside of their own. The objective is to provide the full set of institutional options for its members, removing any feeling that they must choose between living their lives in a culturally comfortable political space and seeking high-quality employment and education elsewhere. So, to the demand for self-determination in the case of national minorities manifests in a demand to have control over a wide range of institutions in a territorially delimited jurisdiction *and* a commitment from the central government to cede control of certain policy areas.

I examine a specific case of self-determination in chapter 4 (the self-determination of Indigenous communities), but here I want to make the general case that political inclusion is served by respecting and supporting the self-determination of cultural minorities. In part, the acknowledgment of self-determination rights is about recognition, which I consider in the next section in more detail: the sustained support of political institutions for recognized cultural minorities creates the foundations for their active and engaged political participation, inside of the boundaries of their cultural community, but also on equal terms with the majority community in shared institutions.

RECOGNITION CLAIMS

The demand for self-determination often travels with a demand for formal recognition. Demands for recognition are typically demands for an official commitment to respecting specific minority communities, often in the form of constitutional or other legislative recognition, as equal or valuable members of the larger political community. Usually, minority groups that demand recognition have been disvalued, or disadvantaged, historically—and official recognition can go some way to acknowledging and remedying this disadvantage. This form of recognition can be granted to Indigenous groups, or self-determining national minorities, in a constitution or via a legislative process (Tully 1995; Patten 2014; Albeck-Ripka 2019).

An acceptance of the importance of recognition stems from a focus on ensuring that *respect* is offered by the dominant group to the minority group. Return briefly to the Māori example. There, the reason the Māori did not support a transition from protected seats to party-list or other proportional representative systems, which the New Zealand Royal Commission proposed (sincerely) on the idea that it would *better* represent Māori interests, was because they felt that the protected seats *recognized* their unique contribution to and role in New Zealand. The establishment of reserved seats for Māori leaders aimed to ensure representation; the protection of reserved seats over time aims to ensure recognition.

Indigenous peoples in Australia have mobilized to demand that they be constitutionally recognized, arguing—just as a political inclusion argument would suggest—that doing so will support the development of trust among Indigenous and non-Indigenous communities, on the grounds that constitutional recognition signals a willingness to extend respect to Indigenous communities (Australian Human Rights Commission n.d.). While there is a worry that recognition in a constitution could be merely symbolic, cultural and ethnic minorities propose that constitutional recognition has the potential to translate into protection from past and ongoing discrimination, and correspondingly more substantive inclusion in political space, as well as public space more generally (DU Correspondent 2018; Albeck-Ripka 2019). In other words, formal recognition can lay the groundwork for a real commitment to remedying the substantive injustices that some cultural minority groups continue to face, by signaling a formal inclusion of that minority group in the overarching identity of the political community.

CONCLUSION

Political inclusion, understood in terms of the importance of *voice* and its effective exercise in shared public politics, is the evaluation metric that should be used to assess a wide range of cultural claims. Cultural claims come in various forms, and they are defended with a range of justifications, some of which appeal to those who in general reject the importance of special treatment for cultural minority groups in political spaces. As a political strategy, having that range is wise; from the perspective of a disadvantaged minority group attempting to gain traction for rights protection, it is valuable to be armed with multiple justifications aimed at the relevant constituencies that will find them persuasive. I have offered, in this chapter, a democratic argument for taking them seriously in general, and then showed that the main clusters of cultural claims are best defended in terms of the objective of securing political inclusion understood in the voice-centric way I defended. But, readers may have noted, I have not yet considered the cluster of cultural rights claimed in support of cultural preservation. These, readers may suspect, are difficult to treat from a political inclusion perspective—I turn to these questions in chapter 4 and suggest that many preservation claims that appear to cause "separation" are, just as the claims considered above, best understood as securing political inclusion.

4

Cultural Preservation and Multicultural Accommodation

IN CHAPTER 3, I DEFENDED most major clusters of cultural claims from the perspective of a voice-centric account of political inclusion. There, however, I did not consider claims for "cultural preservation," that is, claims made by cultural minority groups to preserve their culture in ways that often look like separation and isolation from the larger society, which critics of multiculturalism decry. My thesis in this chapter is simple: nearly all claims for cultural preservation ought to be accommodated, because they too serve to enhance political inclusion by enabling members of minority cultures to raise their voices. In this chapter, I cannot defend every such case, and so I proceed by showing that three major cases of "segregation," justified with respect to some form of cultural preservation, are intimately connected to securing political inclusion over the long term. These are public support for ethnically exclusive organizations, culturally specific schools, and

Debating Multiculturalism. Peter Balint and Patti Tamara Lenard, Oxford University Press. © Oxford University Press 2022. DOI: 10.1093/oso/9780197528372.003.0005

the revitalization of Indigenous self-determination. This chapter proceeds by example, so should not be taken as a full and complete defense of all arguments that are offered in favor of cultural preservation—rather, the chapter's objective is to show how attention to political inclusion can shape the appropriate response to these claims, and to offer, I hope, a guide to considering future cases in a like manner.

WHY ARE CULTURAL PRESERVATION RIGHTS SO CONTROVERSIAL?

Among multicultural rights, rights justified in terms of the importance of preserving, and in some cases reinvigorating, culture are among the most controversial. Why is this? In general terms, the worry is that demands for cultural preservation involve policies that appear to support the separation of cultural groups from the larger society. They include policies that permit the self-government of minority groups; culturally specific educational spaces; taxpayer support for "ethnic organizations" of various kinds, including ethnic language media and community centers; and language support policies, including those that fund teaching minority languages in public schools, and those that require public signage to be in a particular minority language.

When political actors proclaimed that multiculturalism had failed, one key factor was repeatedly cited as evidence, namely, that immigrant minorities chose to live in segregated neighborhoods—ethnic ghettos, they were called—where they could effectively reproduce the communities they left behind, rather than integrate into the larger community (Cassidy 2010; Burns 2011; Vertovec and Wessendorf 2010). Rather than learn a new language and adopt new values, critics claimed, newcomers chose to construct residential spaces in which they could comfortably continue to speak "ethnic" languages and abide by norms and values that had traveled with them, rather than those that characterize their host country. A host of problems allegedly ensued, including low rates of competence in the national language(s), poor economic integration among adults, low educational success among children, and the propagation of worldviews apparently steeped in sexism and misogyny.

The foundation of these objections is a claim about the values that travel with newcomers, which allegedly discourage integration into, and in some cases encourage hatred of, liberal democratic societies. These objections are sometimes infused with hostility toward cultural difference in general, and those who express them are (often fairly) accused of discrimination and stereotyping of cultural minorities. But underneath the frequently problematic way in which these worries about integration are expressed there lies a legitimate worry about what ultimately binds citizens in diverse states. The *worry* is that acknowledging cultural difference, and permitting it to flourish with the use of public funds, will undermine the collective project in which democracies are engaged. It does so by providing space for cultural groups, immigrant and long-standing minorities, to protect and preserve values that are inimical to the broader integration of their members, and so creates and encourages ethnic segregation.

Residential clustering of immigrant and nonimmigrant minority groups is common, certainly. But, those on the other side of this debate, including me, emphasize that structural conditions in host states—that is systemic, institutional racism—bear at least some responsibility for the fact of ethnic segregation. Denying that clustering manifests a resistance among minorities to integration, such scholars propose instead that clustering is caused by political, economic, and social institutions that are problematically exclusionary in ways that make them inaccessible to minorities on fair terms, an exclusionary tendency that is *eased* rather than exacerbated by the appropriate adoption of multicultural policies. This latter account is my view, i.e., in general, accommodating multicultural claims will reduce rather than generate the residential clustering that worries critics of multiculturalism.

As I noted in the introduction, one worry is that multicultural policies that permit and encourage the preservation of minority cultures, especially immigrant minorities, *also* slow their integration, measured with respect to their educational and economic success. I aim to refute this claim by focusing on a range of examples in which cultural groups demand public support to preserve culture. But the point is to show that preservationist arguments cannot simply be rejected on the grounds that they contribute to segregation or isolationism of minority groups: many, if not most, of them are responding to political exclusion and its impact on cultural minorities and in turn support the objectives of political inclusion.

PUBLIC SUPPORT
FOR ETHNIC ORGANIZATIONS

One controversial way in which minority cultural groups aim to sustain themselves over time is via the creation of and participation in ethnically exclusive organizations, for example, Belarusian and Indonesian community associations. An ethnically exclusive organization is one that caters to the interests of, or offers services to, a particular ethnic minority population; sometimes it is directed at achieving political goals, other times at sharing communal holiday celebrations, and other times at organizing collaborative activities like book clubs or cooking classes that are of interest to members of the community. They are often directed at sustaining connections to sending communities and often at supporting the migration of additional members of the ethnic group. One marker of a multicultural state, for example, as defined by the Multicultural Policy Index we described in the introduction, is that it supports—using public funds—key ethnic organizations.

It is of course true that in a democratic state, citizens may freely associate in communities of various kinds, including those that cater to minority ethnic identities in particular, but what is controversial here is the financial contribution of the central state to organizations that, allegedly, support and encourage cultural preservation. To borrow language from the social capital literature, some worry that minority ethnic organizations support only *bonding* among members of cultural groups, rather than *bridging* between cultural groups and the larger community (Putnam 2007; Forbes 2009). That is, critics of ethnic organizations suggest that newcomers should be discouraged from forming and sustaining an "ethnic community," which in their view promotes isolation and discourages political integration in general. Because such organizations are ethnically exclusive, moreover, and so not open to all citizens, they ought not to be entitled to taxpayer support. However, empirical evidence does not support the claim that such organizations promote isolation or discourage integration.

Rather, a significant body of social science literature suggests links between engagement in ethnic associations and measures of political integration, including high rates of political trust, willing compliance with democratic norms and values, and political participation in the form of both voting and more robust activism (Tillie 2004). The organization itself need not be focused on political objectives specifically in order to observe this effect, moreover (Tillie 2004, 536–37). The explanation is the standard one offered in discussions of social capital. Social capital refers to the networks of connections and relations among individuals, which generate shared values and norms, which in turn facilitate cooperation among them, thus permitting them to achieve shared goals (Hooghe 2007). *However*, there is more to the story than this: those who work in collaborative settings to achieve shared objectives also gain a set of skills that can be deployed elsewhere. That is to say, participation in community ethnically centered organizations supports the development of the skills needed to participate in politics and society more widely. Ethnic organizations may sometimes operate in isolation, but the more robust and established of them are embedded in a network of organizations (some of which are also ethnically based), and these connections support further the development of collaborative relations that can translate into specific connections in and interactions with the larger social and political space (Tillie 2004; van Heelsum 2005). There are three additional observations to make about ethnic organizations. First, often their origin is in immigration; that is, they emerge where immigration from a particular ethnic group is substantial, and they emerge to cater to their various ethnically specific needs. Especially in communities where discrimination persists, immigrants may find it easier and more comfortable to join ethnic organizations than organizations with broader mandates (Myrberg 2011, 102). In joining, members gain social connections that can provide multiple practical resources (how to find housing and employment, for example, and where to register to vote), as well as emotional support during the early difficult stages of migration.

Second, as they grow, in membership as well as in terms of their objectives, such organizations become able to integrate newcomers into a larger political system, by furnishing them with essential political skills, and by highlighting where current political deliberations are of relevance to their membership (Galandini 2013). As a result, political actors sometimes cater to or recruit from such organizations, keen to attract their votes or contributions to political activism (Myrberg 2011). They are also sources of group consciousness and so serve as the basis for advocacy around issues of special relevance to the community (Galandini 2013). As a whole, such ethnic organizations support political inclusion, both by encouraging the development of political skills and interests among members, and by drawing mainstream political attention to their priorities and perspectives. Participation in ethnic organizations does not translate into isolation and segregation, but rather acts a gateway to integration in general, and political participation understood broadly. As a result, multicultural states ought to actively support such organizations, since doing so promotes and protects the political inclusion of ethnic communities.

Third, ethnically exclusive organizations often support and produce media—television, newspapers, social media—in minority languages. In defense of the claim for public support, advocates say that it is insufficient to make sure that voting material is available in minority languages; access to information about politics more generally ought to be made available in minority languages, via financial support to ethnic media organizations. Ethnic, or multicultural, media provide essential information to citizens who are uncomfortable in the dominant languages. These media deserve material support to aid the delivery of this information to citizens who would otherwise be at risk of being cut off from the central and dominant political conversations in their state.[1] Even among those who support the provision of electoral materials in minority languages, however, some may object to the provision of more general resources, proposing instead that ethnic communities should manage with support from those whom they

1. This could be a more complicated statement, since only some countries have a norm of state support for media outlets. In states where media is generally supported by the state, of course ethnic media must be included in that support on grounds of fairness; the point I am making here is that, regardless of whether the state ordinarily supports media, ethnic media organizations may be entitled to support for the benefits they generate as I am describing them here.

serve. At issue is whether such media are treated as offering an essential *connection* between minority language citizens and the majority or whether they serve to perpetuate continued isolation of such communities. To take one example, the National Ethnic Press and Media Council of Canada, which represents 650 ethnic language publications and over a 100 broadcasters in radio and television in 60 languages, describes its remit as "a non-profit organization whose mission is to promote and integrate economic, social and culture interest of Ethnic communities into the mainstream of Canadian society" (National Ethnic Press and Media Council of Canada 2012). This organization and other similar umbrella organizations in Canada have been especially vocal during the Covid-19 crisis, arguing that they are the main source of up-to-date health information for thousands of Canadians who require this to be provided in minority languages, and therefore are deserving of relief from the range of Covid-19 relief bills that have been adopted (Howells 2020). Especially with respect to health information, *everyone* benefits where good information is made widely accessible.

Thus, such organizations merit central support for the ways in which they support and encourage, in particular, political inclusion, even as they create and support spaces in which ethnic groups can protect and promote their cultural practices and identities. What of cultural minority organizations and associated media outlets that have explicitly stated goals to discourage integration? I leave aside for the next chapter the question of how democratic states should respond to requests for support where the support is intended to protect isolationism. For now, let me simply say that where such organizations have an explicitly inclusionary goal, they deserve public support in the way I have described.

CULTURALLY SEPARATE SCHOOLS

A second controversial way in which cultural groups aim to sustain themselves over time is by ensuring that their children are educated in the history and values of the group. This education often happens at home, as families relate cultural or religious stories and celebrate holidays together. But, for some groups, this education also ideally transpires in culturally specific school settings, that is, in educational environments that are specifically shaped to ensure that the history and values of a particular group or set of groups infuse the educational curriculum. So-called separate schools are one important cultural preservation mechanism, and many cultural groups demand support from the state in order to support the development and sustaining of such schools. I focus on a case study of the Africentric Alternative School (AAS) in Toronto, Canada, to argue that a commitment to political inclusion drives an obligation for multicultural states to support schools focused on cultural preservation.

The AAS opened in 2012 as a public school in downtown Toronto, the most diverse city in Canada. "Public schools" in Canada are fully funded by the state and are open to all students; although the school opened with the mission of supporting students from African and Caribbean backgrounds, all students are welcome to attend. The idea for a culturally specific school in Toronto emerged from a collaborative effort to confront lower educational success rates among the city's African and Caribbean diasporic communities, measured according to school dropout rates and performance in standard testing. A multiyear consultation among stakeholders produced a report that outlined multiple ways in which the standard curriculum has failed to meet the culturally specific needs of Black students (some, but not all of whom, are recent migrants), who in addition to being poorly served by the traditional curriculum, continue to face racism and violence at schools in ways that hindered their learning (Dragnea and Erling 2008). The curriculum at the AAS teaches the same skills as are taught across in schools Ontario, but makes a special effort to do so in ways that are more connected to the cultures and values of Black students. Its objective, overall, is to support the development of agency among Black students, who will have the confidence and skills they need to effect real change in their own lives and the lives of their communities, which continue to suffer from the effects of racism and systemic discrimination. The school writes of its mission:

> A comprehensive Africentric learning system is an essential and unique approach to educating students of African descent because it recognizes the impact of their history and current reality of structural racism on their learning. Traditional educational models have not been colourblind and African Canadian youth and communities have paid a steep price for the illusion of inclusion. (Levine-Rasky 2014, 204)

The school is "decorated" in ways that emphasize Black contributions to Canadian and global history. The school's history curriculum includes the histories and cultures of African minorities in Canada. One student described learning at the school as "It is like Black History month every month" (James et al. 2014). The school's founders adopted seven principles to use as guidance, drawn from a wide range of African traditions, to match the diversity of student backgrounds: "Umoja, Kujichagulia, Ujima, Nia, Ujamaa, Imani, and Kuumba," which are Swahili for "Unity, Self-determination, Collective Work and Responsibility, Purpose, Co-operative Economics, Faith, and Creativity." These guiding principles were selected to support connections between students with African backgrounds and "traditional African worldviews" (James et al. 2014). The principles guide all aspects of running the school, including the curriculum and school-based activities, with the objective of "cultivating a space for the development of a positive Black identity" (James et al. 2014, 29).

The proposal to open this school drew significant criticism from the Toronto community, with many arguing that it encouraged segregation and that "cultural specificity" has no real role to play in educational spaces. The creation of separate school boards for diverse groups, said critics, encourages divisiveness rather than unity and tolerance among a multicultural student body (Sniderman and Hagendoorn 2007). Some argued, additionally, that the dangers that plague de facto segregated schools in the United States loom large: the collection of low-income students into a school that will, in time, prove to be underfunded and ignored in ways that perpetuate rather than ameliorate unequal educational access and performance (Anderson 2010).[2] Moreover, said other critics, schools are

---

2. In the province of Ontario, 17% of students live in a low-income household; in the 2017–2018 academic year, 34%

not the right place for "cultural learning," which should be left to families and communities and have no place in public spaces that are meant to be open to all on equal terms.

It is important to weigh these objections—of the danger of generating segregation and the claim that cultural learning is a private matter—against the stated objectives of the school, its mechanisms for achieving them, and the particular challenges it aims to overcome. As I wrote earlier, its particular goal is to improve the educational spaces for Black students in Toronto, whose educational outcomes are lower on average than others, in part because of the risk of violence they face in integrated schools and in part because of the systemic racism that continues to pervade them. The mechanism for doing so has been to create a culturally relevant environment, in which students can learn the standard set of skills that they need in order to be successful in the Canadian economic and political space, and in which they can develop the confidence they need in order to contribute effectively to it over the long term. In other words, their stated *objectives* are aligned precisely with those supported by a focus on political inclusion: the cultural focus of the educational space supports the development of the capacities needed to access political spaces, and the confidence students need to do so. One need not agree (although this author does) that the standard curriculum is Eurocentric, that is to say, culturally infused with norms and values that emerge from the histories of European nations, to be convinced that the case for

of students at AAS are from low-income households. See Ontario Ministry of Education 2020.

culturally specific education can be valuable to students who are marginalized in so-called integrated educational spaces.

One objection to this account of culturally specific schools is that, although my defense is credible, it does not generalize to the more familiar example of faith-based schools, which, according to many critics, do in fact encourage and enforce separation from the larger political community. For example, many Muslim schools in the UK have faced criticism for allegedly relying too substantially on religious rather than secular texts, thus not providing students with the skills they need to be successful in the larger British community (Richardson 2014). Such schools are alleged to encourage Muslim students to live parallel lives rather than to engage with secular Britons and to promulgate various norms and values that are believed to be contrary to so-called British values. Furthermore, reports occasionally emerge suggesting that at least some Muslim faith-based schools insist on problematic segregation of girl and boy students (BBC News 2019), suggesting to critics a failure to respect gender equality at the school level. Separate complaints are launched at parents of Muslim children in secular schools who, for reasons of faith, request various forms of gender-specific education, including separate gym classes (Martin 2011). Where separate schools can be demonstrated to be teaching radicalism or encouraging general inequality, or where they refuse to teach the key elements of a national curriculum, they should not in general be permitted to access state support in a liberal democratic state. But the fact that some schools may be guilty of doing so is not an argument for banning them, in general or from accessing public funds, in all instances.

Rather, it is crucial to avoid condemning the idea of culturally specific schools in general terms, where it is clear that some are focused, as is the AAS, on responding to low educational outcomes among a population where, it is believed, conventional schools are inadequate to cater to the population's specific needs, especially in cases where minority students are victims of racism and violence and subject to a curriculum from which they feel detached. Many so-called faith-based schools are responding to the same set of factors as is the AAS: the disconnect that minority students face in conventional schools, the violence and racism to which they may be subject therein, and the belief that a culturally appropriate environment can better support minority students to gain the skills they need. In the British case, multiple so-called Muslim schools (as in the AAS) in fact focus on teaching the national curriculum in a culturally Islamic space (Shah 2012), with the objective of ensuring that students emerge with the skills and confidence they need to engage in the larger economic and political spaces that, unfortunately, continue to stigmatize them. Such faith-based schools are defensible from the perspective of political inclusion.

INDIGENOUS SELF-DETERMINATION

Indigenous communities around the world demand the right of self-determination, in many cases citing their status as original title-holders of the land on which they live, which has been taken from them, generally violently

and without their consent. The right to self-determination that Indigenous groups claim (and which is increasingly, broadly, recognized) is much like the one claimed by
national minorities more generally, in the sense that it is a
demand for Indigenous communities to live regulated by
their "societal culture," that is, to be able to run the full set
of governance institutions, for their communities, in ways
that are consistent with their cultural norms and values.
That said, there are some notable differences suggesting
that the right they claim should not be conflated with the
right claimed by national minorities, like the Québécois
or the Welsh, whose central values and norms are in many
ways the same as those of the dominant majority.

Although it is common to say that Indigenous communities demand self-governance, this demand is a heteroge-
neous one; not all Indigenous communities want the same
form of self-determination, and indeed not all Indigenous
communities want it in the first place; as a result, states
must negotiate separately with each Indigenous group to
develop specific understandings of how this right can be
met. Indigenous communities differ with respect to their
traditional ways of life; their population; their resources,
understood broadly; and, the extent to which their members aim to interact with the larger population, among
many other things. So, the choice to respect the Indigenous
"right to self-determination" requires that states are sensitive to the specific conditions faced by Indigenous communities, and moreover that they be led by each specific
community in determining their specific needs (Borrows
2016, chapter 5).

The importance of protecting and respecting the self-
determination of Indigenous communities is increasingly

recognized around the world. Governments are now negotiating treaties (or acknowledging past ones) with Indigenous communities, and actively reconstructing the boundaries of territorial jurisdictions (for example, as in the case of the creation of the Canadian territory of Nunavut, established in 1999), in ways that permit and encourage Indigenous self-determination. Some Indigenous communities, which aim at self-determination, require support from the government to achieve it, beyond mere legal recognition of their right to do so. In nearly every country that is home to Indigenous peoples, they have been subject to assimilationist and genocidal policies intended to eradicate them, and in many cases continue to be threatened by such policies. Decades of genocidal policies have weakened them substantially, such that any genuine effort to recognize their right to self-determination requires not simply "handing over the institutional reins," as it may do in the case of national minorities, but rather the provision of active and concerned support to rebuild both broken institutions and the capacities of Indigenous peoples to run them effectively—that is, to support the *resurgence* of Indigenous communities (Coulthard 2014). So, there are reasons of "corrective" or "reparative" justice to support the obligations that many states have toward Indigenous peoples, which require them to take seriously the need for states to be partners in institutional rebuilding in and with Indigenous communities.

Notice that the right to self-determination in the case of Indigenous peoples also travels with exemption demands. Many Indigenous communities are defined by ways of life that are deeply connected to the land, and correspondingly their livelihood depends first, on sustaining the health of key natural resources, and second, often, on protecting their secure access to them, sometimes by denying others the right to access them (Moore 2015). It is common, for example, to protect Indigenous access to fisheries or forests, even as others (whose livelihood may also depend on them) are denied such access. Protecting this access for Indigenous communities is especially controversial where the resource in question is at risk of becoming unsustainable because of overuse, for example, in cases of legislation adopted to prevent overfishing, from which Indigenous communities—in the name of protecting their ways of life—are occasionally exempt. For example, controversy erupted recently in several small towns in the Canadian province of Nova Scotia, where Indigenous fishers are permitted (according to a 1999 Supreme Court ruling) to continue to seek a "moderate livelihood" from fishing, even outside of the standard designated fishing season, a designation adopted in order to protect the viability of the fishery as a whole (Googoo 2020); non-Indigenous fishers argued that even the pursuit of a moderate livelihood threatened the fishery as a whole.

Indigenous communities have also demanded the right to exclude nonmembers from territory and, where they apply, from the benefits of membership. For example, in some cases, Indigenous communities deny the right of non-Indigenous people—who have, perhaps, married an Indigenous person, where together they have chosen to live on Indigenous land—to vote in community elections. In others, they have attempted to deny non-Indigenous peoples, without familial relations, to live on their land (CBC News 2014). The justification here is preservation of Indigenous culture, and the argument in favor of exclusion mirrors the arguments that states sometimes make to exclude migrants, whose cultural and religious values appear in tension with those that are dominant in the would-be host society. Note that the analogy is largely imperfect, however, since in the Indigenous case, Indigenous culture remains vulnerable in ways that may justify certain forms of exclusion, whereas it is widely agreed that this additional "vulnerability" consideration is not available to diverse, democratic nation-states. This latter demand, to exclude at least in some cases, likely merits support, on the grounds that the vulnerability of Indigenous communities is real, and created and perpetuated by the colonial governments that govern the territory on which they live. But it is also worth remaining attentive to cases where the claimed right to exclude, when it travels with self-determination, may result in the political exclusion of others who may be long-term residents of an Indigenous community, or in fact believe that they are Indigenous citizens in the relevant way. For example, in some cases, Indigenous communities have adopted membership rules that have excluded Indigenous women who marry non-Indigenous partners (and their children). Of course in most cases, colonial governments pressured Indigenous communities to adopt membership rules of this type (Joseph 2018, 20–23); but where they persist, there are reasons of political inclusion to encourage membership rules that are relatively more rather than less inclusive.

The more general claim, that Indigenous communities are entitled to self-government, as well as public support to revitalize their political communities as self-governing, from which they can then negotiate with colonial governments as equals, is one that is consistent with the objectives of political inclusion that I outlined earlier. In particular, the choice to respect and support Indigenous self-determination permits the building of bridges between Indigenous citizens and the majority population on fair terms. It can, moreover, serve to give a better and deeper voice to Indigenous leaders, who can—on the basis of robust self-determination—speak with authority and legitimacy on behalf of their community members in negotiations with the state.

CONCLUSION

This chapter's objective is to highlight that cultural preservation claims are often deeply connected to political inclusion; that is, they are demanded—and ought to be granted—on the grounds that their accommodation generates more robust political inclusion. As I noted earlier, some scholars find this way of thinking about cultural preservation claims counterintuitive, suggesting that where cultures aim to preserve distinct aspects of their identities and practices, they inevitably generate problematic isolation and exclusion. This intuition guides those who argue that the segregation, and the self-segregation, of ethnic minorities can be traced to the adoption of multicultural policies. I suggested, in this chapter, that the logic underpinning this sort of worry is often incorrect. While there is considerable evidence that the segregation of ethnic minorities—into enclaves that are relatively poorer— is the result of persistent discrimination by the majority community, that claim is tangential to my argument. As evidenced by the cases I examined in this chapter, minority groups request public support to enable the preservation of their culture, and to facilitate the integration of newcomers, in ways that foster engagement of their members with the institutions that are at the heart of democratic politics. Democracy is healthier—that is, it is more inclusive—when this support is provided.

5

Noninterference and Political Inclusion

CHAPTER 4 CONSIDERED CASES WHERE accommodating cultural preservation claims supports political inclusion. However, not all arguments for cultural preservation are even indirectly about political inclusion. On the contrary, some cultural groups make demands of the larger state, in support of cultural preservation, where the objective is plainly to preserve the group as a separate entity that remains, deliberately, at the sidelines of the larger community, interacting with it only when necessary (Spinner-Halev 1999). They are, in Jeff Spinner-Halev's words, partial citizens; they typically engage in some ways with the larger society, in particular by paying taxes in exchange for some key services, but by and large their attention is directed inward toward the sustaining of their community's distinct way of life. These groups claim rights of *noninterference*, arguing that they should be left alone to live their lives as they see fit.

In what follows, I examine the general request for noninterference and then, in some depth, two cases in which exemption requests are made in support of noninterference: exemption from mandatory education, as requested

Debating Multiculturalism. Peter Balint and Patti Tamara Lenard, Oxford University Press. © Oxford University Press 2022. DOI: 10.1093/oso/9780197528372.003.0006

by Amish and Orthodox Jewish communities, and exemption from majority state conflict-resolution procedures, as requested by many religious communities. In both cases, I argue that the majority's response ought to be framed in terms of how best to keep opportunities for political inclusion open and available over the long term, and then that the choice made with respect to requested exemptions may well require compromise on both sides. I suggest as well that a host community must proceed by protecting the basis for trust relations between culturally segregated groups and the majority community, on the grounds that this trust will sometimes be required to facilitate political cooperation in times of emergency. To illustrate the latter, I examine the challenges faced in New York City as it combated the spread of Covid-19 in Orthodox Jewish communities.

WHAT IS NONINTERFERENCE?

Minority cultural and religious groups sometimes demand rights of noninterference so that, fundamentally, they can live a segregated, communal life, regulated by their own values and norms. These are "encompassing" communities, to borrow the language of Avishai Margalit and Joseph Raz (1990). Amish, Mennonite, and Hutterite communities in the United States and Canada have requested noninterference rights of this kind, as have many Orthodox Jewish communities across North America and Israel. Generally, these are communities that support and sustain a range of institutional structures in which their members lives are lived in full: the community regulates their members' educational, familial, and occupational lives. Such communities are often fully *communal* in the sense that all major life events are regulated according to shared cultural norms and values, and the community sets and enforces expectations for members, often in rigorous ways. Often (but not always) property is owned in common, and where it is owned privately, the community generally determines the rules of property ownership, including who may own it and how it may permissibly be transferred to others.

The choice by liberal democratic states to tolerate isolationist groups is largely historical: in Canada and the United States, several such groups migrated from European countries, escaping religious persecution, and they were promised religious freedom in exchange for populating and settling areas of the country that needed cultivating, as part of the political expansionist objectives of leaders at the time (Kymlicka 1995). The toleration extended to them is uncomfortable, however, when these groups eschew liberal democratic values and look upon the larger community with disdain. Yet, some argue, such groups must be permitted to persist without forced integration, either because their religious freedom requires protecting or because states ought not to renege on agreements made in the past. These reasons remain persuasive enough so long as these groups remain isolationist and request only (or mainly) noninterference by the larger state in order to live according to the values they endorse. It may be reasonable, says Spinner-Halev, to accommodate these communities so long as the demands they make on the larger community are relatively minor; conflicts arise in cases where such communities make demands, sometimes significant, on the state, including with respect to reduced protection of key rights, while refusing to accept the burdens that come with doing so.

NONINTERFERENCE AND EXEMPTION REQUESTS

Although they are territorially concentrated, these culturally preservationist communities are nevertheless embedded in larger democratic states, in ways that require at least some interaction. A particular challenge is that in service of the noninterference that is said to be required for cultural preservation, some communities request exemptions from laws that are supposed to apply to all citizens. The exemption requests that they make are quite unlike those that I considered, and defended, in chapter 3. There, I described exemption requests as those that are demanded by minority groups, when particular norms or practices render access to key institutions unreasonably burdensome for them. They are demanded on the grounds of fairness or equal access to social or economic goods.

However, in the cases under consideration here, exemptions are demanded by cultural groups in support of the more general demand for noninterference. In both cases, the motivation is a desire to preserve culture, either a particular practice or the community as a whole. In the cases I considered in chapter 3, the objective was for members of a minority community to secure access to goods offered in the dominant society while receiving exemptions that enable them to both participate in shared political space on fair terms and preserve their commitment to their culture. In the cases I consider in this chapter, the minority community requests exemptions that support cultural isolation. These exemptions are requested as protections from distinct threats: in the cases I considered in chapter 3, the threat of unequal opportunity to access the goods offered by the dominant community on fair terms, and in the cases under consideration in this chapter, the threat of community erosion in the face of the dominant society. Ultimately, the larger community must make a choice about whether and when to insist that minority groups abide by laws intended to apply to all citizens equally, often in cases where basic rights are at stake. Permitting exemptions can give a kind of stamp of approval to the living of lives that are not fully respectful of liberal democratic values; the choice must therefore be carefully made and fair.

Notice that where such demands are made in the name of cultural preservation, and where they are accommodated, they lead to and sustain separation. In these cases, my view that multicultural claims ought to be accommodated where they support political inclusion does not seem to apply. On the contrary, at first glance, the political inclusion argument offers no reason to accommodate such demands. How then should we structure a fair response to these difficult cases, for example, where cultural groups request exemptions from mandatory education or modifications of child labor laws? A fair response must take into account that, although these so-called isolationist groups seek a substantial degree of separation, the separation is inevitably incomplete, in at least three ways. First, isolationist groups pay taxes and correspondingly take advantage of many of the services that taxes provide, including education, healthcare, and infrastructure. Second, there is inevitably movement of members of these groups into the larger society and movement into them from the larger society; some of this movement may even be partial, that is, some members of isolationist groups may wish to remain members while taking advantage of certain benefits or protections offered by the larger society. That some members prefer to remain inside of a culture; that others prefer to exit it entirely; and that others still prefer partial engagement with a minority culture and the larger community is consistent with the dynamic understanding of culture I outlined in chapter 2. Third, because ultimately these isolationist groups are embedded in the larger state, there are moments in which cooperation between them becomes essential.

In what follows, and again by considering a series of cases, I suggest that a focus on political inclusion can nevertheless guide multicultural states with respect to the fair treatment of these communities. In particular, I suggest that the objective must be to protect the terms under which trust can be sustained between these isolationist communities and the larger community. Because of the role trust plays in sustaining democratic practice, there are multiple reasons to protect the possibility of *trusting* engagement, in the present and into the future, between such communities and the larger community. Trust is central to the collaboration on which democracies rely, both between citizens and between citizens and their political representatives. The existence of stores of trust allows democratic legislators to make public policy choices, knowing that by and large citizens will comply with them without aggressive enforcement, and allows citizens to believe that as they comply, so will others.

Achieving and sustaining trust between these communities and the larger state requires striking a precarious balance, which is inevitably delicate. The fundamental principles governing isolationist communities and the larger state in which they are embedded are in unresolvable tension, as all the examples in what follows demonstrate, and compromises may require concessions on both sides. In particular, the compromises require that some exemptions are granted, so long as the exemptions are appropriately limited; both sides may have to concede something of importance and act accordingly.[1]

The compromise that I propose can serve to do something important: it can serve to keep dialogue open with these communities and thereby to protect as much as possible a basis for trust between them and the larger community. One might hope—though I myself do not—that such relations will ultimately forge a pathway forward for such communities to abandon their preservationist preferences and choose instead to integrate into the larger community. Rather, my view is that there are sufficient cases where members of such communities, either as individuals or as communities, must engage on the basis of trust with the larger community, that it is imperative that the larger community act to preserve these trust relations. The reason this job falls to the larger community has to do with its relative power in such cases: the communities I am considering are typically small and vulnerable to outside pressures, which they deliberately resist by living an insular life in the first place.

---

1. I owe this expression—the limits to exemption—to Alice Pinheiro Walla.

Exemption from Mandatory Education

One widely considered case in political theory is the case of the Amish, an orthodox religious community who live communally at the edges of American society, eschewing many aspects of modern life. In the early 1970s, the Amish requested an exemption from mandatory education laws that required students to be in school until they were 16 years old, asking that their children be permitted to leave school at 14. They believed that, absent this exemption, too many of their children would choose to leave the community, and their culture would thereby be threatened. (Burtt 1994). In 1972, the US Supreme Court permitted the exemption, which persists, citing a commitment to protecting their religious freedom (Callan 2006).

The stated objective on the Amish side is the preservation of their distinctive way of life, which they believe is mandated by God. Additionally, it is conventional to believe that parents may permissibly shape the environment in which their children are raised, so long as they do not thereby inflict major physical or emotional harm. But critics had suggested that the fact that children, educated to 16 years of age, were more likely to leave the community was a reason to refuse the exemption request: in virtue of their being citizens of a liberal democratic state, Amish children (just as are all children) are entitled to the education they need in order to make an autonomous choice (Arneson and Shapiro 1996). This felt imperative, to provide Amish children with a full basic education, stems from the view that, in democratic states, there are certain rights—and the right to education is one of these—to which all citizens are entitled and which the state must

protect (Gutmann 1987). For critics, if the result of protecting rights equally (in the domain of education access)
is that children choose to exit a community, so much the
worse for that community.

Much turns on whether depriving Amish children of
two years of education constitutes "major harm," but it is
valuable to notice that forcibly intervening in families to
enforce mandatory education (for example, by marching
children to school against their parents' wishes) is certainly
deeply harmful. Consider a separate request by Amish
families, who cited the cultural importance of work in
their communities, to permit children aged 14–17 to labor
in dangerous workspaces with their families. In response,
the American Fair Labor Standards Act was altered in the
early 2000s to permit this. Granting the education exemption may be uncomfortable for liberal democratic states,
for the way it concedes that some children will permissibly
be restricted from education that is believed to be valuable
(and indeed, a basic right). However, exemptions from safe
workspace requirements are less defensible, both for the
physical harm to which children are subject—in 2013, an
Amish teenager's arm was cut off in a workplace accident,
for example—and for the implausibility of requiring children to *work* in such dangerous spaces in the name of cultural preservation (Greenhouse 2003; KPC News 2013).

Since education (but not remedies to permanent physical injuries) can be pursued later in life, an appropriate
compromise may be one that trades reduced education
for Amish children for the collaboration to protect viable
rights to exit for Amish community members who, once
they reach adulthood, prefer to leave. This compromise is
not perfect, but it may be defensible. Here's what the exit

option might look like. In communities where property is owned in common, an exit fund can be made available so that potential exiters are not forced, if they exit, to leave penniless, but rather would have some at least minimal resources to survive in the larger community (Spinner-Halev 1999). As well, the dominant community must be prepared to welcome exiters with the resources they need in order to make the transition from living in these insular, religious communities to living in the wider community with the challenges this entails for those who are not familiar with its workings (Holzleithner 2012; Kukathas 2012, 1992). The latter demand, that the larger community focus on creating a space in which exiters can land, and find culturally sensitive support in their efforts to become self-sufficient members of the larger society, is required by a commitment to political inclusion. So, a commitment to political inclusion of exiters demands the protection of a viable right to exit as a condition of permitting exemptions from other democratic principles in some cases.[2]

As I indicated earlier, the reason to think seriously about a principled way in which to respond to isolationist groups is that, after all, the separation of these groups is not complete. There are inevitably cases where individual

---

2. I say in some cases on purpose. There will be some cases, like this one, where the balance of evidence suggests that liberal states ought to accept reduced rights protection for members of culturally isolated groups. However, this will not always be the case. In situations where violence and abuse of children or women are believed to be essential to preserving the community, the liberal state must step in to protect the abused. However, the choice to intervene to protect rights must always be done in a sensitive way.

members or families need to interact with services offered by the larger community, in which they are at substantial risk of having their cultural norms and values violated or undermined as a result of their individual vulnerability in those circumstances. I have in mind cases where individuals and families must exit their group to seek medical care or specialized educational support. Such interactions are filled with friction and, as a result, opportunities for undermining trust relations into the future.

For example, in the late 1990s, residents of the town of Kiryas Joel, an Orthodox Jewish community in Orange County, New York, faced the challenge of securing high-quality educational opportunities for its special needs children (Spinner-Halev 1999). Ordinarily, children in Kiryas Joel attend religious schools run internally, in consonance with the community's religious convictions, but they did not possess adequate resources to educate children with special needs. The community's leadership asked for state support, which was offered—the children were invited to attend secular schools and to be educated together with other special needs students, following a secular curriculum. Initially the community was satisfied with the solution, recognizing that they were relying on state support to offer education to their children. But, over time, it became clear that the secular school was largely unwilling to treat the religious convictions of the students respectfully. One student was apparently dressed as Rudolph for a Christmas pageant, and others were taken to McDonald's for lunch, in spite of their well-known dietary requirements. Ultimately, the children were withdrawn from the school. In this case the minority community was willing to compromise in order to secure a publicly provided basic right for its children, so long as the dominant community was willing to display some basic respect for their religious convictions, which it proved unwilling to do. An opportunity for inclusion was lost and, even worse, trust was thereby undermined.[3]

Exemption from the Majority Community Legal System

Some minority groups request exemptions from the majority community legal system, especially with respect to conflict resolution. These exemptions often pertain to family law, and less often to some elements of criminal law. Indigenous communities argue that the dominant criminal system is not only biased against them (and evidence suggests bias against Indigenous citizens in Canada and elsewhere is pervasive) but also fails to engage with Indigenous wrongdoers in culturally sensitive ways; Indigenous communities demand the right to punish Indigenous wrongdoers in ways that are culturally appropriate and thus, in their view, more likely to achieve the desired effect.[4] Similarly, Roma communities are often

3. This case was ultimately complicated and involved the creation of a separate school district, which allowed public funds to be diverted to schools reserved for members of Kiryas Joel—a choice which the US Supreme Court ultimately ruled unconstitutional. See Grumet and Caher 2016.
4. This statement is deliberately vague, since the precise goals in "punishing" wrongdoers are distinct in majority and many Indigenous communities, with a more substantial focus on seeking forgiveness and rehabilitation in the latter. See, for example, Melton 1995.

governed by informal systems of justice, which manifest in culturally specific ideas of punishment and rehabilitation (Caffrey and Mundy 1997).

The demand to regulate family life, that is, to be exempt from the laws that govern family life in the larger community, is controversial. Early in the political theoretic deliberations on the merits of multicultural rights, Susan Moller Okin wrote a provocatively titled essay asking whether "multiculturalism was bad for women" (Okin 1999; Shachar 1998). Listing the myriad ways in which cultural groups use their power to control the lives of women (and children) and to impose on them cultural demands that demonstrate and reinforce their inferiority, by permitting or encouraging the violations of their rights, Okin drew attention to the dire consequences of accommodating multiculturalism where doing so amounts to accepting the unequal, rights-violating treatment of women. She highlighted, as well, the ways in which "cultural norms and traditions" are often defined by men of power in such cultural groups, with the purpose of controlling women; these men assume leadership positions that are recognized as legitimate by the outside community, when in fact their views are not (necessarily) representative of the women and children who, Okin worried, suffer as a result.

In the Canadian province of Ontario, such worries came to light over the use of the 1991 Arbitration Act, an act that permitted organizations of various types to regulate their own conflicts, as a way to take pressure off an overburdened legal system. As part of the arbitration process, parties to a dispute were asked to agree on an arbitrator, whose decision would be binding so long as it was not in conflict with Canadian or Ontario law. Among those deploying the act to resolve family conflicts were originally Christian and Jewish groups, who selected arbitrators from among their religion's leadership. Attention was directed toward this usage in 2005, when a Muslim lawyer in Toronto publicly declared that a so-called Islamic Institute of Civil Justice would henceforth use the provisions of the Arbitration Act to resolve Islamic familial and other disputes as directed by the principles of sharia law. Although he had no authority with which to make or enforce this claim, he said publicly that Muslims would be required to submit to these Islamic arbitration panels to remedy private disputes, on pain of being labeled a bad Muslim. His public pronouncement raised worries that Muslim women would be forced by (male) religious leaders to succumb to religious arbitration founded on the worst (and most stereotypical) interpretations of sharia law (Korteweg 2008), which would most often resolve familial conflicts in ways that severely disadvantaged women.

In response, the Ontario attorney general and the minister responsible for women's issues asked for a systematic assessment of the use of arbitration in religious disputes in general (Boyd 2004). The resultant report advised that arbitration guided by Islamic legal principles was both legally permissible in Ontario and ought to continue, with the proviso that the province had "a society-wide obligation to ensure that women would be able to address unfair decisions in any type of arbitration" (Korteweg 2008, 436). The report suggested further the adoption of amendments to ensure "oversight and education on the principles of religious arbitration and

Canadian family law. . . . The education measures were to ensure that people would understand the legal ramifications of their decision to arbitrate, know their rights to appeal if they did not agree with the arbitral decision, and comprehend the relationship between religious law and Canadian law" (Korteweg 2008, 436–37; for a similar conclusion, see Eisenberg 2007).

Provincial leadership did not heed the recommendations of the report and instead amended the act to deny religious groups the right to access arbitration. But the recommendations demonstrated the possibility of reaching a compromise, suggesting that religious arbitration could proceed so long as the majority community's legal system retained jurisdiction to ensure that all rights were protected and any individual who accepted arbitration to resolve a dispute was adequately informed about the process and the rights she retained even as she participated in it.

In most liberal democratic communities, Muslim minorities are not "isolationist" cultural groups, of course. But the report on the Arbitration Act, even though it was spurred by an irrational fear of sharia law, signals that there are ways in which minority groups and the majority community in which they are embedded can reach an acceptable compromise. Such a compromise is respectful of the fact that although women are often disfavored in religious communities, they may prefer remaining *inside* the community to alternatives. It gives them resources with which to combat, if they desire, inegalitarian elements of their cultural communities (Deveaux 2006), even as they value their religious cultural context and desire to live in accordance with their edicts.

TRUST IN TIMES OF CRISIS

There is an important reason to approach exemption requests, where they are made to support cultural preservation for isolationist groups, with caution and care: it is crucial to sustain trust relations between them and the larger community so that, where needed, the communities can be relied upon to work together to combat a shared crisis. There are inevitably situations in which cooperation between the cultural group and the larger community is demanded, in ways that ask for sacrifices on both sides, in order to achieve a common objective. Such sacrifices are more likely to be accepted where trust relations have been preserved and protected over time.

The collective response to Covid-19 provides an example. In the fall of 2020, as the second wave of the virus washed over New York City, its government adopted emergency legislation to slow its spread, including limits on the size of gatherings. Yet, an ultra-Orthodox Jewish community in Brooklyn repeatedly held gatherings flouting these limits, including a 2,500-person gathering for a funeral for a rabbi, who himself had died of Covid-19; in gathering for the funeral, the leaders of the community cited the importance of traditional ways of responding to tragedy in the community. By the time the funeral took place, the police had already broken up a bat mitzvah and a yeshiva (Jewish day school), citing the dangers of spreading Covid-19. The mayor of New York City expressed extraordinary frustration in a variety of public media and allegedly instructed police to "proceed immediately to summons or even arrest those who gather in large groups" (Stack 2020). This aggressive response was met with anger inside the Orthodox

community, which cited its religious freedom as justification for flouting emergency orders.

In flouting the regulations adopted in New York City
to reduce Covid-19 transmission, the community threatened not only its own health, but also the health of all
those with whom members come into contact; for example,
many of its members interact with the wider community
for economic reasons. Correspondingly, New York City was
justified in refusing to authorize gathering exemptions, in
the name of protecting public health. Leaving aside a history of distrust between Orthodox Jewish communities
and the state government (for example, as demonstrated
in the breach of trust described in the earlier case I considered), in this particular instance there are suggestions that
attempts to engage the community in the collective fight
against Covid-19 transmission were not culturally sensitive. One report observed that although several Orthodox
communities speak only or predominantly Yiddish, as late
as September 2020, no Yiddish speakers were employed on
New York City's contact-tracing team. Then, having realized this challenge, the city opted to blast messages in
Yiddish throughout Orthodox Jewish communities, even
those where other languages (English, Russian, Hebrew)
were the dominant languages. There are signs that the city
is learning: "There are encouraging signs, like an internal
push for more testing in the community: fliers in Yiddish
went up in Brooklyn, alerting people to testing sites, and
rabbis issued warnings about the perils of large gatherings."
Yet, says one rabbi, after a meeting that had concluded with
a commitment to collaboration, the city nevertheless sent
emails that he described as "bullying," threatening to shut
down yeshivas, a threat that is particularly concerning

in communities where many homes do not have internet access (Bellafante 2020).

What this case demonstrates is that, where external circumstances require collaboration in order to combat a substantial threat, such collaboration may be more readily offered where efforts (by the larger community) are made to engage in a culturally sensitive, politically inclusive manner. Choosing to work with community leaders to emphasize the threats that are collectively faced, and having a conversation about ways that cultural events can be celebrated while also protecting the community itself from threats, will do more to preserve trust and encourage cooperation than will the use of force to threaten such cultural moments.

CONCLUSION

The multicultural edict to respect cultural claims so long as they are connected to a political inclusion objective does not stop, but rather shifts in form, when the challenge arises from a demand for cultural preservation in the form of isolationism rather than inclusion. In these cases, political inclusion requires attentiveness to the ways in which political relations can persist between minority cultural communities and the larger community, which is carried out by respecting the autonomy of cultural communities, ensuring the inclusion of individual members who wish to join the larger community fully or partially, and maintaining collaborative relations between the groups when they must interact. The demand for this way of proceeding stems largely from an incomplete separation between cultural communities and the larger community; the people who move between communities, and the fact of shared spaces and interactions and sometime even political (or health-related) objectives, produce the obligation to keep political inclusion options at the center of dealings between culturally isolationist groups and the larger multicultural state.

6

Shared Public Culture
in Diverse States

I ARGUED THAT DEMOCRATIC STATES are morally required
to accommodate many cultural claims in order to ensure
that the political voices of members of cultural minority
groups are genuinely heard. A commonly expressed worry,
however, is that an acknowledgment of such a wide range
of cultural claims only serves to emphasize how citizens
differ from each other rather than what they share in common. It therefore undermines the solidarity that is meant
to bind together members of a diverse democratic community. Similarly, many worry that if the importance of
respecting a wide range of cultural claims is acknowledged,
all projects that aim at building solidarity among citizens
are doomed because they problematically "homogenize"
the diversity represented by cultural groups. For those who
hold these views, not only does a robust multiculturalist
approach undermine solidarity, but any attempt to build
solidarity violates the commitments that multiculturalism
is supposed to hold. In this chapter, I agree that communal
solidarity is important to a well-functioning democracy
and that attempts to build solidarity both can and must
be sensitive to the cultural diversity that characterizes

Debating Multiculturalism. Peter Balint and Patti Tamara Lenard, Oxford University Press. © Oxford
University Press 2022. DOI: 10.1093/oso/9780197528372.003.0007

democratic states. I begin with a brief elaboration of the two worries I just mentioned and then offer an account of the content of a *shared public culture* which communities can build robust multicultural solidarity.

SOLIDARITY IN MULTICULTURAL STATES

Democracy requires substantial cooperation of its citizens. This point is important: a democracy can deliver many goods to its citizens because it can forgo aggressive enforcement of laws. It instead relies on citizens' more or less willing cooperation with a range of laws and policies, including income tax filings, payment of transit fares, compliance with road safety regulations, and so on. It is of course true that the cooperation on which democracies rely is, in some sense, enforced; that is, citizens can be and are penalized when they violate law. It is also true that, because democracies rely on the more or less voluntary compliance of citizens, they are at liberty to direct resources that would otherwise be spent on enforcing compliance toward providing a wide range of benefits (Lenard 2008). The space in which this is clearest is with respect to redistributive policies that ask that citizens pool resources to provide many important goods, including especially education and healthcare, in common to all citizens (Miller 1995). But, say some, the solidarity that is key to supporting a willingness to participate in redistributive schemes emerges from a belief, among citizens, that they share something important in common, and whatever this "something" is, it is undermined by robust multicultural policies that highlight what citizens do *not* share instead of what they do. This worry does not usually lead scholars to abandon multiculturalism entirely, but rather to argue in favor of prioritizing a shared national or public culture over multicultural demands for rights where they conflict.

The choice to prioritize nation-building efforts, however, encounters its own objections—usually citing historical nation-building efforts—that such efforts are inevitably problematic for the ways in which they force homogenization of values, norms, interests, and practices on a diverse population (Abizadeh 2002; 2004). Historically, such efforts were perhaps more aggressive than they are now—banning minority languages or denying full citizen rights to religious minorities—but these efforts remain morally problematic for forcing citizens to think and act in ways that are not necessarily consistent with their beliefs. The particular worry is that the values and beliefs that nation-building efforts impose on citizens stem from "ethnic" views of what a nation is and should be. An "ethnic" nation is one that is founded on a shared history that is characterized by common ancestry and religion, in ways that make it nearly impossible for newcomers to be accepted as full and equal members. For many of those who decry nation-building, any nation-building effort is inevitably ethnic in some form, however much it tries to deny it; even the nation-building efforts of supposedly secure and diverse states have ethnic overtones, for example, in the public displays of Christian religion around its major holidays.

The only acceptable option for these critics is a fully civic nation, one that demands of citizens *only* that they are committed to the sustaining of democratic institutions, the liberal principles that underpin them, and the decision-making taken therein (Yack 1996). The challenge this civic nationhood view faces, however, is commonly known in political theory as the "particularity" problem—it is widely believed that while citizens ought to be respectful of all democratic institutions certainly, they ought to be *particularly* respectful to the state in which they are members. This unassuming claim implies that some sort of explanation is needed for the source of this special respect that citizens do in fact show to the democratic states in which they are members, and civic nationhood does not provide that explanation. Whatever one believes explains people's deeper commitment to their own states than all others, and whatever the moral defense of that commitment, it ought to heed the worries expressed by those who accuse all nation-building projects of being ethnic at their core. It must avoid attempts to support and enforce a shared public culture that relies on ethnic, religious, or ancestral requirements that are impossible for newcomers to adopt, even if they wanted to do so.

So neither the ethnic nor the civic view of nations seems right. In what follows, I aim to give an account of a *shared public culture* that I believe can meet the challenge posed by the particularity problem without running afoul of the critique made by those who are critical of all forms of nationalism. Notice that I am moving away from the language of nationalism, which has too often distracted political theorists from the key questions, which are these: Are there any good reasons to believe that a robust and solidaristic democratic political community can be sustained among individuals who share *only* a commitment to liberal principles and democratic institutions? Or is it more plausible to believe that *something* must provide the foundation for solidarity among citizens? If the latter, is it possible to construct that "something" in a way that is consistent with ensuring that cultural claims are respected in a democratic state? I argue, yes, it is possible to construct a shared public culture that can support widespread solidarity *and* respect cultural claims in a democratic state.

Recall my invocation of John Rawls, who describes a society as one of "willing cooperation among equals." This *willing* cooperation is key. Of course, on scales as large as a society, incentive structures can be created to encourage cooperation, for example, by increasing the costs of refusing to cooperate or by decreasing the risks of doing so. Democracies increase the costs of refusing to cooperate, most commonly, by investing in enforcement and increasing the penalties of noncooperation; those who cooperate because they wish to avoid penalties are cooperators, but they are perhaps not *willing* cooperators. But here is my central contention: cooperation is more likely to be *willing* where citizens can trust that others, also, cooperate. Trust is an attitude toward others, a belief that they can be counted on in various ways to do what is expected of them; when we extend our trust to others, we are expecting them to reward our trust by acting as we expect or hope they will (Baier 1994). The better we know others, the easier it is to trust them (or not). In democratic states, however, the objective is not to attempt to recreate the trust that characterizes intimate relations; rather it is to construct the conditions that render trust among strangers more likely. To the extent that trust extends between citizens, and between citizens and their elected representatives, cooperation is more likely. It is more likely because the risks—of cooperating when others do not, and then of

suffering the consequences of being the lone "sucker"—
are decreased.

How so? Trust between people operates as a facilita-
tor of cooperation: cooperating to achieve a common goal,
especially where that cooperation requires accepting an
initial cost, is more likely to be willing where there is widespread trust (Gambetta 1988). Taking this conversation
out of the abstract, consider that redistributive social programs, including, for example, universal healthcare, child
tax benefits of various kinds, and income assistance for the
relatively less well off, rely on the willingness of citizens
to participate in them: the link is not straightforward, of
course, since there are penalties associated with refusing
to pay the taxes that are directed toward such programs.
But there is a good deal of social science evidence suggesting that where citizens have relatively *lower* levels of trust,
their willingness to participate in these kinds of cooperative programs is also lower. In those places, more people
support political parties and policies that reduce the obligations citizens have to contribute to these programs
(Lenard and Miller 2018).

What I have written is not determinative, certainly,
but I hope it is sufficient to indicate the plausibility of the
claim that *trust*, where present, facilitates the cooperation on which democracies rely. Trust in others lowers the
risk of cooperation, by giving would-be trusters information on which to base their choices to extend or withdraw
cooperation. Where does trust come from, though? Trust
has many sources in large, diverse, democratic communities: some people are more naturally trusting than others,
and some people are more resilient in the face of betrayed

trust. As well, social science evidence suggests that multiple factors influence whether someone is trusting: more educated people are more trusting, for example, as are those who are wealthier (Inglehart 1999). Members of minorities—cultural, ethnic, and racial—are often less trusting than members of the majority, explained in part by a history of marginalization and dispossession at the hands of the majority (Williams 1998; Krishnamurthy 2015; Patterson 1999).

In what follows, I suggest that in addition to these factors (and in some cases for the same general reasons as these factors), the presence of a shared public culture supports trust among a citizenry. A shared public culture is the set of norms, values, and practices that define a particular community. Recognition that different societies each have their own shared public culture answers the "particularity" challenge. While democratic societies share important features, including a commitment to protecting the equal basic rights of all citizens, they differ with respect to their defining norms, values, and practices, and these differences shape the ways in which in their state's democratic obligations are carried out. That is, it is meaningful to say that there is an "Australian" way or a "South African" way to do things, which makes sense to citizens given the norms, values, and practices that define these states. The widespread knowledge that there are shared norms, values, and practices reduces the *risk* of extending trust, and is thereby a source of trust in democratic societies (Festenstein 2005).

To repeat the challenge facing advocates of nation-building as a way to create solidarity, for a shared public culture to be genuinely *shared*, it must be accessible by all members of a state, including cultural minorities. A shared public culture is accessible if its central features can be adopted by cultural minorities *without* requiring them to sacrifice norms, values, and practices that are particular to their own culture. Here is an easy example: a shared public culture that borrows heavily from Christian religious commitments is not accessible in the right way, because it demands that non-Christian minorities give up something that they value in order to be included fully. Similarly, a public culture that appears to require, or assume, a shared ethnic background is not appropriately accessible. The key features of "ethnic" nations clearly do not meet the requirements set out here. In the face of this conclusion, however, it is crucial not to conclude that a fully civic nation is the only alternative. Rather, I shall suggest that there is a great deal of "cultural" content on which a shared public culture can, should, and in many cases does rely, in order to foster trust relations among all citizens, including cultural minorities (see also Gustavsson 2019; Nielsen 1996; Shulman 2002; Reeskens and Hooghe 2010). In what follows, I identify five content clusters that are available for creating or revising public cultures that aim to be accessible on fair terms among a diverse citizenry: note that public cultures are *actually existing*, and so what follows operates not only as an assessment of what content is permissible for public cultures, but also as a set of guidelines for public cultures that ought to be revised in the direction of greater inclusivity. Emphasizing and building these public cultures can support the trust that is key to sustaining robust cooperation in the presence of diversity.

THE COMPONENTS OF A SHARED PUBLIC CULTURE

I aim to describe clusters of *cultural* content, elements of which can permissibly be combined into a genuinely shareable public culture.[1]

Cultural *markers* make up the first cluster of permissible content. A cultural marker identifies a particular culture, in ways that can be trivial or significant. Anyone who has spent time in Australia's largest cities knows that every commercial space is home to what feels like an infinite number of cafes, so many that it feels impossible to outsiders that they can all find sufficient customers to stay afloat. The centrality of the cafe to at least urban Australians is well known. As well, most states have iconic artists, athletes, authors, animals, and even jokes, and these can be cultural markers. Wildfires are devastating communities around the world, and when they spread through Australia last year, key stories and images about the harm caused focused on wildlife, and especially the fate of koalas. The famous Canadian clothing company Roots chose the beaver, Canada's national animal, as its logo, to signal its identity; Canadians often report to each other the experience of explaining to Americans that certain famous actors or musicians that Americans claim as their own are, in fact, Canadian. A state's cultural markers can emerge via deliberate political processes (as, for example, is the selection of national animals) or organically (as artists or athletes come to be treated as representative), and they can last

---

1. This discussion is drawn from Lenard 2020; see also the discussions in Gustavsson and Miller 2020.

for decades or can be fleeting. Ultimately, what makes a marker a marker is that it is identifiable by a significant proportion of group members as theirs in some way.

Second, states are also often marked by *significant historical moments*, broadly understood. These are moments that can link members together, ranging from sports victories to entering and emerging from political crises to military successes and defeats. They can be recent or historical, and like markers they can be fleeting or enduring. The recent mosque shootings in New Zealand linked New Zealanders together in solidarity with the Muslims who had been victimized, which manifested in pride in the compassion and resoluteness of their political leader in that time of crisis. South Africa's emergence as a constitutional democracy founded on equality, from decades of apartheid, continues to define it, and the same is true of Rwanda's still rocky path toward reconciliation from a horrific genocidal war.

Third, *cultural norms and practices* shape the interaction between citizens in public spaces. All communities have "ways of being" in public space, including rules for queuing, or passing each other on the street, or whether jaywalking is accepted. In some, often Middle Eastern, spaces, job applicants show respect for potential employers by refusing to make eye contact; in North America, refusing to make eye contact is a sign of shiftiness, and looked down upon in job interviews as a sign that someone is not serious about the job or lacks self-confidence. Greetings are culturally specific as well. Leaving aside how Covid-19 has impacted human interaction, residents of many European countries greet friends and colleagues with kisses (sometimes two, sometimes three, on alternating cheeks); others greet with hugs, bows, or handshakes. Britons are often relatively reserved, whereas Italians are more effusive, in greetings and in general (hence the humor associated with which countries find "social distancing" guidelines associated with reducing Covid-19 transmission more or less difficult to accommodate).

Fourth, *modes of public and political interaction* can also mark distinct communities. The main modes of political engagement are often culturally specific: in some states, public protest is normal, while in others it is normal for collective action to take place in the form of letter-writing campaigns. Of course, much depends on what is perceived to be more likely to have the desired effect, but certain ways of interacting can become normalized over time as what "we" do when political engagement is called for. Formal political practice also has a cultural inflection. All democratic states protect the right to vote, but in some states it is normal that voting is compulsory, whereas in others compulsory voting would be rejected as a rights infringement. States differ moreover with respect to the acceptability of denying the right to vote to some citizens (felons, for example), whether election day should be a national holiday (or how many hours off citizens are entitled to in order to vote), or whether it is obvious or a source of contention that minorities are entitled to special representation in legislative spaces. These are all legal or political choices, of course, but the way in which they are normalized as part of a political conversation is culturally moderated. Additionally, a state's political conversation is often culturally inflected. The sometimes fraught relationship between francophone and anglophone communities underpins many political disputes in Canada; the appropriate place of Christian religious beliefs in politics (in the face of a supposed constitutional separation of religion and state) is a constant source of conversation in the United States; and the appropriate place of Britain in a united Europe, historically and presently, was central to the conversation around the desirability of "Brexit." These are all recurring and constant themes in their respective states.

Finally, states are often defined by *values that are culturally inflected*. While in the abstract, liberal democratic states are defined by a commitment to the same set of basic rights and liberties, states nevertheless make choices not only about which rights to prioritize when they come into conflict, but also the way in which these conflicts are manifest; these choices are infused with cultural specificity. For example, all democratic states recognize that freedom of speech or expression is fundamental to effective politics, but some states are more reluctant to restrict it than others. It is common in the United States to permit a wide range of speech acts that are criminalized elsewhere, for example, with respect to hate speech (heavily restricted in Canada) or Holocaust denial (illegal in Germany). Political scientists will recall a disciplinary specific brouhaha raised when the American Political Science Association announced its intention to hold its annual meeting in Toronto: some (self-conceived radical) political scientists objected, saying their freedom of expression would be limited by the choice to meet in speech-restricting Canada.

While values can be an inclusive component of a shared public culture, in practice, even liberal democratic values are frequently interpreted in exclusive ways. One might say, for example, that "secularism," or the separation of church and state, is a classic liberal democratic value. In principle, there is no reason to believe that a practicing Muslim cannot also endorse secularism as a political ideal, and yet in the French context the invocation of secularism, in particular in restricting certain practices in public spaces, is often interpreted as deliberately excluding Muslim citizens by targeting the practices that they hold dear. So, it is not sufficient to say that "liberal democratic" values, with their contextually specific interpretation, will be inclusive in ways that serve the building of a shared public culture. Context also matters.[2] With that warning in mind, in any given place, particular values from among those that define liberal democracies have special resonance for historically contingent, but nevertheless meaningful, reasons.

The purpose of articulating these five clusters is to signal that there is *ample* content from which to build a culturally specific "shared public culture" that is nevertheless fundamentally accessible to cultural minorities. States are not forced to choose between being an ethnic nation that is not appropriate for diverse states and being a civic nation that is devoid of defining particularities. Rather, there is a third option that may be formulated from the desiderata I have noted, which permits a culture to be inflected in ways that are contextually specific and meaningful to its members on that basis, without being oppressive to cultural minorities. The content fluctuates over time. Some of its individual components have "staying power," whereas others are fleeting. Moreover, its individual components

2. I owe this example to Alasia Nuti.

can be more meaningful to some than others, some components are more generalizable than others, and many will be the subject of ongoing contestation in the public space. Fundamentally, what makes any of the content just described meaningful is that it is recognized as such by members of a shared public culture, and this recognition can be grudging or enthusiastic.

HOW DOES A SHARED PUBLIC CULTURE FACILITATE POLITICAL INCLUSION?

Having described how a shared public culture is possible even in multicultural democracies, I turn now to the way in which it serves to respect and encourage the political inclusion of cultural minorities.

First let me respond to the objection that any attempt by the state to adopt and support development of a shared public culture is, ultimately, a "state sponsored project of cultural assimilation," which is coercively imposed on unwilling cultural minorities (Abizadeh 2002). If this critique is correctly directed even at what I have described as the permissible content of a shared public culture, then the project of creating and encouraging a genuinely inclusive shared identity will, obviously, have failed.

My response to the particularity objection previews my response to this objection: we must *fill in* the content of the shared public culture rather than reject state-specific content altogether. The critics are right to be skeptical of the content that nation-states have relied on historically to build and support solidarity, but they are wrong to conclude that the project is impossible and therefore ought to be abandoned. The five categories I have described, of accessible content on which public cultures can draw, provide a foundation for building solidarity without exclusion. A shared public culture that is built on this content is not neutral by any means; but it should be available and accessible to all members of a citizenry *without* requiring that they give up something of cultural import. It is neither appropriate nor desirable that the project of creating and enhancing a shared public culture be abandoned; a diverse and democratic citizenry will function better, in the sense of being better able to produce the goods that are supposed to come from democratic rule, if there is a foundation on which solidarity can be built. So, while I agree with the critics that a shared public culture, if it is genuinely not shareable, could only be imposed on cultural minorities in a coercive way, my objective has been to identify content that can be adopted by all members of diverse citizenry in noncoercive ways.

These comments raise another possible objection with which I would like to engage. This is the objection that, since many cultural minorities are immigrants to a state, the only way that they can adopt the content of a shared public culture is via coercive means—the coercion operates by signaling to newcomers that, if they reject the content, they will not be treated as full and equal members of the community. It is crucial to distinguish between forced assimilation—the requirement that cultural minorities give up all or much of what is culturally distinct about them in order to be treated as a member—and asking newcomers to learn about and, to the extent possible, adopt the distinctive shared public culture of their new home.

If states are defined by distinctive, accessible shared public cultures, then newcomers can permissibly be asked to learn this content and, to the extent possible, adopt it as their own (Carens 2005). As any newcomer knows, adopting local practices about punctuality, queuing, and traffic safety takes time, and is not always seamless, but this adaptation is expected as part of the migration process. Newcomers do some of their learning in informal spaces, among friends and family and as they interact in a range of social and economic spheres. As well, where a state takes the lead in *informing* newcomers of the cultural norms in a new space, for example, via citizenship guides, classes, and their connected tests, and explaining their origin, it is not a coercive one.

This example dates me, but when my American partner began to contemplate a move to Canada, I said to him, here is a key piece of information about Canadians: "All Canadians know that Paul Henderson scored the winning goal against the Soviet Union in the 1972 hockey Summit Series." He did not experience the learning of this piece of Canadian trivia as oppressive; he experienced it as quaint. The point is, it is wrong to assume that immigrants are coerced if they are asked to become informed in key ways about the country they have joined, and it is wrong to say that immigrant cultural minorities resent having to do so as a condition of their admission to full membership in a society. On the contrary, so long as the content of what newcomers must learn is not objectionable in the ways that ethnic content is, it can largely be absorbed by newcomers in nonproblematic ways (Kymlicka 1998).

A critic of my view might highlight that the hockey example is trivial (to which I would respond, yes, that is the point—the cultural content of one state appears trivial to outsiders, and that explains in part why it is not harmful to share with newcomers), but observe my outline of acceptable cultural content also gives space to shared values. A focus on shared *values* is problematic, a critic might think. This objection states that the focus on *values* is necessarily exclusionary, and no state ought to demand that newcomers pledge to adopt a new set of values. But this is a mistaken claim in the context of democratic states: democratic states are underpinned by a common set of values, which are defensible and just. It is reasonable to expect that newcomers to democratic states, who grew up in nondemocratic states, adopt democratic values upon migrating. Indeed, evidence suggests that newcomers from nondemocratic states have little trouble with this transition, and generally agree that democracy is the best form of government (Bilodeau 2014; White et al. 2008). Moreover, what I argued was not that a particular set of values is demanded by a shared public culture. Instead, I argued that the implementation of these values is subject to "cultural inflection"—the modes of political protest look different in France and the United States, for example, although both countries have strong traditions of protest—that is, they are interpreted differently across cultural contexts, informed by specific histories and current circumstances.

So, then, how can a shared public culture support political inclusion? The first way in which it does so is by securing inclusion for all members of a diverse citizenry, in ways that I have already described. It provides a foundation for the trust and solidarity that support democratic rule and, more importantly from an equality perspective, the willing cooperation of citizens in redistributive programs that protect equality of all citizens. The shared public culture does this work for all citizens, not just cultural minorities. Among some scholars of diversity, there is a reluctance to concede that the *sharing* of key traits can support trust relations. The reluctance is well founded, because, historically, traits that were said to be essential for communal trust were not accessible to newcomers, by being grounded in religion or ancestry, and the same kind of claims are still made by anti-immigrant political parties and their supporters. But, as I have suggested, even though some traits of a population are not shareable (and thereby exclude cultural minorities who cannot exhibit or adopt them), the sharing of traits in general can still serve to build trust relations in a diverse society. One can wish that majority communities were easily comfortable with differences however they manifest, and that they would thereby respond by extending trust to all newcomers with ease; but that is wishful and naive thinking, which ignores the reality that trust is more likely to be extended and more likely to be robust when it stems from a foundation of shared *something*. I have detailed the parameters of the content of a public culture than can be genuinely shared among citizens of a diverse citizenry and which will thereby reduce the barriers to extending trust among citizens, some of whom have unfamiliar (to the majority) cultural practices.

Now, the history of public cultures has been exclusionary, *and* there is ongoing evidence that although many democratic states are increasingly open to the diversity of norms and practices that travel with immigrants, they can and do remain stubbornly resistant to inclusion claims by cultural minorities (Eisenberg 2020a). It is therefore insufficient to merely declare my job is done, having outlined appropriate cultural content for the building and sustaining of a shared public culture. Public cultures are actually existing—we are not at liberty to build them from scratch—and in many cases continue to exclude cultural minorities, implicitly and explicitly. What can we do about that, to make it more likely that public cultures adapt into genuinely shareable public cultures over time?

Here is the complicating context: all present public cultures contain elements that do not meet the key requirement I have outlined, namely, that they are adoptable by cultural minorities without their giving up something of value to them. The persistence of Christianity's influence in the public culture of Western democratic states is a clear example, as newcomers arrive with commitments to other religions. Members who share a public culture come to be *aware* that a key component of that culture is exclusive in this way when cultural groups make this case. It is normal, and to be expected, that cultural minorities will encounter resistance to their claim that a particular feature or set of features excludes them.

A commitment to political inclusion however requires, for one thing, that all contributors to the shared public culture in democratic states—including citizens, political actors, media, civil society organizations, and so on—recognize the ongoing and dynamic nature of their shared public culture. No one segment of a democratic society "owns" the shared public culture, which is in some sense genuinely and simply "in the ether." As a result, demands for shifts in its content can be demanded from, and stem from, any one of these segments. A shared public culture naturally shifts in response to a range of factors, including newcomers and the practices and norms that travel with them, and these shifts over time should be expected rather than (necessarily) resisted. For another, a commitment to political inclusion requires that a type of deference be given to those who claim to be excluded by a particular marker or set of markers. This deference, I believe, should be in the form of a kind of informal veto given to minorities claiming that certain markers are exclusionary. By informal veto, I mean a commitment to listen to the excluded when they say they are, in fact, systematically excluded. Let me flesh out what this means, given that there is no one public space in which citizens determine once and for all the markers that come to be adopted as part of the state's public culture, and given that the emergence of a marker is often spontaneous and contextually specific. The content of a shared public culture is the subject of discussion in *public*, which is to say in political spaces certainly, but also in widely consumed media. To say, then, that there is a veto to be given to cultural minorities is not a formal claim, as much as it is a commitment to listen to their voices, as I described in chapter 2, in a genuine way when they are claiming exclusion from a particular marker (Chin 2019). I argued in chapter 3 that a demand for cultural accommodation was most likely to be justified where respecting it produces greater political inclusion. Where the demand is justified in terms of producing greater political inclusion, I argued, states have a duty to accommodate the claim.

Why should there be a commitment to deferring to a cultural minority? Why should cultural minorities be treated as having particular authority in disputes like this? For one thing, they are best placed to evaluate the costs of adopting a marker—that is, since I said earlier that the objective is to identify markers that do not require minorities to give up something of value in order to adopt it, where they claim that they would otherwise have to do so, the cost is too high. What if a cultural minority claims that a particular democratic value is too high a bar, for example, with respect to gender equality, and contend instead that women should be denied education, or required to marry at a young age? In that case, if the value that is contested is one that derives from core democratic commitments, the majority community may legitimately persist in insisting on its adoption—the core democratic commitments are about inclusion, so cannot be overridden even where they are contested. This acknowledgment *should* relieve critics who (erroneously) argue that certain immigrant groups are disdainful of democratic values—often, members of orthodox religions are accused of being insufficiently respectful of gender and sexuality equality in democratic states. But this is an exception to the general rule I am articulating here: where cultural markers are contested by minorities, which they can contest in both political and discursive spaces, their contestation ought to be treated as a presumptive reason to modify or abandon the questionable marker. In a multicultural state, cultural minorities are to be the judge of the adoptability of the marker, and of the costs of doing so, as much as possible.

Democracies need trust to survive, and to thrive, among their citizens and between citizens and their political representatives. While public cultures have historically been onerous for newcomers to adopt, multicultural democracies can reap the benefits of communal solidarity without the excluding cultural minorities, many of whom are immigrants. To do so, all segments of a shared society ought to strive to enhance and support the accessible portions of their culture while listening carefully to minority groups' statements of which parts are inaccessible. Stable, functioning, and *particular* multicultural democracies are the prize to be won.

CONCLUSION

In this final chapter, I have argued against the claim that a multicultural state must abandon efforts at shaping a cohesive and solidaristic public culture. Rather, the trust that a diverse democracy relies on to produce the democratic and redistributive goods its citizens expect is in substantial ways derived from a public culture that is shared. Trust and the cooperation it encourages are stronger when based on a robust foundation, which can be provided by a genuinely shared public culture. I argued against the claim that the only option in a diverse state is to assume that collaboration stems from shared commitment to abstract liberal democratic ideals and instead articulated some clusters of possible content that can be used to make up an accessible but still particular shared public culture.

In the real world, of course, no public culture consists of only acceptable content, and the content itself is contested. Where the contestation arises because cultural minorities object to specific markers, claiming that they are politically exclusive, they ought to be treated as having a presumptive veto power. This presumption, that cultural minorities can and do appropriately identify markers that are excusive, and that they must be *listened* to as a condition of full political inclusion, must guide attempts to resolve disputes over a public culture's content. It is my view that a shared public culture is consistent with robust multiculturalism in a democratic and diverse state so long as efforts are persistently made to ensure that the components of a public culture are acceptable—especially efforts made by cultural minorities to shape it in the direction of inclusivity.

This chapter concludes my positive argument in favor of a maximalist understanding of the requirement that states accommodate claims of culture. In chapter 2, I offered an account of culture and the multiple rights that are claimed in its name. In chapter 3, I argued that although there are many possible defenses of multicultural accommodation claims, the best defense of such claims rests on the importance of political inclusion, understood in terms of providing a context in which all citizens, including cultural minorities, can make their voices *heard*, that is to say, expect not only to speak but also to be listened to respectfully by co-citizens. In chapter 4, I tackled the most controversial of multicultural claims, that is, those that appear to support separation rather than integration, and argued that for the most part even these claims can be defended from a political inclusion perspective. In chapter 5, I considered cultural preservationist claims that ask for separation explicitly. I argued that although the claims themselves are not justifiable with respect to their contribution to political inclusion, a genuinely multicultural state must consider these claims from the perspective of inclusion nevertheless. Accommodating certain cultural rights may leave open avenues for inclusion for individual members who may wish to exit these communities, and can foster trust relations between communities, to ensure that collaboration between them can be relied upon in cases of emergency. So, even in these cases, I argued, attention to political inclusion guides us toward an attitude of accommodation, even of cultural preservationist claims that press for support for separation. Finally, I suggested in this concluding chapter that, even in the context of a state that affirms its duty to respect cultural claims, it remains important to think seriously about what its *glue* is, and so I argued that the promotion and protection of a shared public culture can be justified. But, I said, the content that is adopted to construct and sustain this shared public culture must be genuinely accessible, and so I delineated five clusters of possible cultural content from which such an accessible shared public culture can be built.

Part II

AGAINST MULTICULTURAL

MINORITY RIGHTS

Part II

AGAINST MULTICULTURAL MINORITY RIGHTS

7

Introduction to Part II

LET ME START WITH WHAT may seem like a deflationary claim: minorities should not be treated differently to majorities. Neither minorities nor majorities should receive special treatment. Those who wish to argue against multiculturalism and minority rights because of the importance of majorities will likely not be satisfied with this egalitarian claim. But mine is a liberal argument, in which the claims of any individual to follow their unique ways of life are as important as those of any other member of the polity. No one has an obvious claim to special treatment. In fact, the special treatment of minorities that multiculturalists argue for is only justified because of the special treatment of majorities. That is, if majorities did not enjoy a relative advantage over minorities, then the special treatment, in this case minority rights, would not be justified. In fact, this is my main argument: *remove majority privilege and thereby avoid the need for minority rights.*

By "majorities" I don't necessarily mean in a numerical sense, but those who belong to the dominant groups in a society. So a "majority" might include the English-speaking Anglo-Saxons in the United Kingdom, who are a numerical and cultural majority, or under apartheid, the white population of South Africa, who were not a numerical majority

Debating Multiculturalism. Peter Balint and Patti Tamara Lenard, Oxford University Press. © Oxford University Press 2022. DOI: 10.1093/oso/9780197528372.003.0008

but shaped institutions to their advantage. It is when a set of institutions (courts, schools, hospitals, dress codes, safety regulations, etc.) favor the majority way of life that we start to see claims to help minority ways of life. Classic examples in the multiculturalism literature include turban-wearing Sikhs seeking exemptions from compulsory construction site and motorcycle helmet laws, or Jews and Muslims seeking exemptions from humane animals-slaughtering laws. In these cases there is a set of institutions that favor the majority, and minorities seeking their own alternatives. There are many possible cases here, covering issues as diverse as clothing, language, noise, opening hours, and so on. What is similar, though, in these cases is that there is a certain dominant way of doing things that does not easily accommodate those who do things differently. The "certain way of doing things" in these cases almost always favors a majority. So wearing a helmet at work, while perhaps annoying at times, is easier for non-Sikhs than male Sikhs. Or having your meat slaughtered a particular way is usually not of major consequence to those who are not Orthodox Jews and Muslims, who want their food to be kosher or halal. Claims for minority rights almost always arise because of an institutional background that favors majorities. If the institutional background made it equally easy for minorities and majorities to perform particular things, no claim for minority rights would arise—or at least no claim that would be entertained as legitimate.

As my title suggests, I want to argue against multicultural minority rights. This gives me three options. My first option is that I could argue that multicultural minority rights are *trivial*, that polities have a "certain way of doing things around here" that all citizens need to conform to.

Perhaps I could add that not being able to work in the construction industry or ride a motorbike—as is the case for
turban-wearing Sikhs—because of one's convictions is a
choice: there are plenty of other jobs and modes of trans-
port to choose from (Barry 2001). We all make choices in
life based on our convictions and desires. This naturally
rules some activities in, and some out. My fear of heights
may rule me out of being a being a roped-up high access
window cleaner, but it seems unreasonable that I demand
scaffolding be put up on all buildings so I can still clean
office windows and mitigate this fear. Similarly, I may wish
to follow my dream and open a cafe, but my hatred of early
morning starts means that I won't. In this sense, it seems
entirely reasonable, to use Peter Jones's term (Jones 1994),
that I bear the consequences of my belief and desires, even
when I may have little or no control over these beliefs and
desires. On this line of argument, minority ways of life
are harder (at least in some aspects), but everyone's life is
constrained by their beliefs and desires and it is hard to
see why or how the world should or could be changed to
accommodate our varying beliefs and desires. The majority
have laid down a "certain way of doing things around here,"
and as long as they have not explicitly or prohibitively discriminated against minorities, then minorities, while having some of their beliefs and desires thwarted, will still be
able practice their unique ways of life.

Now while I think it is true that people should bear
the consequence of their beliefs and desires, and so I do
not think scaffolding should be put on all buildings or my
cafe subsidized to avoid early starts, I don't take this line
of argument. This is because something, at least initially,
seems unfair when sets of beliefs with similar weight and

importance are treated differently. Of course, a "certain way of doing things around here" will be almost unavoidable, but why should this be the result of majority beliefs and desires? If there is some independent justification— such as the high cost of doing things differently, or the efficiency of the current arrangement—then perhaps those with divergent ways of life will just have to put up with it. But without a sufficiently weighty independent justification, then we are just privileging the majority and their beliefs and desires.

This leads to the second possible argument I could take, which is that the majority has a *right* to protect its way of life in a polity, even when this proves very restrictive for minority ways of life (Koopmans 2018). Why shouldn't the result of democratic decision-making or shared cultural history determine the institutions and practices of a polity? People have spent generations shaping their institutions, and these are supported by a majority of citizens. On the previous argument in the turban/construction site example, there were certainly other occupations available. On this line of argument such a consideration is irrelevant. If the majority, or their representatives, decide on a course of action, it is fine to enforce it on minority ways of life. Here, for example, it is entirely legitimate to ban burkas in public, as at least 15 countries have done (including France, Austria, Denmark, Belgium, the Netherlands, Tajikistan, Latvia, Bulgaria, Cameroon, Chad, the Republic of the Congo, Gabon, Morocco, Sri Lanka, and China). Going out in public is a pretty basic part of a human life, so there are not really other viable options for those who want to wear face coverings in public. It is not like the turban/construction site example, which simply limits which activities you can do. This need not be racist, even if some of the real-life cases may well be. The rule is not "no Black people" or "no Muslims" in public, just "no face coverings." Yes, it suits the majority citizens, but it does not fully exclude others, it just asks them to assimilate. We see similar reasoning behind Québec's Bill 62, passed in 2017, which bans a person whose face is covered from delivering or receiving a public service. I don't take this line of argument because, at least from a liberal perspective, there needs to be limits on majority decision-making and the role of tradition. While these are undoubtedly important, liberals are resistant to the pressures of conformity, especially when it is coerced. Instead, they preach toleration of divergent ways of life rather than banning them. That is, just because something is distasteful, objectionable, or even potentially harmful to its participants, this does not mean it should be outlawed. For toleration to be a meaningful practice, the majority need to put up with practices they may not like.

If I don't argue for majority rights or that nobody has a right to have every option open to them, what do I argue? Let me outline the third possible argument against multicultural minority rights, and this is the one I will take. Like the minority rights theorists, I take seriously the claims of those who want to do things that background institutions make difficult to achieve. There is something wrong when minorities have a relative disadvantage that makes their ways of life harder to practice than those of the majority of citizenry. But instead of arguing for minority rights to counter their relative disadvantage, I argue that their relative disadvantage is removed when institutions reduce the privileging given to majorities. That is, if the issue is relative disadvantage, then remove the advantage given to majorities. In other words, I argue for *neutral institutions which provide no significant advantage to either majority or minority*. As I will show, *this position has significant benefits over the alternative of multicultural minority rights*. It avoids the problems that have plagued minority rights, such as reification, misrecognition, and entrenching power inequalities within minority groups, all while not only addressing the valid concerns of those who have rightfully focused on minority accommodation, but also providing more freedom for all of us.

In my part of this book, I am deliberately ambivalent on what culture, and thus what "multicultural" means. I simply assume that *we are all different*, and that the things some of us want to do or be will be significantly different from the way the majority of people in a polity will do them. These differences might be because of religion, cultural background, identity, or other related reasons. I take this to be the issue at the core of multiculturalism: the fact that some ways of life experience a *relative institutional disadvantage*. The question is what to do about it.

The relative institutional disadvantage that is of most concern is public, and involves institutions like courts, schools, military, government departments, police, government services, and so on. There is, of course, disagreement on where the public/private distinction should be drawn, with some pushing for all forms of social life to be considered public, and others insisting on a distinct private sphere. This disagreement over what is public and what is private plays out in the multiculturalism debate too. Those with a more expansive view of what is public see multiculturalism as not only an issue for what have traditionally been considered public areas (courts, schools, etc.), but also for private business, civil society organizations, and sometimes even personal interactions as well. My discussion of relative institutional disadvantage will mainly focus on the narrower understanding of "public" (courts, schools, military, government departments, police, government services, and so on), but it is fully applicable to a wider understanding if the reader desires. (I discuss intercitizen relations in chapter 11.)

I will use the shorthand *ways of life* to describe differences, which will include beliefs, desires, practices, history, and identity, that put some people at a relative institutional disadvantage. So when I talk of *multicultural minority rights*, I am talking about the differentiated rights given to some minority ways of life in order to counter their relative institutional disadvantage. There will be other contexts for minority rights (and I discuss these in chapter 10), but my focus is on the case for minority rights when ways of life experience relative institutional disadvantage, in other words, "multicultural minority rights."

Within this multicultural context, I argue both for liberal neutrality in general, and for a particular form of it I call *active indifference*. This is where neutral institutions are not just "set and forget," but actively try to remove majority advantage in order to be equally accommodating to as wide a range of ways of life as possible. Outside of the multicultural context—such as in the case of Indigenous people—I argue that active indifference may still play a role, but other justifications, such as sovereignty and historic injustice, provide a very different context.

My argument proceeds as follows. In chapter 8, I explain what I mean by *neutral institutions*, and in the process explain the importance *of neutrality of justification* and *neutrality of intent.* Both forms of neutrality are required in order to achieve minority accommodation and address the relative institutional disadvantage commonly faced by minorities. But as I show, multicultural minority rights theorists also subscribe to these forms of neutrality—even if they don't say so.

Chapter 9 provides my main argument against multicultural minority rights. I introduce a narrower understanding of neutrality than chapter 8, which I call *active indifference.* This separates me clearly from multicultural minority rights theorists. Like multicultural minority rights, this form of neutrality is also active in recognizing and responding to the relative institutional disadvantage of minorities, but responds by *removing majority privilege rather than adding minority privilege* in the form of multicultural minority rights. As I argue, active indifference not only avoids the problems of multicultural minority rights—problems such as reification and essentialism that are acknowledged by the advocates of multicultural minority rights—but has the added advantages of offering more freedom, in terms of both fewer restrictions and more opportunities.

Chapter 10 looks at the issue of *national minorities* such as Indigenous peoples. While I have argued against *multicultural* minority rights, I have not said anything about national minorities. In this chapter, I show that while there is significant overlap between multicultural minority rights and the rights of national minorities, these issues are distinct. This is mainly because national minorities usually have additional grounds for claiming rights, commonly in the form of issues of sovereignty, historical injustice, and a desire for political autonomy. Where there is relative institutional disadvantage, active indifference may still play a role, but because there are additional—nonmulticultural—grounds for differentiated rights, they may still be granted. But crucially, just because they *may* be granted in some cases for national minorities does not justify their need in the case of multicultural minorities.

Chapter 11 takes a slightly broader look at the issues of multiculturalism, and in the process moves beyond institutions. This chapter looks at the role of citizens in accommodating minorities. I examine two different multicultural virtues: respect and appreciation of difference and tolerance of difference. I argue that, perhaps ironically, respect and appreciation of difference are not as accommodating of minority ways of life as tolerance of difference, and nor are they as neutral toward the different ways of life that exist in contemporary diverse societies.

8

We Are All Neutralists Now!

NATHAN GLAZER ONCE FAMOUSLY DECLARED that "we are all multiculturalists now," with the implication that the debate is now about what type of multiculturalism is applicable in which contexts, rather than whether multiculturalism was applicable at all (Glazer 1998). In this chapter, I hope to show that, at least for those concerned for minority accommodation, we are all neutralists now, with the real debate being about what type of neutrality and in what contexts. By this I mean, perhaps ironically, that those who advocate for multicultural minority rights are actually in favor of neutral institutions—as they should be. Neutral institutions are the fairest way of accommodating minority ways of life. Of course, how we think neutral institutions should operate is a matter for debate—a debate I take up in the next chapter. Here I simply want to explain what neutral institutions are, and why all of us who are concerned for minority accommodation actually support them—despite protestations to the contrary.

As Lenard and I noted in our introduction, one of the dominant political arguments against multiculturalism has been a majority rights view. But the main position multicultural theorists themselves were, at least originally, arguing against was some sort of liberal neutralism. That

Debating Multiculturalism. Peter Balint and Patti Tamara Lenard, Oxford University Press. © Oxford University Press 2022. DOI: 10.1093/oso/9780197528372.003.0009

is, they rejected the idea that the state's institutions provided a neutral, or at least fair, background for differing cultural backgrounds.

Charles Taylor, whose theory of identity recognition was crucial for minority rights, writes that "the ideal of 'benign neglect' is a myth. Government decisions on languages, internal boundaries, public holidays, and state symbols unavoidably involve recognizing, accommodating, and supporting the needs and identities of particular ethnic and national groups. Nor is there any reason to regret this fact. . . . The only question is how to ensure these unavoidable forms of support for particular ethnic and national groups are provided fairly—that is, how to ensure that they do not privilege some groups and disadvantage others" (Taylor 1994, 43).

Will Kymlicka, whose work "liberalized" minority rights, writes, "The supposedly neutral set of difference-blind principles of the politics of equal dignity is in fact a reflection of one hegemonic culture. As it turns out, then, only the minority or suppressed cultures are being forced to take alien form. Consequently, the supposedly fair and difference-blind society is not only inhuman (because suppressing identities) but also, in a subtle and unconscious way, itself highly discriminatory" (Kymlicka 1989a, 115).

And finally, Tariq Modood, whose sociological approach to minority rights has been dominant in the United Kingdom, writes that "multiculturalism is clearly beyond toleration and state neutrality for it involves active support for cultural difference, active discouragement against hostility and disapproval and the remaking of the public sphere in order to fully include marginalised identities" (2007, 64).

This argument against the possibility of neutral institutions and practices accommodating minority ways of life was the starting point for multicultural minority rights in political theory. But, as I will argue, granting minority rights as way of countering relative institutional disadvantage is actually to be guided by neutrality. And claiming that institutions unfairly favor the majority is using the critical power of neutrality to challenge these institutions. So multicultural minority rights are not anti liberal neutrality, but are guided by the ideal of neutrality. Later on I will argue that multicultural minority rights are not the best form of neutrality, and that we should instead just remove relative majority privilege, but here I want to show this important point of often unnoticed agreement between those arguing for and against minority rights.

NEUTRAL INSTITUTIONS

The basic idea of neutrality is to show no relative favor or disfavor to the things being treated neutrally. This means that neutral institutions should not favor any particular way of life; neither majority nor minority. So a state could be neutral to people's religions by either supporting no religion, or supporting all religions equally. In either case, there would be no relative favor or disfavor toward people's religions. Or to use another example, a sports-funding body would not be neutral toward people's sporting interests if it just focused on the most popular sports, rather than on all sports. Once again, neutrality requires showing no relative favor or disfavor to the things being treated neutrally.

The reason neutrality matters in a liberal polity is that it is a way of treating each of us and our different interests and ways of life equally and fairly. By showing neutrality toward people's ways of life means that no one's particular way life is seen as more important than anybody else's way of life. It is not that neutrality in itself matters, but neutrality is a way of treating all of us equally and fairly—it gives all of us an equal opportunity to live our lives as we see fit. Liberals disagree deeply on what equality of opportunity entails. But whether one thinks it involves constant government interference and redistribution, or that it simply involves a removal of pertinent obstacles, neutrality will help realize this important value. In sum: neutral institutions show no relative favor to our different ways of life, and this matters because it treats all of us equally and fairly.

While this is the ideal of neutrality and its value, there is nevertheless considerable skepticism toward neutrality. A common reaction is something like "Well, that's all well and good, but all institutions show *some* relative favor— none of them show *no* favor. Surely there is no such thing as complete neutrality!" This is absolutely right. Neutral judges favor the law, neutral umpires favor the rules, and neutral countries (in international relations) favor themselves. But this is just a fact about neutrality. It is always relative to a particular range of things. The judge is neutral among the parties before her, the umpire between the sporting teams, and the country between warring powers. The same is true of institutions; they will also only be neutral among a specific range. In other words, neutrality is a range-concept. That is, there is always a specific range that an agent (such as a state) is neutral between. There will always be things outside of this range. In liberal states, this range of neutrality is, at minimum, ways of life that are consistent with justice. No liberal state will (or should) be neutral toward ways of life that seek to harm others (Cohen 2014). For example, the liberal state will not be neutral toward extremist groups and those who want to undertake "honor" killings (Ercan 2015). Liberal states, at minimum, uphold justice, and so will certainly not be neutral on this. The widest possible range of neutrality in a liberal state will include all justice-respecting ways of life. If a way of life is *not* justice-respecting, liberal states will not be neutral toward it. This discussion of range is important. Not only does it show that we need to specify the particular range an agent is neutral among, but it deflates the common criticism of neutrality: that there is no such thing as complete neutrality. This criticism is true but only trivially so. No state can or will be neutral about absolutely everything. To use this as a criticism misunderstands the concept of neutrality.

There is a second sense in which there commonly is skepticism toward neutrality. The range point above might be accepted—that neutrality is never absolute, but relative to a particular range—but it still might be argued that no real-world actor is ever really neutral even in this way. That is, they either just pay lip service to it, or their own bias means it is just not possible. Once again, this is true, but it is also not a strong criticism. Neutrality is a political ideal. Like justice, equality, democracy, freedom, and so on, it is an action-guiding ideal. This means that, assuming it is the right ideal (and I think that it is), it is something we aim for. But being an ideal, it is something that will never be perfectly achieved in real-world cases—especially complex

ones where the range involves more than just two competing sporting teams. All ideals are like this—they tell
us where to aim and guide our actions. But either because
they must be balanced with other ideals and concerns, or
because the real world is not the ideal world, we never perfectly achieve them. Take democracy: no actual democracy
is perfectly democratic according to any of the ideal conceptions. But that doesn't mean our ideal conceptions are
wrong or even flawed. This just means that our conceptions
of democracy are ideals. Neutrality will be no different.

MINORITY ACCOMMODATION

I need to be more specific about what I mean by "neutral
institutions." We can distinguish between two different
understandings of neutrality in this context: *neutrality of
justification* and *neutrality of intent*.[1] Both of them will be
necessary if the aim is to achieve minority accommodation
in diverse societies.

---

1. There are other possibilities—and labels—for types of neutrality, but these two are sufficient for the point I want to
   make here. For other views, see De Marneffe 1990; Kymlicka
   1989a; Patten 2014; Arneson 2003, 193. Neutrality of outcome is commonly added to the list—this is the idea that no
   matter what our ways of life and our choices, we should all
   be able to live them equally. I haven't included this here as it
   seems too strong an ideal for any liberal approach to these
   issues—and almost no authors take it seriously, merely
   mentioning it before dismissing it.

Neutrality of Justification

If institutions are neutrally justified, they are not justified by the rightness of any particular way of life. A paradigmatic example of a nonneutral justification would be a state church that exists because it is believed to be the correct understanding of God. Theocracies, such as the one in Iran, are not neutral in this way. Their institutions are not justified neutrally, and their existence is justified via a particular way of life. John Rawls's "political liberalism" is probably the best-known example of neutrality of justification (Rawls 2005). Here Rawls argues for the importance of an institutional structure that uses no particular way of life to justify its rightness. Rawls wants an institutional structure that is neutral to all reasonable conceptions of the good. In his "political liberalism," the principles of justice that regulate a polity must be consistent with public reason, which is the form of reason that is not particular to any one conception of the good, and can reasonably be shared by all citizens.

Justificatory neutrality (although not always of the Rawlsian variety) is not really questioned by multiculturalists. In fact, most liberals hold that institutions should not be justified by the rightness of any particular way of life, but only by more general principles, of which the most well-known are principles of justice (Clarke 2014). There is, of course, plenty of debate about exactly what these principles should be, and so there is disagreement about the content of justificatory neutrality. But a great deal is agreed upon, such as that using religious justifications, for example, is not neutral in this way. So, once again, neutralist liberals are not neutral about everything. Justice is something they will not be neutral about, but they will be neutral among all ways of life that are justice-respecting (ways of life that do not undermine, threaten, or contradict justice).[2]

Neutrality of justification should be accommodating of minority ways of life. When an institution is justified by a majority way of life—such as a dominant religion—it

---

2. Not all liberals consider themselves neutralist in this way. There are other liberals, "perfectionists," who think it is okay to promote some ways of life—usually those that encourage autonomy. These are ways of life that encourage and allow critical reflection and do not close off future options for their adherents. That is, they think it is okay to justify institutions (and their practices) through the *rightness* of autonomy. But even these "nonneutral" liberals don't think using the rightness of *any* particular way of life to justify institutions is fine. Only certain nonneutral values can be used for justification. Perfectionists simply think that promoting autonomy (encouraging thoughtful choices and having things to choose from) is legitimate. People can choose all sorts of things that are consistent with autonomy, and the perfectionist liberal is (or should be) entirely neutral among these many choices—whether it be studying at university, doing stunts in movies, or joining the priesthood. In this sense, there is still actually neutrality of justification, it is just in a narrower range. Because there is no such thing as an entirely neutral justification (cf. Larmore 1987, 53–55), debates over neutrality/perfectionism are always about how wide the range of neutrality should be (Wall 2010). Or to put this another way, the debate is about which justifications are legitimate, and which are not. "Neutralist" liberals' simply have a smaller number of legitimate justifications, and thus a wider range of neutrality, while perfectionists have more legitimate justifications and a narrower range of neutrality.

will almost certainly favor those of this majority, and likely disfavor minorities. So if one cares about minority accommodation, one should certainly care about neutrality of justification.

In a liberal polity, it is not that common for an institution to be explicitly justified through the rightness of religion, or something equally strong. But there are plenty of cases where assumptions about what is a good life justify institutions. In many cases, it may be that the assumptions that favor the majority may not be reflected upon. A policy on uniforms might, for example, be about "looking smart," where "smart" is clearly tied to an aesthetic that suits the majority. Many minority rights activists spend their energy showing that important institutions have the rightness of the majority way of life built into their practice, and in a way that is often unreflected upon. It is this bias that needs correcting, and a properly neutral justification, and likely changed practices, put in its place. Here, for example, there might be a realization that there is more than one way to look "smart"; new uniform options might be introduced and/or exemptions for members of certain cultures to modify their uniform.

My point here is that neutral justifications matter for minority accommodation (Zellentin 2012). And it is not just that we need to worry about explicitly nonneutral justifications such as religion, but also more subtle ones that perpetuate outdated social and cultural norms. These more subtle nonneutral justifications may take some more digging to expose, and may not be consciously enforced by those in charge of our institutions. But nonneutral justifications stifle minority accommodation and need to addressed.

When fully realized, justificatory neutrality may seem very accommodating of minority ways of life. A preference for a majority way of life cannot be used to justify an institution, and so minority ways of life cannot be disadvantaged in this way. As important as a neutral justification is, it may still lead to significant burdens for minority ways of life.

Here we can look at France's 2010 "burka ban." This is a law that "no one in the public area may wear an outfit designed to conceal his or her face." Note that this law is entirely phrased in neutral language and avoids discussing either religion or the superiority of any way of life (Brown 2020). Likewise, the 2013 proposed law in Québec to prohibit public sector employees from wearing conspicuous religious symbols targeted Muslim headscarves and Sikh turbans, while allowing smaller Christian crosses. This, too, was given an entirely neutral justification that it would foster public confidence in these employees and show the state and its agents as being neutral (Brown 2020). Similarly, the 2009 Italian defense before the European Court of Human Rights of the requirement to have crucifixes in all state schools also attempted a neutral justification. Crucifixes were argued to represent "principles that could be shared outside of Christian faith" (Pierik 2012). Likewise, in 2000 Christiane Ebrahimian lost her job in a French public hospital because she refused to remove her headscarf at work, a decision upheld by the courts as it was "necessary to preserve the principles of the secularism and neutrality of public services" (Gentile 2020).

For a more historical example, we can look at Jean-Jacques Rousseau in *The Social Contract*, who ends up arguing for a civil religion, not from any particular theological position, but because such a religion would bind people together and align their interests in the right sort of way to allow the freedom that democracy provides (Rousseau 1762/1998). This type of state religion also has a neutral justification. In all these cases, neutral justifications—whether genuine or not—impede minority accommodation. In other words, a neutral justification—while important—will not always lead to the accommodation of minority ways of life, and may even be directly opposed to them. If we are concerned with the accommodation of minority ways of life, neutrality of justification will not be sufficient, even if it is necessary. We need more than neutral justifications if we want minority accommodation.

There are two ways of dealing with the problem that apparently neutral justifications may inhibit minority accommodation (and both will be required).

First, we need to *look at what a neutral justification actually implies*. In many cases, a neutral justification can lead to more than one way of doing things. Just because something is justified neutrally does not mean it is the only possible action that could be justified this way.

In the case of crucifixes in Italian schools, the Italian defense argued that it is important to have symbols of the shared principles of "non-violence, the equal dignity of all human beings, justice and sharing, the primacy of the individual over the group and the importance of freedom of choice, the separation of politics from religion, and love of one's neighbour extending to forgiveness of one's enemies" (*Lautsi v. Italy* 2009, cited in Pierik 2012, 23), If, for a moment, we accept that this argument is sincere, it still seems possible to either have other much less loaded

symbols of these shared principles than Catholic crucifixes, or to include a range of symbols from other religions
as well.

In the example of Rousseau and the civil religion, we
might ask, what form does the religion actually need to
take to achieve its goal? Perhaps it is very strict and inconsistent with all other religions. Or perhaps it is very open
and consistent with all other religions. Here John Locke's
seventeenth-century support of attempts to reform the
Church of England prove instructive. Locke supported
those arguing for "comprehension," that is, broadening the
church and making the rituals of the church as minimal
and accommodating as possible so that many more people
could conform (Kaplan 2007, 132–33). This was toleration
as "comprehension." Toleration as "indulgence" was for
those few who could not still conform (Cranston 1987,
111–12). Thus Locke accepted the need for a civil religion,
but thought it should be done in a way which was effectively
neutral to most Protestants (he famously was certainly not
neutral to atheists and Catholics—[Locke 1689]). To make
this point more generally, it is one thing to have a civil religion, but it can take different forms, some of which may be
very accommodating of diversity, and some which may not
be. It might also be possible to have more than one civil religion, or at least grant special status to minority religions.
This would be a form of minority rights. Indeed, as a form
of toleration, granting special status to minority religions
would resemble the Ottoman millet system, where minority religions were granted substantial autonomy over their
own affairs despite Islam being the religion of the empire
(Nimni 2007).

Just because an institution's shape is neutrally justified does not mean it is the only form that the institution can take and still meet this neutral justification. Of course, taking a form that disadvantages particular minorities may well be intentional—and this seems a fair reading of the 2013 Québec law and the 2010 French "burka ban," among others. This leads to the necessity of a second form of neutrality: neutrality of intent.

Neutrality of Intent

Here the intent of the institution is what matters; *there should be no intention of favoring one way of life over others.* For minority accommodation to be achieved, institutions should not intend to favor any particular way of life. It is quite clear in both France's "burka ban," and the Québécois attempt to ban conspicuous religious symbols, that there was nonneutral intent. So while both jurisdictions were careful in how they phrased and defended their new laws, the broad exemptions that were provided for face coverings in the French case "on grounds of health and professional reasons, or if it is part of sports, festivals or events of an artistic of traditional nature," and to smaller Christian religious symbols in the Québécois case clearly demonstrate nonneutral intent (Brown 2020). Minority accommodation is best achieved when institutions have both neutral justification *and* neutral intent.

Considering we are talking about institutions here, it is worth clarifying "intent," which is something we usually apply to individuals, and not institutions. How can an institution *intend* to be neutral? In some cases it is very easy to gauge intent: the apartheid system in the former

South Africa clearly did not have neutral intent. Whites were clearly intended to be favored over other races. But in other cases, determining intent might seem much harder. Does a strict school uniform policy (perhaps one with very particular headwear requirements) really intend to favor students from majority backgrounds? Or is this just an unintended outcome? It may be very hard to tell. Perhaps those who drew up the policy did not think about this issue, or perhaps they were aware but did not think it important. And, of course, maybe they really did intend to favor a particular way of life. This problem is, of course, compounded by the difficulty of knowing the real intentions of those who set up institutions.

Many institutional founders may say one thing while knowing very well that the institution will actually do something else. This would seem a reasonable interpretation of the "separate but equal" doctrine in US constitutional law, which, when created in the 1890s, allowed racial segregation to not be seen as violating the Fourteenth Amendment of the US Constitution (which guarantees "equal protection" under the law to all people). Because of the difficulty of knowing the real intent of an institution, I want to suggest a particular way of understanding "intent" in this context. On this understanding, an institution is not neutral in intent when it both *knowingly* and *avoidably* favors one way of life over others. Both of these need explanation.

Let me deal with "knowingly" first. It is true that some institutions do not *knowingly* favor one way of life over others, even if this is what they actually do. So, for example, a parental leave policy or a family tax policy may end up favoring traditional gender roles. Often this is because if parental leave is given to the birth parent, then this reinforces her role as the caregiver and her partner's as the breadwinner. Likewise, tax or transfer policies can make it seem ineffective for her to return to the workplace, as childcare will cost the equivalent of her wage, and the family may deem it more rational for her to remain in the caring role—a role we know is reinforced over time (Okin 1999; Mahoney 1995; Balint, Eriksson, and Torresi 2018). But this may not have been the intention of those who constructed these policies; they simply may have wanted to address an important need in the community. However, once activists or policy specialists have indicated that these policies *do* favor traditional gender roles, and this has been stated repeatedly, then they are *knowingly* nonneutral.

One may want to go further and argue that those in power should be regularly conducting research into the impact of their institutions, and that this is a duty. But this additional, and perhaps more controversial, point is not necessary. All that is required is that there is clear knowledge. Whether this knowledge is originally produced by those from the inside or the outside of the running of the institution does not matter. In the sorts of cases usually discussed in multiculturalism and minority rights, this knowledge is clearly present. Minority claims are often repeatedly and vociferously made. One may also want to go with a "should have known" or culpable negligence interpretation of "knowingly." This seems reasonable, as those in power should at least be aware of the more obvious consequences of their laws, policies, and institutions. But I am happy for this understanding of "knowingly" not to be included if the reader feels it a step too far. There will be enough cases covered with the first understanding of "knowingly"—that is, those in power have been clearly and repeatedly told—to allow for changes in favor of minority accommodation, at least in the common examples discussed in multiculturalism and minority rights.

Let me now turn to "avoidably." Many institutions, once made aware of their nonneutrality, can take steps to avoid it. For example, governments could change their tax and transfer arrangements, or decide not to have a civil religion, or institutions could change their uniform policies. What matters is whether there are alternative options. That is, just because something has always been done a particular way does not mean it must continue. Neutrality of intent can often be met by changing and modifying practices. And if practices can change, then nonneutral intent is avoidable, or at least reducible. Here, some of the classic examples from multiculturalism should prove instructive. Police forces in Western liberal democracies can still protect the people even though their members now wear turbans or other alternative head coverings; things that would have been unthinkable just a short time ago. Likewise, children can still be educated in a common curriculum even when that happens in a religious setting, or predominantly in another language. Clearly, there are different ways of doing many things that still meet the neutral justification and purpose of the institution. That is, the institution can change to be more accommodating. This change can either involve removing majority privilege (for example, overturning a "burka ban"), or granting minority rights (for example, allowing a Muslim school student to wear a headscarf to school). Of course, institutions (like most of us) are reluctant to change, but as these and countless more examples show, change is possible, and so they can often *avoid* being nonneutral.

I have used "avoidably" here to acknowledge that there may be cases where nonneutrality is unavoidable. My argument is not that minority claims should always be met. And this is true whether the claims seem minor or very significant. Sometimes, institutions that make some ways of life harder than others are (seemingly) unavoidable. One popular example here is of lingua franca, or national language. While national languages may knowingly be nonneutral to some ways of life, they *may* be unavoidable. Those in favor of national language/s usually argue they are necessary for efficiency, social cohesion, and social mobility (for example, Barry 2001). That is, we need to speak the same language in order to have services delivered efficiently, a feeling of being "one people," and so people can move through society and not have their opportunities limited by their birth. Here I think it is worth noting that the necessity of a single national language seems overstated. Many countries have two or three national languages, including Canada, Switzerland, and Belgium, and these multilingual countries are often highly prosperous and winners of "most livable" city and country awards. There may be a practical limit on the number of national languages that can be employed and still meet the goals of having a national language, although South Africa has 12 languages. In the case of a lingua franca, one can rightfully be skeptical of many claims. Nevertheless, it is likely that at least some institutions in multicultural polities may not be able to avoid being entirely nonneutral in this area.

It is not enough to simply play an "unavoidability card." Any claim to unavoidability needs to be properly examined. The question is whether the institution can still meet its goal and avoid being nonneutral, or at least reduce its nonneutrality, if it does things differently.

CONCLUSION

In this chapter I have shown how neutral institutions (in terms of both justification and intent) can accommodate minority ways of life, and that nonneutral institutions can, albeit reluctantly, change to make these accommodations. This change can take two basic forms. First, it may involve removing majority privilege, for example, dismantling state religions, overturning bans on head and face coverings, or removing religious symbols from state schools. Second, it might involve directly redressing minority disadvantage while leaving everything else unchanged. Here an institution may grant minority rights—the police, for example, may decide that looking "smart" can involve turbans and headscarves in the same color as standard uniform headwear, and allow these for Sikhs and Muslims. Or a state may decide the history and centrality of its state religion is too important to abolish, and instead extend recognition and privileges to other major religions as well. These are examples of multicultural minority rights as forms of neutrality toward people's ways of life.

As this discussion shows, and it is worth highlighting, neutralizing action may actually involve minority rights! Favoring the majority is nonneutral, and so adjusting an institution to add favor to the minority is a neutralizing action. In this sense, minority rights are a form of state neutrality. The reason I stress this is that it seems multiculturalists actually endorse neutrality in practice, if not in name. In this sense, we have come full circle— my argument for neutrality (so far) is entirely compatible with an argument for minority rights. Given the argumentative framework set out earlier—where minority rights were directly opposed to liberal neutrality—this point is significant in itself. Liberal neutrality does not fail to accommodate minority ways of life—even if they require minority rights. Nevertheless, in the next chapter, I want to go further and argue for a form of neutrality that does not require minority rights at all, and this further position *is* opposed to minority rights. Here I will argue that the first way of realizing neutrality—removing majority privilege—is the best way of gaining minority accommodation, as it avoids many of the pitfalls of granting minority rights and has its own unique advantages in the form of more freedom for all of us.

9

Neutrality
without Minority Rights

SO FAR I HAVE BEEN arguing that when an institution
that is public in the relevant sense knowingly and avoidably favors a majority and disfavors minorities, there is a
strong case for change that addresses this failure of neutrality. But I have been deliberately ambiguous whether
this neutralizing change should involve either minority
rights or the removal of majority privilege. In this chapter I describe the removal of majority privilege as an ideal
form of neutralizing change that does not require granting
minority rights, and show how it is an ideal that can be,
and indeed is, regularly achieved. I will call this form of
neutrality *active indifference*, and show why it is superior to
minority rights for accommodating minority ways of life.
Active indifference involves removing privilege from the
majority rather than adding minority privilege when there
is known and avoidable nonneutrality.

Let me start with the example of police uniforms in
order to show the difference in these two approaches to
minority accommodation. Patterns of migration in the
second half of the twentieth century meant that when
groups such as orthodox Sikhs or Muslims wanted to join

Debating Multiculturalism. Peter Balint and Patti Tamara Lenard, Oxford University Press. © Oxford
University Press 2022. DOI: 10.1093/oso/9780197528372.003.0010

the police forces in many Western countries, they found some of the uniform requirements a barrier to entry. What usually occurred (sometimes after an unnecessary delay) was that provisions were made to allow Sikhs or Muslims to wear turbans or headscarves in the color of the uniform, or to have facial hair, among other possibilities. Sometimes this was expressed very specifically, as in the United Kingdom: "Sikh officers and uniformed staff may wear a black or dark navy blue turban with a modified cap badge. Muslim officers and staff may wear a black or dark navy blue headscarf" (College of Policing n.d.). At other times it was expressed more generally without naming any particular groups. For example, in Texas, the Houston Police Department's uniform code reads, "A employee who believes that for religious reasons he should be allowed to deviate from the dress code policy may request an accommodation from the Chief of Police" (Houston Police Department 2020). But whether expressed specifically or more generally, both forms require recognition of particular identities as well as minority rights.[1] This is the minority rights approach: an individual needs to be from a recognized religious group in order to access the exemption from a general rule. This requires some measure of *authenticity*. You need to be from a recognized group in order to

---

1. Usually not all religiously styled requirements were accepted. "Pastafarianism" (or the Church of the Flying Spaghetti Monster—an initially parodical religion), for example, is usually excluded from such provisions. There are some cases of people being allowed to wear colanders on their heads for identity photos, but these are the exception rather than the rule (Martin 2020).

access these exemptions from the usual police uniform requirements. That is, there has to be some measure as to whether you really do meet the specific requirements. Only once this authenticity has been accepted is an individual able to access a minority right in the form of an exemption.

This recognition and exemption approach, precisely what is favored by those who argue for minority rights, does grant more minority accommodation than doing nothing. But it is not the only way to proceed. For while granting exemptions and minority rights can be a form of neutrality, so too is removing and changing barriers altogether. A neutralizing alternative is to do away with exemptions altogether—this is active indifference. If a police force can still function with some members wearing turbans, some wearing headscarves, and some beards, then this seems to show that the general rules in place are unnecessarily restrictive. There is no need for an exemption from an unnecessarily restrictive rule; much better is to remove the rule altogether. Why not just say turbans, headscarves, and beards are now permitted without the need for recognition? Orthodox Sikhs and Muslims would still be accommodated. There would then be no need for minority rights, recognition of identity, or measures of authenticity. All that is required is an understanding that existing arrangements are nonneutral, and for a new set of more neutral arrangements to be put in place that expand the possibilities for diversity. Once these possibilities are expanded, then no exemption or recognition is required. In this case, there is simply a new set of broader uniform requirements.

This expansion of possibilities without recognition is neutrality as active indifference. It is active because it follows the knowingly and avoidably criteria of neutrality of intent. It is indifferent because it actively strives to favor neither majority nor minority, but does this by removing rather than adding privilege. It is also a clear and feasible alternative to granting minority rights in order to achieve minority accommodation.

Examples of active indifference are easy to generate. Another example is the running of elections. Several countries have polling days on Saturdays (New Zealand, Australia, Malta, and Latvia among them), but Saturdays are a strictly observed Sabbath for Orthodox Jews. This looks like a barrier for Orthodox Jews discharging their civic duty in these countries, and suggests the institution in this form is not neutral. Let us assume that the intent of choosing a Saturday was to make it is as easy as possible for people to vote (as it is on a weekend), and so maximize voter turnout. Given this barrier for Orthodox Jews, it would seem we need to do something in order to make the institution more neutral. We have two competing options: multicultural minority rights and active indifference. The recognition and minority rights approach should recommend granting Orthodox Jews an exemption—perhaps they would be offered the opportunity to vote on another day altogether, or be allowed to postal vote. This would be neutralizing in their case. But if it is possible to have voting on more than one day or to postal vote, then this suggests the institution can serve its purpose (collecting the voting intentions of citizens) without making everyone turn up on the same day. Applying active indifference may mean keeping the Saturday polling day, but opening up pre-poll and postal voting to all of us without recognizing any particular group identity, including

Orthodox Jews. In fact, active indifference is standard practice in most of these countries. They have pre-poll and postal voting without the need for recognition or minority rights. So what is now the standard practice would not actually be the recommendation of multicultural minority rights advocates. There is no need to recognize Orthodox Jews as a particular group in order to accommodate them, or any similar groups of people.

Or consider the example of publicly funded schooling for ethnic and religious groups. Here we seem to have three broad options in dealing with minority ways of life. The first option is a nonneutral majority-privileging view, which does not aim to accommodate minority ways of life. This is a common schooling experience for all with little room for diversity. Here there is a common curriculum, national examinations for all schools, public funding for all schools, and precise criteria for all teachers and schools. The French schooling system would seem a good example here. The second option is a recognized-group approach, where only a few particular groups that meet the necessary criteria are able to set up their own publicly funded schools. In Britain, for example, religious groups can run state schools. There are Catholic, Church of England, Jewish, Muslim, and Hindu state schools, all of which, as publicly funded state schools, need to meet national standards, but are (reasonably) free to teach what they want in religious education, can require conservative, religiously appropriate school uniforms, and may use religious criteria in the hiring and maintaining of staff. The third option is much more decentralized, with some common curriculum but with significant local community decided variation—such as the role of school boards in the United States.

For those concerned with minority accommodation, the usual problem with the common experience model is not only that some minorities will struggle to be accommodated by it, but that it will be shaped in the majority's image. That is, the common experience is not neutral in intent, even if it has neutral justification. A common schooling experience may include the language of instruction, history, religious instruction, and uniform requirements. The two other schooling approaches address this nonneutrality of the common schooling experience. On the recognized-group approach, some groups are given permission and public funding to set up their own schools that address their needs. These schools still need to teach to a core curriculum, but can also teach particular religious values, culture, and languages. In this way, this is a neutralizing option for these recognized groups, who are granted a particular set of minority education rights. For example, prior to 2010 in the UK these groups had to be particular organized religions, and no other group was recognized.

But, as I have been arguing, the fact that an education system can function with different groups doing different things suggests that uniformity is not so necessary. So rather than grant just a few recognized religious or cultural groups the autonomy to run their own government-supported schools, why not loosen the restrictions on the common core and allow any group that can meet educational standards the right to run their own schools? Indeed, this seems to be the intention, if not the practice, of the Dutch Constitutional Right of "Freedom of Education" (Article 23), whereby any group should be able to set up its own publicly funded school if none already exists—be it religious or not (Wolf et al. 2004). This second way of realizing neutrality is in fact invited by the minority rights approach. If a system can function with minority rights, then it can likely function with mainstreaming these very provisions. Once again, the choice is between multicultural minority rights which involve recognizing groups with particular characteristics (usually religious in this case), and active indifference, which requires recognition only of capability, and not ethnicity or culture. Both approaches allow for minority accommodation, but active indifference avoids recognition of identity altogether.

Let me say a little more about active indifference and how it differs from multicultural minority rights. "Active indifference" is intended to capture the idea that an institution should be indifferent between the range of ways of life of those who are subject to it. But this indifference cannot be "set and forget." It requires the institution to respond to unjustified failures of neutrality by broadening its range of indifference—institutions should be indifferent to as many different ways of life as possible. The label is not as important as the concept that when nonneutrality is realized and it is avoidable, there is a strong justification for broadening the range of neutrality by removing relative majority privilege, rather than adding new forms of minority privilege.[2] It is an active form of "hands off" neutrality (De Vries 2020; cf. Laegaard 2020). But certainly not the

---

2. I have described active indifference elsewhere as "difference-sensitive neutrality" (Balint 2015). But this label also seems appropriate for the neutrality followed by those who prefer multicultural minority rights—they too are difference sensitive.

form of "benign neglect" maligned by multicultural minority rights theorists, and it is neutrality of intent as it should be understood. That is, if neutrality of intent is to realize its goal of not intentionally favoring any particular ways of life, then this is the best way for it to operate.

In the cases so far, I have shown how nonneutrality can be addressed by active indifference, as well as, of course, by multicultural minority rights. But sometimes, neither active indifference nor multicultural minority rights will be appropriate. This is for two reasons. The first reason is that sometimes minorities will not be accommodated by neutral institutions and rightly so. Neutral institutions will certainly not accommodate all ways of life. For example, several minority ways of life (including, but not limited to, some Native Americans and Rastafarians) can involve taking mind-altering drugs. Nevertheless, and irrespective of their legality, the laws that prohibit driving under the influence of such drugs should neither be abandoned nor exemptions given to these ways of life. These laws are justified neutrally on the importance of not causing harm to others. In this sense, there is no nonneutrality that should be addressed.

Second, even when there is known and avoidable nonneutrality, this does not automatically mean that neutralizing actions should take place. Neutrality and minority accommodation is an ideal that should be aimed for, but it is not an ideal that will always be met. This is because there may be other values in play. It may be known that an institution is nonneutral and it could also change to be more neutral, but other values, such as security or efficiency, will justify its current design and resist change. For example, perhaps having a national language is nonneutral, and changes could be made to counter this nonneutrality. But the importance of efficiency means the national language remains in place. In philosophical terms, the case I am making is only pro tanto, and not *all things considered*. The case for neutralizing change is strong, but it may be outweighed by other values. I should stress this is an issue for active indifference *and* multicultural minority rights.

Nevertheless, the claim for neutralizing change is weighty, and is not simply overridden by these other considerations. This means that it remains action-guiding even when outweighed. Active indifference—and indeed neutrality more generally—is an action-guiding ideal, not a binary property. So if the argument for a national language wins out, this does not mean there is no place for minority languages. Neutrality in the form of active indifference should still limit the extent that this majority language is promoted. The promotion of this nonneutral (in intent) goal should be limited to achieving its neutral justification, and should certainly not be maximized. How this balance should be struck is a contextual question, but it is clear where the balance has failed. One need only look at the modern European history of nation-building (Weber 1977), which commonly involved the deliberate wiping out of regional dialects and the punishment of those who continued to speak them to see a clear case of when neutrality was not a guiding, if outweighed, ideal. My point here is simply to address the location of neutrality within the pantheon of things we hold as important. So while it is an ideal (in either the form of active indifference or minority rights form), it is an ideal that will necessarily be balanced with other things held as important.

THE ADVANTAGES OF ACTIVE INDIFFERENCE OVER MINORITY RIGHTS

My argument here has been that if an institution can function with minority rights, then this suggests they are not needed, as the institution can just broaden to accommodate diversity without such recognition. But I am yet to show why this broadening is preferable to simply granting minority rights. That is, if both approaches are neutralizing and accommodating of minorities, then it may seem the question of which approach to take is context dependent, and perhaps there is nothing wrong with minority rights after all. On this reading, all I have shown is that neutrality and multicultural minority rights are compatible, and not that we should do away with multicultural minority rights altogether. In this section I want to show both what is problematic with multicultural minority rights, and what is advantageous about removing majority advantage rather than adding minority advantage. In other words, why what I have called "active indifference" should be the preferred way of expanding the range of neutrality. I will break the relative advantages of this broadening approach to neutrality into two groups. The first involves avoiding many of the costs and risks of recognition; the second involves providing more freedom for all of us.

Avoiding the Costs and Risks of Recognition

The first set of advantages of active indifference is that the costs and risks of recognition can mainly be avoided.

These risks are not only argued for by those critical of multicultural minority rights, but agreed upon by those who argue for minority rights (Eisenberg 2013; Modood 1998; Phillips 2007; Hayward and Watson 2010). These problems with the recognition of cultural identities—acknowledged by those arguing both for and against multicultural minority rights—can be divided into four broad categories.

The first is the problem of trying to decide who exactly is entitled to a particular minority right. To work out who is entitled to a particular minority right, we need to know *who actually is a genuine member of the minority group.* Minority rights, by definition, are not for everyone, just members of particular groups. So should membership of a group and entitlement to a right simply be given to all those who self-identify as members? Or do they need to be recognized by an authority from that particular group? Or is there some objective criterion on which genuine membership lies? (Killmister 2014). While being recognized as a member by the group authority seems more authentic than simply accepting those who self-identify, it can leave those with less orthodox understandings of the group out in the cold. The problem here is that being a "member" (or not) is subject to the internal politics of the group, something that is often controlled by older, more conservative males. On the other hand, if being a member is simply self-identified, this may be viewed as allowing opportunists who are not "genuine" to take advantage of minority rights. And finally, there is the possibility of an objective list of membership criteria. While this approach specifies specific independent criteria, it is unlikely to capture all of those who meaningfully self-identify, nor will it easily capture cultural change—identities and cultures change significantly over time. As Federico Zuolo describes, because of the difficulty of marking out clear groups to give rights to, we have a problem of "normative vagueness" (Zuolo 2014); that is, we lack the necessary precision on which to fairly allocate multicultural minority group rights.

Moreover, and compounding this problem of membership, is the question of *which groups count*. That is, which types of "cultures," or at least which salient features, are worthy of recognition and subsequent minority rights? What sort of groups actually matter for multicultural minority rights? Do we need members to have "sincerely held" beliefs or at least strong identification? In Canada, for example, public and private organizations are legally obliged to offer "reasonable accommodation" measures to those whose conscience is significantly burdened by a prima facie neutral rule (Maclure 2020). Or is something less strong still okay? Does it matter how easily members of a culture could actually change their practices to fit in with existing institutions? That is, while some groups may claim a practice is essential and could not be altered, it may actually be capable of change (and often has changed over time). For example, the laws of kashruth mean that Orthodox Jews who eat meat require that an animal is not stunned prior to slaughter. But Orthodox rabbis in Sweden, Norway, and Switzerland have accepted legislation requiring stunning prior to slaughter with no exemption for ritual slaughter (Singer 1990, 54, cited in Barry 2001, 35). Or to give another example, even the issue of Sikhs and helmets seems less straightforward given the patkas favored by many Sikh sports people, including cricketers who wear them under their batting helmets. These questions are not clear-cut, and minorities will, understandably, usually couch any claims in the strongest terms: that is, that the practices they require exemptions (or other rights) for involve sincerely held beliefs and are essential to their way of life (cf. Barry 2001). Active indifference can avoid these problems of determining suitable groups and members for recognition.

This leads to the second problem acknowledged by those working in minority rights, and this is that *the political recognition of identity has a direct impact on that identity*. That is, politics can help construct, or at least shape identity (Song 2007; Shachar 2009; Hayward and Watson 2010). As Sarah Song writes, "Cultures vary in the degree of fluidity, contestation, and permeability, but even in relatively closed societies the content of cultures is not determined purely 'from the inside.' Rather, cultures are shaped by interactions and struggles with other cultures . . . [and] . . . also by concerted state action" (2007, 36). Song provides the example of the three major tribes in Nigeria being recent political constructions, and the example of the way the government played a crucial role in defining what counts as a tribe and its effects on the Wampanoag Indians of Mashpee. But there are almost as many possible examples of the impact of states on identity as there are recognized identities.

When a group is recognized, this action can fix what it is to be a member of that group, and do so in a way that may fix or reify that identity. Why is this a problem? Well, we know that identities in the real world are fluid and changing things. For almost all of us, we only need to reflect on the changes in our own identities in recent years to see some strong and significant changes. Different parts of our identities become more important, and what each identity means changes over time. The political construction and fixing of identity are sometimes described as the problem of essentialism. Political attempts to describe the contents of a culture—something that is required for multicultural minority rights—can create an essentialized and reified version of the culture (Bessone 2012). This essentialized version does not admit internal difference, or change, or disagreement, and can cause the cultural group to become a cage where its adherents have a fixed set of characteristics (Zuolo 2014). Once again, this is not an external critique of multicultural minority rights, but one fully accepted by minority rights theorists. Avigail Eisenberg, for example, writes that "the best approach to good decision making is not always the one that avoids essentialism . . . advocates of minority rights must discover how to mitigate the risks" (Eisenberg 2013, 159, 175).

Not only can recognition (mis)shape identity, but *this can restrict the freedom of members of minority cultures.* This is the third generally accepted problem with multicultural minority rights, *the minorities within minorities problem* (Eisenberg and Spinner-Halev 2005). Here those with divergent views or less power can be disadvantaged and vulnerable when a group is emboldened to determine its own membership criteria and/or its identity is fixed to the advantage of its more conservative leaders. This, for example, has been a concern in granting more autonomy to religious groups in family disputes. Here, as well as in other cases, where cultural groups are granted power or rights, women in particular may be more vulnerable to adverse outcomes (Okin 1999; Phillips 2007; Shachar 2009). Shachar calls this the "paradox of multicultural vulnerability," which is the "the ironic fact that individuals inside the group can be injured by the very reforms that are designed to promote their status as group members in the accommodating, multicultural state" (2009, 3). This is because many minority groups—especially, but not only, religious groups—have very conservative views on family and gender roles. Giving community leaders and spokespeople more power can just reinforce this issue to the detriment of women and those with more progressive views. Shachar gives the example of Israel's family law policy, where family law is determined separately for Jews, Muslims, Christians, and Druze, leaving women potentially subject to intragroup controls based on their own group's traditions (Shachar 1999). Once again, by eschewing recognition, active indifference can sidestep these problems.

Finally, there is the fourth problem, that of *misrecognition*. Recall that Taylor's argument (following Hegel) for proper identity recognition stresses the dangers of having your identity incorrectly recognized (Taylor 1994). It is not just that your identity needs to be recognized correctly and as worthwhile, but that misrecognition of identity causes serious damage. The problem here is that if identities are fluid and complex things (which nobody in this debate denies), then they may be hard to accurately capture. On top of this, we live in large, modern states which are filled with multiple, overlapping, fluid, and complex identities. It will be very hard for these states to know and properly understand this complexity, let alone react to it constantly and accurately. Recognizing identities, which is essential for multicultural minority rights, requires knowledge and understanding of these identities.

But given the dangers of misrecognition, it seems better if we can avoid recognition by the state altogether, rather than trust the state to recognize our identities correctly. Recognition must be done correctly, but this seems very hard to do. Thus, somewhat ironically, one of the key problems with multicultural minority rights is that the requirement for recognition of identity can involve the dangers of getting it wrong—the very thing it is trying to avoid. My argument is not that the recognition required for multicultural minority rights can never be done correctly, nor with the required agility to adapt as people's identities change over time. Instead, I am arguing that this precision and agility is difficult to achieve, especially from an entity as large and cumbersome as a modern state (cf. Joppke 2017). My argument is comparative: in a case where a minority way of life needs accommodating, if we have a choice between multicultural minority rights and active indifference, then active indifference is more likely to avoid the pitfalls of multicultural minority rights while still delivering the advantages. The challenges of identity recognition are not insignificant, and as their own advocates argue, the costs of getting it wrong are serious. In a comparative sense, active indifference with its lack of recognition is much better at mitigating this risk.

Neutrality, as active indifference, can avoid these important practical problems because it does not require this level of fine-grain distinction. Active indifference does not require a state or its agent to have specific criteria for who is granted differential rights in which circumstances—something multicultural minority rights does require. When minorities, or their advocates, challenge a practice as not accommodating their way of life, the question should first be whether the challenged practice has neutral justification, and then whether the goals of the practice can be achieved in a more neutral way. My argument is not that the claims of culture are trivial—far from it—but that they cannot be adequately distinguished from other similar claims. Moreover, when they can be met, it is easier and less risky to meet them in the negative (by removing an obstacle) than in the positive (by granting a positive right to culture). Active indifference thus avoids the four main problems associated with multicultural minority rights, problems which are agreed upon by those arguing both for and against multicultural minority rights.

More Freedom for All

The second set of advantages of active indifference over multicultural minority rights is more positive in nature. In a case where a minority way of life needs accommodating, if we have a choice between multicultural minority rights and active indifference, then active indifference will not only avoid the pitfalls of recognition, but will bring additional advantages. Because the broadening of active indifference does not pick out any particular group or individual, not only is a "would-have-been-recognized" minority member now accommodated, *but more freedom is offered to all.* If freedom is understood as either having fewer restrictions or having more options to choose from, then broadening an institution provides more freedom for everyone. By removing barriers and equally distributing opportunities among all of us, this freedom is evenly and fairly distributed across the community. This freedom is both immediate, in the sense that we now have fewer restrictions, and potential. Let me explain further.

It is immediate in the sense that we can now participate in an institution with fewer restrictions. So to go back
to the voting example, when postal and pre-poll voting is
introduced, everyone, and not just Orthodox Jews, can
now exercise their civic duty in a wider range of ways. We
are all now free to vote before Saturday, allowing all of us
to fit this civic duty into our lives; perhaps we usually work
on Saturday, are planning on being away, have children's
sporting commitments, or just feel like a lazy day. These
reasons do not need to be examined for authenticity, and
individuals are free to use whichever voting method suits
their circumstance. Active indifference has enabled more
freedom for both Orthodox Jews *and* for all of us and our
own particular ways of life. The lack of restrictions of active
indifference is thus equally distributed; we all have unnecessary barriers removed, even if we do not take advantage
of them. Yes, many will argue that these barriers are most
significant for Orthodox Jews, but this need not be a zero-
sum game. This way of dealing with minority accommodation equally, and dare I say, fairly, distributes this form of
freedom.

This freedom is also potential. While some options,
such as wearing a turban to work, may not be options many
of us care about now, and we may not feel this possibility
adds anything to our lives, they offer new opportunities
should we wish to exercise them in the future. While the
obvious case here is one where there is a future conversion
to Sikhism, there are many more possibilities. Perhaps, for
example, in the future you might decide to join a brand-
new religion, and a broader set of institutions will likely be
more accommodating. In the voting case, it will not matter
when your Sabbath is if pre-poll voting is permitted. And

in the schooling case, you will not need to be recognized as a religion, only as educationally competent, in order to run your own school. Active indifference thus leaves more options open, even if they are not options you might consider valuable right now. If equality of opportunity matters, it should matter not only for options you want right now, but for options you may (or may not) want in the future. This is what a comprehensive view of fair equality of opportunity requires.

Institutions that broaden rights, rather than provide minority rights, not only avoid the pitfalls of recognizing minorities, but provide many advantages. They allow all of us, not only the immediate targets of such broadening, to be freer than before, but the lack of recognition more easily allows, to use John Stuart Mill's term, "experiments in living," and for individuals to literally try things on. Broader institutions do not grant rights only to particular groups to do things differently—such as eat different foods or wear different uniforms or have different safety requirements—but allow these possibilities for everyone. This means that we all have more options to choose from in our lives; something that those who are concerned with individual autonomy hold as valuable. This means that active indifference should be appealing to both classical *and* autonomy-focused liberals. Active indifference has fewer restrictions (important for classical liberals) *and* more easily allows individuals to change their life plans (important for autonomy liberals). This means that if we change our preferences and beliefs, then we will not necessarily have to change our institutions.

Let me give one final example that brings both the advantages of avoiding the problems of multicultural minority rights and the increased freedom of active indifference together. This example is institutions, such as almost all militaries, that require short hair for men but allow women (and sometimes Sikhs and Rastafarians) to have long hair neatly tied up. If women, Sikhs, and Rastafarians can have long hair tied up neatly, then it seems functionality can be met with long hair, after all. That is, short hair is not actually necessary. If long hair was simply allowed, then this would avoid the problem of needing to recognize and decide who is a woman (or a Sikh or a Rastafarian). This would also be more accommodating of nonbinary or transitioning gender identities. Indeed, such an approach is clearly possible. The Patrol Guide of the New York City Police Department is very explicit, stating, "All regulations regarding the appearance of members' hair apply equally to male and female uniformed members of the service" (New York Police Department 2020). It is worth noting that this openness to diversity, albeit often for capability reasons, is something that several militaries are actually at the forefront of, even if they still have strict hair policies. For example, the Australian Defence Force "strives to make the most of the skills and talents of all personnel and aims to reap the capability benefits of having a diverse workforce through embracing and supporting all personnel, including LGBTI persons," including during transition (Australian Government 2019). While the Canadian Armed Forces policy stresses that every member has a right to define their own gender identity (Harris 2019), allowing long hair would be entirely consistent with these diversity policies.

Simply allowing long hair if it is neatly tied up when on duty would allow more freedom for anyone to have long

hair, with less reification of identity, and allow more possibilities for those interested in identity fluidity. The lack
of recognition of identity would avoid an unnecessary
gender binary and provide more freedom to all involved;
women, men, trans and intersex persons, religious Sikhs,
Rastafarians, and simply the fashionable. While multicultural minority rights do offer minority accommodation,
active indifference offers greater accommodation with less
associated problems, and with significant advantages.

DOES "CULTURE" MATTER?

So far I have been arguing that where a particular way of
life is relatively disadvantaged by an institution, it is better to reform the institution and remove a relative majority advantage than to add a minority right to that way of
life. In this sense, I have been firmly on the same ground
as minority rights activists and have deliberately used
their, mainly religious, examples to show there is a better way to achieve the goals of minority accommodation
than minority rights. I have deliberately accepted the usual
premises about which cultures matter for multiculturalism. I was seeking to make a clear point against multicultural minority rights and so used widely accepted cultural
examples. But now I want to bring out the implications of
my argument so far for this traditional understanding of
culture. In the previous section I argued that it is hard to
tell which cultures actually count significantly enough for
institutions to change to accommodate them. This was the
debate over who is a member, what sort of identification
is required, and how "sincere" or "authentic" a belief must

be. But these problems also seem an issue for active indifference, as well as for multicultural minority rights. In the case of active indifference, for whom should we remove majority privilege?

My simple, and perhaps radical, answer is *anytime there is unjustified majority privilege*. If an institution is knowingly and avoidably nonneutral to someone's way of life (and there are no sufficiently outweighing considerations), then action should be taken. As I also noted in my introduction to this part of the book (chapter 7), I do not take a position on what "culture" in "multicultural" means. There I stated that what mattered was when people's ways of life suffered a relative institutional disadvantage, there was the question of what should be done about it. The reasons for people's different ways of life are many and varied, and are likely to differ markedly both between persons and in the same person over time. I suggest, then, we make no distinction. If someone wants to do/be something but is limited by an institution, and if that institution can still meet its neutrally justified purpose, then there is a case for change. It matters little if their way of life is religious or otherwise. Institutional barriers that restrict our freedom need justification, and justification that is neutral between ways of life. Anything else is an unjustified impediment. Put bluntly, we should not worry about "culture," but simply impediments to people's ways of life and their freedom.

This very broad understanding of "ways of life" is entirely consistent with my argument for the advantages of active indifference. This lack of distinction among more or less worthy ways of life both avoids the problems of multicultural minority rights and has its own unique freedom-realizing advantages. Nevertheless, for those concerned about its feasibility, let me make two points. First, in practice active indifference will require some level of activism. Recall that institutions need to be *knowingly* nonneutral. They are unlikely to second-guess our unique needs, and so those who protest the loudest will most likely be those who are accommodated. For those who think the strength or sincerity of particular ways of life should matter for accommodation, then in practice this will be a proxy for their concern, as those with more flexible ways of life may not bother pushing for accommodation. This is not to say that those whose way of life might be newer or less a matter of conscience do not have claims for accommodation, just that the *knowingly* barrier will likely work against them. In real life, politics matters. Nonetheless, when institutions do change, they should take the opportunity to look beyond those making the loudest claims and see how they could also be more accommodating to others. If we return to the Orthodox Jews and voting example, Orthodox Jews and their advocates may provide the trigger for change, but that change should look at who else may experience a relative institutional disadvantage and strive to accommodate them as well—and the solutions of pre-poll and postal voting offered earlier do a good job of doing this work.

Second, for those who think this argument is too radical and that we need to only offer accommodation for certain types of ways of life, active indifference remains the best guiding principle here too. It is still better to accommodate a particular minority by removing majority privilege than by granting minority rights. One does not have to accept such a broad understanding of ways of life for active indifference to be a better guiding principle than multicultural minority rights. If you have a preferred criterion for triggering multicultural accommodation (for example, conscience, religious belief, sincerity, etc.), then simply use this as another layer to justify change. Exemptions for recognized Orthodox Jews in the Saturday voting case are not as good as simply allowing pre-poll and postal voting. Granting minority rights in a case of relative institutional disadvantage remains inferior to removing majority privilege whatever the criteria for triggering accommodation. This is the case whether one is concerned only with accommodating deeply held religious beliefs, or with "mere preferences." In both cases, minority rights are not the best path to accommodation.

OBJECTIONS TO ACTIVE INDIFFERENCE

I have argued that in cases where multicultural minority rights have been granted, the institutions could have just opened up this possibility to anyone. That is, if the institution can function with minority exemptions (or similar), it can function if these exemptions are simply opened up entirely to all of us. One objection here might be that in at least *some cases there are limits* to the amount of accommodation that is possible. On this objection, then, it is okay for multicultural minority rights to apply to a few people, but active indifference opens things up too far. Perhaps a small number of people voting early or wearing turbans is okay, but not if this becomes more widespread. On this objection, minority rights and exemptions are acceptable, as they are usually too few to threaten the main function of an institution. But opening things up entirely may well undermine the institution's purpose altogether.

Here I am a little skeptical of how often this would actually be the case. For example, in allowing voting to be spread over a significant period, some democrats might object to the end of the "festival of democracy" that is a single voting day, when everyone meets their fellow citizens and feels like they are collectively deciding their future together. But there are other ways of achieving this feeling—for example, a voting window of a few days to a week would presumably be sufficiently similar. The Czech Republic and Slovakia, for example, vote over two days. And under Covid-19, most elections were deliberately spread out over a longer time period. Yes, the nature of the institution changes, but its essential character would be maintained. We would no longer have a single day, but could still participate in the election period, and still meet fellow citizens at pre-poll voting. Once again, the question is whether a neutral justification can be met in a different way that is more neutral in intent than the status quo.

Or take the case of uniforms. In all the examples so far, it is really hard to see how generalizing the uniform exemptions would undermine the institution's purpose. Almost no uniform, no matter how "traditional," has remained unchanged over time. They have, at minimum, had variations in size, fit, sleeve length, and so on, and have often changed to accommodate the inclusion of women. The Australian army, for example, has changed its uniform many times in recent years—mainly driven by modernization and health and safety issues—but the "rising sun" badge has been highlighted as the core of the uniform and something that should always be maintained.

Nevertheless, even this central symbol has gone through seven iterations since 1902, the most recent in 1991.

The changes required for minority accommodation are just a new set of variations. Perhaps if the proposed changes would undermine safety, the variations will need to be reconsidered and some minority accommodation may not be possible, or perhaps will need to be limited to only a few people. But even if safety is used to trump minority accommodation (either in terms of minority rights *or* active indifference), the question still needs to be asked whether this goal could be achieved in another way. To give an example, the wearing of beards is outlawed in many militaries because of the need to attach gas and oxygen masks securely. And although many militaries do allow exemptions for religious purposes, this does not mean this particular safety justification should not be re-examined. Take the British Royal Navy, where, when safety equipment is required, beards "shall be modified in such a fashion as to accommodate the type of equipment to be worn," rather than simply banned (Wells 2019). It is possible to examine institutions more deeply and realize greater accommodation is feasible without undermining the institution's purpose. So perhaps there are limits in some cases, but these seem exceedingly rare, and all too often an institution can actually change its practices and its purpose can still be met.

Another objection might focus on *the lack of recognition entailed in active indifference*. When an institution is broadened, the new opportunities created are not limited to particular people. So if an institution now allows the wearing of headscarves as part of its uniform, this would allow anyone to wear a headscarf—whether they be orthodox

Muslim, fashion conscious, having a bad hair day, or just trying it out. There seem to be two possible parts to this objection to the lack of recognition entailed in active indifference.

On the first part, there may be concern over equalizing the opportunities of those with deeply held religious beliefs with those whose concerns seem more trivial. In this example we have equated those having bad hair days, the fashionable, and orthodox Muslims. It may seem there are some very important differences being overlooked here. But while it may be true that orthodox Muslim women will have stronger feelings about this new opportunity than the fashion conscious, one should not so quickly discard nonreligiously motivated desires. As most of us are aware, the extremely fashion conscious take how they look very seriously indeed. But more importantly, this is not, as I noted earlier, a zero-sum game. No one needs to lose out when this broadening happens; all compatible desires can be met—no matter how seriously they are held by their adherents, or how trivial they are viewed by outsiders.

On the second part of the objection, there may be concern that people will use these broadening measures to either make fun of minorities—perhaps wearing a turban to work "as a joke"—or that it will enable cultural appropriation. That is, provisions for those with deeper needs will be appropriated by others, and this appropriation will be offensive and wrong. While all actual (and not simply claimed) cases of cultural appropriation are wrong, even if often trivially so (Lenard and Balint 2020), there is a separate question of what should be done about it. This issue seems more of an ethical than a political concern. If there is a wrong done here, it is outside the usual boundaries of state power, which usually focus on particular kinds of harms. That is, we need to allow that people will do the "wrong" thing, and that others through their free speech will point it out to them, likely halting this sort of behavior. People have a right to do wrong, and can likely expect others to call them out on it (though they can still ignore them).

A final objection might focus on *how achievable active indifference will be*. It might be argued that because I say I do not think liberal neutrality will always be reached, especially as active indifference, then we will still need minority rights anyway. Or it might be argued that because I am not giving an all-things-considered judgment, in the end we will just need minority rights after all, and this is just more academic/ideal theory "unicorn speak." It is true that in the real world reducing majority privilege will be challenging, and the politics of it very difficult indeed. But such an objection is overstated. What I hope to have shown is the real strength of liberal neutrality, and that when competing claims are weighed against it, it will not so easily be swept away. I hope to have shown that if there are cases where active indifference cannot apply, they are much rarer than initially thought. Creative solutions are possible which meet the neutrally justified intention of an institution and which lead to the successful accommodation of minority ways of life. Let me also stress that, as many of my examples show, active indifference already happens in real life—institutions can, and do, change to be more accommodating. And they do this without recourse to multicultural minority rights. So arguing for active indifference involves no more "ideal theory" than arguing for multicultural minority rights.

A second response to this objection is slightly more technical. This is a methodological point on *how we deal with competing claims*: in this case, the ideal of neutrality and values (such as democracy) which push against it. The wrong view, I think, is that one claim simply overrides the other. If values were simply overridden, then classic trade-offs like privacy versus security, or justice versus efficiency, would mean one of these (presumably privacy and justice) would no longer remain action-guiding. But that just seems plain wrong. When new "terror" laws are introduced to protect our security, or tax systems introduced that make it easier to collect revenue, that doesn't mean the outweighed value—in these cases privacy and justice—no longer plays a role. These values still limit what is permissible and so continue to guide action. That is, even though a value is outweighed in the final decision, it still has weight. We do not (or should not) live in a world where one value overrides other things we also hold as important. All-things-considered judgments involve balancing these values. In the case of liberal neutrality in the form of active indifference, it may not always be possible to realize it in full—either because of real-world constraints such as democratic politics or because other values have more weight. But this does not mean active indifference as an ideal should not remain action-guiding. It should continue to guide and constrain the actions of our institutions.

So my response to the objection that active indifference is simply an unrealizable ideal is twofold: first, neutrality (without minority rights) is a highly robust response, and one that I hope to have shown can, and actually does, make accommodation of diversity possible in the real world right now. Joppke and Torpey (2013) show how this is essentially the legal-moral status quo in more and more Western European states and in North America. Second, in cases where other values win out, neutrality can still guide and constrain action. If, for example, majority identities need favoring (perhaps for reasons of social cohesion or to help the realization of social justice), then one of the things stopping them being maximized is the impact on minority identities. That is, the interests of those with divergent ways of life (whether right now or as future options) limits, but doesn't stop, the promotion of majority identity. Likewise, if the need for minority rights arises, then they too should be limited by the values imbued in neutrality as I have described it.

CONCLUSION

In this chapter I outlined and made the case for liberal neutrality in the form of active indifference as the best way to deal with issues of minority accommodation. Put simply, if the problem is majority privilege, then remove that privilege. This approach to minority accommodation is much better than multicultural minority rights as it avoids the classic problems of granting minority rights, as well as offering more freedom for all of us. This chapter concludes my main argument against multicultural minority rights as the best way to achieve minority accommodation. Nonetheless, two issues remain, and I take these up in the next two chapters. The first concerns Indigenous peoples and other national minorities. I have deliberately avoided discussing these groups so far as their claims seem to be about more than multicultural minority accommodation. The second is whether multiculturalism is about more than just relative institutional disadvantage. On this question I look at whether we need to look beyond institutions to achieve minority accommodation, and if so, in what ways.

10

National Minorities, Indigenous Peoples, and Historical Injustice

MY ARGUMENT FOR NEUTRALITY AS "active indifference" has hopefully demonstrated that multicultural issues can be resolved without recourse to minority rights, and that minorities can be accommodated when their desired actions are consistent with the neutrally justified purpose of an institution. Institutions can, and should, do things in different ways, and this ability to change and reflect removes any need for multicultural minority rights. Note, though, that I am not arguing that minority rights are *never* justified, just that they are rarely, if at all, justified in multicultural contexts, that is, contexts of relative institutional disadvantage. There may well be other contexts in which minority rights are justified, and in this chapter I explore some of these contexts.

Within the multiculturalism literature, several issues are commonly lumped together which should be separated out. Much of the early multiculturalism literature, particularly the Canadian work of Taylor and Kymlicka, started from the importance of granting substantial rights

Debating Multiculturalism. Peter Balint and Patti Tamara Lenard, Oxford University Press. © Oxford University Press 2022. DOI: 10.1093/oso/9780197528372.003.0011

to national minorities, and lesser cultural rights to immigrant groups. Added into the mix here was discussion of minorities that had faced persistent historical injustice. Indigenous people usually filled both these positions; they were national minorities *and* had faced historical injustice. But Indigenous people were not the only target here. Also included were groups like the Québécois in Canada, the Welsh in the United Kingdom, and the Catalans in Spain. Here arguments were mounted to provide these nations within multination states a distinct set of rights. These rights might take the form of language rights (often in the form of schooling, but also street signs and so forth) or political rights (in the form of political autonomy or clear representation at the national level). In the case of Indigenous peoples, these claims for language and political rights (the New Zealand Māori, for example, have both), were supplemented with cultural rights (including hunting exemptions, among other things), as well as strictly redressive rights (for example, targeted welfare and quotas for education or professional roles).

As noted in our joint introduction to this book, Kymlicka's seminal work distinguished between "polyethnic" and "national minority" rights. Multiculturalism since then seems to have split along these lines, with many Canadians (and other theorists from multination states) focusing on national minorities, and others such as European and Australians focusing instead on what Kymlicka called "polyethnic" rights. Not surprisingly, perhaps, my focus has been on polyethnic rights—albeit broader in scope. What I want to suggest in this section is that there are different things going on here, not all of which are usefully considered as "multiculturalism," despite some obvious overlaps. The reason I make this point is to show that the existence and perhaps necessity of minority rights in some contexts does not mean they are also required in multicultural contexts.

In what I call *multicultural contexts*, we have relative majority privilege—usually manifested as restrictions on what minorities want to do/be, while in the case of *national minorities*, we usually have people who have never ceded sovereignty, and/or face continued discrimination, and/or regions that seek more control over their governance, and all this usually on top of the relative majority privilege. I reserve "multiculturalism" for the cases where background conditions favor the majority, and people who live divergent lives have restrictions not faced by the majority; no more and no less. So multicultural minority rights are there for cases of relative institutional disadvantage. For people such as national minorities who have never ceded sovereignty, or have faced persistent historic injustice, or who wish to govern themselves, this might look like multiculturalism, and even overlap with multiculturalism, but it adds a different set of issues. The question in these other cases is not only whether the particular individuals or groups are restricted in being who they want to be or doing what that want. It is not simply about inclusion or integration, or having a polity that treats everybody the same—the usual motivators of multicultural minority rights. But in many cases it is about a specific, and often profound, set of wrongs; and wrongs that do not simply go away when minority rights are provided. In fact, inclusion and integration may not even be the goal of many rights for national minorities (for the New Zealand case, see O'Sullivan 2006). These historic wrongs do not only apply to Indigenous people. Other national minorities, including the Basques, Bretons, Scots, and Québécois, have been subject to forceful assimilation and have been discriminated against to varying degrees (Kymlicka 2000). These specific wrongs also, of course, apply to victims of slavery and genocide, as well as cases of persistent racial and gender discrimination.

Note, too, the way we talk about these wrongs, especially, but not only, with Indigenous peoples. In these non-multicultural contexts, they are always described as injustices by those who think there is a wrong. This is not usually the case for multicultural minority accommodation, where failure to accommodate might be unfair, or fail some test of recognition, or fail to adequately integrate.

Moreover, the sorts of minority rights that are granted in non-multiculturalism cases are often quite different. When addressing persistent historical injustice, for example, minority rights are commonly redressive and are intended to be temporary; that is, to only be in place until the injustice is addressed. Minority rights that seek to redress a specific historic injustice (such as slavery) or a pattern of discrimination (such as in the case of gender or race) are intended to be phased out when justice is served—even if that looks a long way off. The most well-known cases are of "affirmative action," which, it has been argued, is intended to be ultimately group-destroying, rather than group-affirming (Sabbagh 2014), that is, for the salience of the group to no longer matter in terms of relative disadvantage or harm. This is very different to multicultural minority rights, which are intended to be much more permanent and address a permanent relative institutional disadvantage.

When we look at national minorities, the political rights that they may be granted also seem very different from standard multicultural minority rights, and are about democratic decision-making. When regional in nature, such as where a group is concentrated in one area (such as the Welsh and the Québécois), these can be understood as federal-like. Federations grant a great deal of autonomy to subnational units. These subnational units often develop their own identity, and often put this before, at least on par with, the larger nation-state. This could be said of New York in the United States, or Queensland and Western Australia in Australia, for example. These subnational units are certainly not "nations" in the same way as the Québécois or Catalans, but they have a distinct identity, and one that is realized in a great deal of political autonomy, including in key areas for identity and culture such as education. Regional autonomy is nothing new or peculiar. States will always need to decide what should be the appropriate subnational units—an act that usually involves accepting historical boundaries around particular polities that have evolved their own distinct identity and, it should be added, an act which usually strengthens identities. The case of Scotland seems apt here. Scottish claims for more autonomy, although sometimes linked to identity and cultural issues, are much more about seeing a better material future in the European Union than in the United Kingdom (Scottish Government 2019).

The exception here is where the subnational units or national minorities are not territorially concentrated. Some countries, such as New Zealand, have dealt with this by putting in reserved seats in parliament, in this case for Māori. Others have tried consultative bodies, such as the Aboriginal and Torres Strait Islander Commission in Australia from 1990 to 2005. These moves are not so easily understood in a federal-type structure, but they seem about deep structural disadvantage (many countries, for example, reserve seats for women in their legislative bodies) or a tacit acknowledgment of issues of sovereignty and legitimacy. Another complication is when national minorities exist across more than one state, such as is the case with the Sami, who live across Norway, Sweden, Finland, and Russia (Vitikainen 2020).

My point here is simply that *multicultural minority rights are very different from these other forms of minority rights.* It is not just that the types of rights granted can be very different, but so too is their justification. National minorities, when they have valid claims, can rely on something other than just relative institutional disadvantage and claims for inclusion and integration. What matters for national minorities, particularly in the form of Indigenous peoples, is usually that their forebears never ceded sovereignty to those who now make these laws and institutions (Ivison, Patton, and Saunders 2000; Ivison 2015) and had their lands taken over without consent (Simmons 2016). Focusing on Indigenous people, Ivison writes, it is important to distinguish the claims of Indigenous peoples "from the claims of other minority groups, such as migrants or refugees, because they are challenging the extent to which their incorporation into the state (and its subsequent consequences) was just. The question of legitimacy looms much larger with regard to indigenous peoples than it does with other minority groups" (Ivison 2008).

To this question of legitimacy is also commonly added persistent historical disadvantage, as well as arguments from contemporary socioeconomic disadvantage too (Brock 2002; Waldron 1992). These additional arguments are not present in standard multicultural cases, which rely much more straightforwardly on relative institutional disadvantage. It is these additional arguments that are doing the real work in cases where differentiated rights are granted to national minorities.

ACTIVE INDIFFERENCE AND NATIONAL MINORITIES

In the case of national minorities it will not always be easy to separate out which issues spring from historical injustice, which from a desire for political autonomy, and which from relative institutional disadvantage, and, of course, which have all in play. Indigenous issues, for example, commonly involve issues of sovereignty, autonomy, and culture. Nevertheless, my suggestion is that whenever relative institutional disadvantage is the issue, then active indifference should always be the preferred solution, and while this may not solve all issues for national minorities, there are cases where it can work.

One such example of active indifference working in an Indigenous context is in the court system. In Australia, it was realized that many Aboriginal and Torres Strait Islander peoples found mainstream courts inaccessible or alienating. This affected access to justice, and resulted in some of the principles underpinning criminal justice—including deterrence, punishment, and rehabilitation—having a lesser impact on Aboriginal and Torres Strait Islander defendants (Australian Law Reform Commission 2017). In most Australian jurisdictions, specialist courts, which aim to be inclusive and culturally appropriate, and provide different approaches to sentencing, have been developed in response (Australian Law Reform Commission 2017). While in most jurisdictions defendants need to be recognized as Aboriginal or Torres Strait Islander to participate, this was not the case in the Northern Territory when Community Courts were operational there, with both Indigenous and non-Indigenous offenders able to participate (Bradley 2005; Thalia and Crawford 2013). The Northern Territory system was consistent with active indifference.

Because Indigenous issues often involve more than just relative institutional disadvantage, active indifference may not always satisfactorily resolve the issue. Take the example of Indigenous hunting and fishing rights. This is where Indigenous people have been granted a right to hunt or fish particular protected species and/or in places, such as national parks and marine reserves, where these activities are usually prohibited. In Australia, for example, this provision in some form exists in all states and territories, usually with a proviso that it is "for the purpose of satisfying . . . personal, domestic or communal needs, or for educational or ceremonial purposes or other traditional purposes, and which do not have a commercial purpose" (Fisheries Management Amendment Act 2009 (NSW)). Sometimes there is the further proviso that these activities are permissible only when undertaken using traditional methods, such as in Queensland, where the "taking [of] marine products or fauna by traditional means for consumption by members of the community . . . [is] . . . not . . . liable to prosecution" (for example, section 77, Community Services (Aborigines) Act 1984).

The fact that the general norm in the countries with Indigenous hunting and fishing rights is the protection of certain species, and limiting the areas where these activities can take place, means that without these hunting and fishing rights, many Indigenous people would not be able to hunt and fish particular species in the places where their forebears did. This is usually framed as a right for the preservation of culture (Patton 2016; Ivison, Patton, and Saunders 2000).

As I have suggested, the first attempt to resolve this issue should be to see whether hunting and fishing availability could just be broadened for everyone, rather than offer minority rights—that is, to implement active indifference. While this is possible, it would seem to push against some important conservation values; allowing, for example, all of us to hunt whales (in Canada and the USA) or dugong (in The Torres Strait and Northern Australia) would likely drive such species back toward extinction, and undermine what seems a pretty good justification for the hunting restrictions.

The fact that broadening hunting and fishing availability for everyone would undermine a shared value would seem to suggest that hunting of endangered species and/or in national parks should simply be outlawed—after all, not everyone can do whatever they want. But this case is, of course, different. It is not just that without these exemptions, Indigenous people cannot do something they want because of a relative institutional disadvantage, but in most cases sovereignty was never ceded and socioeconomic disadvantage persists from continued and long-term discrimination.

It is these additional arguments that need to be evaluated in any decision about potential Indigenous hunting rights (as well as similar claims). My aim is not to vouch for their veracity of these arguments, but to simply point out that it is these arguments that justify rights in these cases, and not relative institutional disadvantage per se. That is, while it is true there is relative institutional disadvantage for many Indigenous people when it comes to hunting and fishing, and many other areas too, the reason they may end up with minority rights is because of their unique history and/or contemporary socioeconomic disadvantage—something that is not true in cases of multicultural minority rights.

It is also worth noting here how the underlying values—in this case nature conservation—are still operational. That is, these conservation values still limit the extent of any minority right. So not only are non-Indigenous people not allowed to hunt particular species or in particular places, but the way Indigenous people are allowed to exercise such rights is usually limited. These rights are almost always for "noncommercial" purposes, often with clear maximum catch limits, and sometimes requiring "traditional methods."

One obvious objection here might be that Kymlicka's argument for minority rights for Indigenous peoples (and other national minorities) does not seem to require these arguments from legitimacy and historical injustice. Recall that for Kymlicka Indigenous peoples and other national minorities should have minority rights because they need a "societal culture" to have a meaningful context of choice in which they can sufficiently exercise their autonomy

(Kymlicka 1995). But this argument does not do enough by itself to grant different rights to national minorities than to other minority groups. Kymlicka needs to add in a distinction between immigrant groups who *chose* to enter a society, and national minorities who did not (Kymlicka 1995). It is this choice-sensitivity that does the real work of granting significantly stronger rights to Indigenous peoples and other national minorities. This is a type of luck egalitarianism or "luck multiculturalism" (Quong 2006), where justice requires people to only bear the consequences of things they actually chose. And it takes us back toward the questions of legitimacy and historic injustice. Once again, being involuntarily incorporated into a state is the major factor. Otherwise immigrants would also be entitled to their own societal culture, especially immigrants such as refugees whose migration was not particularly voluntary.

In all cases where there is relative institutional disadvantage, even when there are also issues of legitimacy and/or historic injustice, neutrality in the form of active indifference should be applied in the first instance. This may resolve the issue itself with nothing else required. For example, language in schools may be resolved in this way. If schools were simply allowed to choose their own language of instruction, or at least their primary language of instruction, then the minority languages of national minorities may be able to be preserved. We would not need to grant an exemption for particular languages, but simply allow school communities to determine their own primary language. There may be cases, though, where active indifference does not resolve the issue and there is not a good case for neutralizing change. Perhaps having schools choose their own language of instruction clashes with a neutral justification on social mobility. If the minorities seeking accommodation are national minorities or Indigenous people, then issues of sovereignty and historic injustice may come in to play and may independently justify minority rights and outweigh a concern for social mobility. In these cases, just because active indifference does not lead to minority accommodation, it does not mean there should not be minority rights, but they will not be *multicultural* minority rights.

CONCLUSION

Minority rights can, and have been, used to address many issues: from the treatment of Indigenous people, to discrimination against racial minorities, issues of sex and gender, a desire for political autonomy, and of course issues of cultural disadvantage. What I have tried to suggest is that multicultural minority rights should be kept distinct. While it is hard to pinpoint exactly what is "multicultural," I have suggested it involves relative institutional disadvantage without additional questions of legitimacy, sovereignty, historic injustice, sustained socioeconomic disadvantage, or a desire for political autonomy. Without these additional issues, and perhaps even with them, active indifference should be able to solve the issue of minority accommodation without recourse to minority rights. When these issues are present, as is most obvious in the case of Indigenous peoples, then minority rights may be justified, but crucially not because of relative institutional disadvantage.

Many readers may wish to run all these examples of minority rights together. But multiculturalism does not have to include all minority issues—and it does not usually include issues of gender identity, for example. I hope to have shown that separating out minority issues in this way is helpful, but I have explicitly not done this along lines of "culture." Also, none of this is to suggest that minority rights are the best way to address issues of historical injustice or nonceded sovereignty—indeed the problems with minority rights do not suddenly disappear in this space either. My argument is just that these issues are, and should be, analytically distinct. And thus potential minority rights in the case of national minorities do not justify multicultural minority rights. Here active indifference is still the best path for minority accommodation.

11

Multiculturalism and the Demands on Citizens

MY ARGUMENT SO FAR MAY seem to have reduced multiculturalism to "relative institutional disadvantage," and the response to this disadvantage to a choice between either minority rights or active indifference—with my argument favoring active indifference. Many readers may wonder, though, if this is too narrow a picture of multiculturalism. I would agree that it is. A diverse society, if minority cultural accommodation is to be achieved, will require not only institutions that accommodate, but an accommodating society. That is, the burden of accommodation will fall on all of us too. In this chapter, I want to look at what this burden entails, and in the process argue against the position that this burden requires an appreciation and respect for different ways of life. Once again, if the aim is minority accommodation, which it should be, then, perhaps surprisingly, an appreciation and respect for different ways of life is not the best way forward. Instead I argue for tolerance of difference as being more accommodating of all ways of life. This argument is connected to my argument for neutrality. I will argue for a burden on all of us that is the most neutral toward our differing ways of life, and so consequently,

Debating Multiculturalism. Peter Balint and Patti Tamara Lenard, Oxford University Press. © Oxford University Press 2022. DOI: 10.1093/oso/9780197528372.003.0012

the most accommodating. This means that neutrality is a relevant guiding ideal for both the design of public institutions *and* the demands on citizens.

TOLERANCE AND RESPECT

Intercitizen relations matter in multicultural polities. One might have the best and most accommodating institutions and policies, but if these are not supported by the majority of citizens, then minority accommodation will fail. By support, I do not just mean that the majority needs to not undermine these institutions at the ballot box by voting for political parties and candidates that actively resist minority accommodation, such as seems to be occurring in the current trend to right-wing nativism, populism, and anti-immigrant political sentiment (Eisenberg 2020a; Parvin 2020). I also mean that citizens need to be accommodating in the myriad of ways they have power in their daily lives; whether that be as employer, landlord, fellow bus passenger, or another role.

In this second sense, it might be tempting to just say that there should be strong antidiscrimination legislation and that is all that is required. But this will not be enough. Antidiscrimination legislation will unlikely be able to cover the many varieties of diversity on which people can unjustifiably be discriminated against. Moreover, relying on antidiscrimination legislation has too much faith in law to shape behavior. Yes, law does shape behavior and our attitudes too (for example, Myers 2014). But law also leaves plenty of gaps; both because law cannot cover all possibilities, and because it can be very hard to enforce. In an area as complex as how we treat each other, there is plenty of room to hide our true justifications and explain our poor behavior away. Take, as one of many possible examples, housing discrimination against African Americans. Despite the introduction of the Fair Housing Act in 1968, and its amendment in 1988, surveys have consistently shown widespread and often blatant discrimination against African Americans (Roscigno, Karafin, and Tester 2009). It is worth noting that this failure to achieve nondiscrimination is in the seemingly more straightforward area of race, rather than the more complex and shifting area of culture.

In real multicultural jurisdictions it is, at least partly, because of these issues that policymakers have realized that minority accommodation cannot simply be a matter of law. Our attitudes and behavior toward each other matter too. This move toward focusing on intercitizen relations has become much stronger this century. For example, in Britain "community cohesion" became a key focus, particularly after the Oldham and Bradford riots of 2001 and the subsequent Cantle Report (Home Office 2001). British multicultural policies moved from what was previously more of a rights and representation agenda (as a response to the race riots in the 1980s, among other things) toward a very strong and overriding emphasis on community relations, and with it the responsibilities of "active citizenship" (Kundnani 2002; Burnett 2004; Thomas 2007). In Australia, multicultural policy over the last decade or so of the twentieth century shifted from emphasizing what the state should do, to placing much more emphasis on individual duties (Levey 2001), a trend which has continued.

This trend is common in education (Drerup 2019; 2018). Here, when dealing with the issues of diversity, there is an attempt to instill the right civic virtues in our future full citizens to enable the full accommodation of minority groups. While the focus in education is on children, for adult citizens we too are often exposed to campaigns to assist minority accommodation as well as publicly funded festivals and events. I do not want to challenge the intent of policymakers in trying to assist the accommodation of minorities—and we unfortunately know too well what can happen when people's discriminatory attitudes and behavior go unchecked. Instead, I want to look in this chapter at what might be required from citizens in diverse societies, and what types of attitudes and behaviors should be encouraged.

One path that is commonly taken here is to encourage deep understanding and respect for the differences that exist in a particular polity, with the presumption that if we only understood and appreciated our diversity more, then there would be less discrimination and more minority accommodation. In political theory, for example, James Tully writes: "The condition of self-respect is met only in a society in which the cultures of all others are recognised and affirmed by others, both those who do and those who do not share those cultures" (1995, 190), and Joseph Raz writes that "multiculturalism insists that members of different groups should appreciate and respect the other cultures in their society" (1994, 72–73).

In policy, Canada's (now superseded) "Federal Immigrant Integration Strategy" stated: "Newcomers are expected to understand and respect basic Canadian values, and Canadians are expected to understand and respect the cultural differences newcomers bring to Canada" (Citizenship and Immigration Canada 2001, 4). In law, the Community Relations Commission and Principles of Multiculturalism Act 2000 (of the Australian state of New South Wales) reads: "All individuals and institutions should respect and make provision for the culture, language and religion of others within an Australian legal and institutional framework where English is the common language" (New South Wales Parliament 2000, Part 1, Section 3, Principle 2).

So *respect of difference* can, and has been, encouraged as a norm of good citizenship by educational authorities, policymakers, and legislators. Respect of difference might just mean respecting the rights of others even if they have different ways of life, or it might mean actually respecting those ways of life (Balint 2013). These examples seem to point to the stronger understanding, at least as the ideal, that we should engage with the different ways of life in our community, learn more about them, and appreciate their unique and positive aspects. That is, that we should actually respect those ways of life. This norm of good citizenship seems to entail not just respecting other people's rights to act and be different, but the actual content of that difference.

An alternative approach to respect for difference is that citizens need to *tolerate each other's differences*. That is, instead of learning about and appreciating the diversity that exists in a polity, citizens instead need simply to not hinder the activities of those they object to. Of course, they may decide to respect and value particular differences, but they do not need to. With this alternative norm of good citizenship, all that is required is that when they have strong views on other citizen's ways of life, and the sort of views that may lead them to fail to accommodate the followers of these ways of life, they restrain their power and treat these other people equally. So, for example, if a landlord has particular religious worldviews, and is confronted by a prospective tenant whose way of life is counter to these views, the landlord needs to treat the tenant equally (would they be a good tenant? Can they pay the rent? etc.) and not act on their objection. This alternative places a demand on citizens to tolerate each other's difference. As I want to show in this chapter, this is preferable to the demand that citizens respect each other's differences.

It may seem very obvious, but it is worth stressing: citizens are human beings who all hold differing and contrasting views on what is a good life. Indeed, it is these very views that make intercitizen accommodation so challenging. In the cases where there are failures to accommodate, this is usually because of a negative judgment of the other's difference. Tolerance of difference simply says that we should not act on that judgment. Tolerance of difference is a minimal demand that leaves entirely open the attitude we might have towards our fellow citizen's ways of life. It simply requires nonhindrance; that we do not act on our objection to block minority accommodation.

To some readers, this may seem undesirable. If tolerance of difference is the minimal demand, then we still have people judging each other badly and having the power to interfere in each other's lives. This is a common critique of tolerance. For example, Tariq Ramadan writes (2010, 46–47):

> Toleration is intellectual charity on the part of the powerful . . . and we must get beyond it. When standing on equal

footing, one does not expect to be merely tolerated or grudg-
ingly accepted: that others endure and "suffer" one's presence is inadequate for oneself and detrimental to them.

Michael Walzer writes: "To tolerate someone else is an act
of power; to be tolerated is an acceptance of weakness,"
before then adding "We should aim at something better than this combination, something beyond toleration,
something like mutual respect" (1997, 52). And Adeno
Addis argues that "the toleration model...'nourish[es] false
charity' towards minorities" (1996, 112–53, 142). What we
need is to explore institutional structures and processes
that would simultaneously allow us to affirm and respect
plurality while also cultivating some notion of solidarity.
This *despotism challenge* to tolerance seems to have become
somewhat of a sociological, or at least critical theory, ortho-
doxy (Balint 2017). Much better, it is argued, is respect for
difference.

But if the aim is accommodation of minority ways of
life, then encouraging tolerance, and not respect for difference, is preferable. This is because tolerance actually
allows for more accommodation of diversity than respect
for difference. If someone now respects and appreciates a
particular difference, they no longer find it objectionable.
This may seem a good thing. But this change has already
narrowed the range of diversity. While this may not seem
problematic at first, the reason we have policies that push
for respect and appreciation of difference is because we
have divergent ways of life. If we encourage citizens to no
longer object to each other, then a significant amount of
this diversity is gone—perhaps so much so that "diverse
society" would be a misnomer.

My point is not that anything goes and that all ways of life should be tolerated, but instead that a diverse society should contain ways of life that can tolerate each other. And importantly, allowing greater diversity does not automatically impede minority accommodation. We know that tolerance of difference is possible—our societies are full of people who object to each other's ways of life, beliefs, and opinions, but who still manage to tolerate each other. Think, for example, of the religiously devout who work alongside those following other religions or no religion at all. Respect and appreciation are not necessary for minority accommodation. It is true that those with objections can fail to tolerate, but it is hard to see how encouraging them to respect and appreciate the things they despise is the most likely path away from such intolerance and toward accommodation. A more realistic and manageable step would simply be to encourage tolerance. Encouraging tolerance acknowledges that citizens have objections, but says they need to be careful not to act on them. For those with objections to particular ways of life, tolerance will appear a much more feasible option than moving straight to respecting and appreciating the very things they think are deeply wrong.

Asking citizens to respect and appreciate each other's differences is burdensome. It is also potentially contradictory. It is burdensome because citizens have their own views and they have their own ways of life. When we ask them to respect and appreciate, especially when this contradicts their own beliefs and ways of life, this is a lot to ask. A classic case would be between those whose tenets see human fetuses as life that should not be harmed, and those whose tenets see women as having full autonomy over their own bodies. Respect and appreciation among those on opposing sides of the abortion debate would seem almost impossibly burdensome. It would also fail to take people's differences seriously. It is in this way potentially contradictory. If respect and appreciation matter because we need to understand people's uniqueness in order to properly accommodate them, then asking them to do things that contradict their beliefs seems deeply problematic at best, and entirely contradictory at worst. That is, it fails to take their differences seriously—the very thing it is supposed to do.

In contrast, tolerance of difference is not as burdensome as it requires acts, not attitudes. It is also not contradictory. It takes people's differences seriously, and only asks that they refrain from action in particular circumstances. It is true that it does ask the intolerant not to act intolerantly, and for some this will be a big ask, but it allows a great deal more diversity than respect and appreciation.

For many of us, respect and appreciation of difference is possible (and perhaps even enjoyable) in many cases. But it is quite likely that these are cases where we would not have failed to accommodate. That is, respect and appreciation will not be such a big ask when we would have accommodated anyway. I might, for example, be encouraged to learn about and appreciate the practices of my local Italian community. But if I already had no objections toward them or their practices, then I am unlikely to have been a barrier to their accommodation. Let me stress that it is the hard cases, where accommodation is not likely, that should be the real test of multicultural practice. It is in these hard cases, where individuals and groups have deep animosity toward each other, that approaches to accommodating intercitizen relations need to be tested. Here, once again, tolerance of difference seems a more likely candidate, as it seeks more realistic change.

It might seem that my argument is overstated. What, you may wonder, is the harm in encouraging citizens to respect and appreciate each other's differences? It is not being coerced, but simply encouraged as good civic practice. Surely, you may wonder, it makes the world a richer place, and may make it a little more accommodating. In many ways I agree. It is interesting to learn about other ways of life and to appreciate their uniqueness. But that is not, or should not be, the main aim in fostering more accommodating intercitizen relations. Such a view is clearly a conception of the good—that is, a way of life itself—and if the state is to be neutral (as I have argued it should be), then promoting such a view without neutral justification violates this neutrality. It is up to individuals how they spend their time, and surely this is just one valuable option among many. It is a cosmopolitan view of diversity that works well for liberal-minded individuals, but it is not a neutral view.

Given that we know diverse societies are made up of more than just liberal-minded individuals—otherwise they would not by definition be diverse—there is another problem with promoting respect and appreciation as an ideal. This is because respect and appreciation are much easier for liberal-minded individuals than for those with more divergent differences. If an ideal citizen is a respecting and appreciating of difference citizen, and one whose differences can be respected and appreciated, then properly divergent ways of life will face assimilatory pressures (Balint 2013, 2011). Cultures will need to accentuate their most acceptable parts—usually things like their cooking and their dancing—and downplay their more difficult parts—usually their values and beliefs. Doing this risks turning diversity into simply an aesthetic category, completely trivializing values and beliefs. This encouragement of respect and appreciation either unjustifiably leaves out some citizens altogether from this respect game, or unjustifiably assimilates them into a comfortable cosmopolitan mainstream. I say unjustifiably because there is no necessary link between failure to respect and appreciate and failure to accommodate. As I have already said, respect and appreciation are not necessary for minority accommodation. All of this narrows the range of diversity, and in its own way fails to accommodate.

One final objection may be that I have mischaracterized "respect." It is true that the phrase "respecting and appreciating difference" can play on the ambiguities in "respect." Respect can involve valuing something as worthy, or feeling awe—this is "appreciation-respect," and it is the way we might respect an artist's work. Or it might involve just acting in a way that upholds a particular status—this is "recognition respect," and is the way we might respect a judge in a court of law (Darwall 1977; see also Ceva and Zuolo 2013; Seglow 2020). The other ambiguity with respect of difference involves the object of respect. As I mentioned earlier, it might be the content of the difference that should be respected, or it might be the right to be different itself that should be respected. If all that those who are pushing for "respect of difference" were saying was that everyone has a right to be different and we should not interfere with this, then we are simply back to talking about tolerance of difference. Because we respect a right, we need to tolerate the content of that right. For example, respecting someone's right to free speech will (when the speech is objectionable) involve tolerating the content of that speech (Ferretti 2018). But it is clear from the earlier statements that much more is often asked and aimed for. And this "more" commonly involves appreciation-respect of the content of the difference, and this is a very different thing. It is both more onerous and much less accommodating.

CONCLUSION

Respect and appreciation of difference are not particularly neutral. They seemingly promote a conception of the good and place pressures on divergent ways of life which have the potential to narrow the range of diversity. Tolerance of difference, in contrast, is more accommodating. It enables a much greater range of diversity, and is more neutral toward people's own values and beliefs. In promoting greater tolerance, it does not matter what people think or feel; they simply need to accommodate. This allows people to have a range of attitudes toward the diversity they encounter—whether it be a deep objection, indifference, or even respect and appreciation. All that matters is their action. Yes, this is still demanding, and will not solve all cases of failed accommodation, but it is both more neutral and more accommodating of diversity, and so should be preferred.

The problem of minority accommodation is not just one of relative institutional disadvantage. How we treat each other matters too. This raises the question of what multicultural civic virtue should be promoted. There has been a tendency to push for respect and appreciation of difference seemingly because if we have a positive attitude to diversity, then we will accommodate. I have instead argued for tolerance of difference. Promoting tolerance acknowledges that people may have objections to other ways of life, but asks them to refrain from acting on them. Not only is tolerance of difference more neutral than respect and appreciation of difference, but it is more accommodating and allows a greater range of diversity. That is, promoting tolerance of difference is the best way to achieve minority accommodation.

12

Conclusion to Part II

THOSE CONCERNED WITH MINORITY DISADVANTAGE
and accommodation have generally seen neutrality as the
enemy; as a false principle that simply maintains the status quo and its power over everyone else. In the words of
Iris Marion Young (1989, 116, 169): "The standpoint of
the privileged, their particular experience and standards,
is constructed as normal and neutral," with the problem
being that "formally neutral rules and policies that ignore
differences often perpetuate the disadvantage of those
whose difference is defined as deviant."

Or in the even stronger words of Tim Nieguth
(1999, 113):

> In the context of an unequal distribution of societal power
> among ethno-cultural groups, there are only two approaches
> for the state to address cultural diversity: privilege and rec-
> ognition. . . . state neutrality is a myth; states cannot nor-
> mally expect to act in a fashion that is culturally neutral.
> Approaches to the management of cultural diversity which
> are founded on the ideal of state neutrality effectively con-
> tribute to the perpetuation of power differentials, and thus
> to the maintenance of privilege.

But neutrality is not conservative; it is a radical principle
that can tear at majority privilege and open up the way for

minority accommodation. When those in power defend the status quo and its privileging of majority ways of life, it is the ideal of neutrality that has the critical power to attack and undermine that privilege. Neutrality is the friend, not the enemy, of disadvantaged minorities.[1]

While many actions that stifle minority accommodations may be cloaked in the language of neutral justifications, this in itself is not neutrality. It is not neutral to ban burkas in public, or to stop public sector employees from wearing conspicuous religious symbols, or to ban a person whose face is covered from delivering or receiving a public service, even if such provisions are shrouded in neutral justifications. A neutral justification is necessary for minority accommodation, but it is not sufficient. Intent matters too.

Institutions that knowingly and avoidably favor majority ways of life are not neutral in intent. As I have argued, in most multicultural cases, the "knowingly" condition has been clearly met by disadvantaged minorities and their advocates vocally pointing out this relative privileging. As for "avoidability," I have argued that the purpose of the institution can often be met if things are done differently—just because something has always been done a particular way does not mean it must continue. Our institutions can, and do, change over time.

---

1. It is interesting to note that parallel arguments from advocates of women's human rights and LGBTI rights also express frustration with the limitations of "difference blind universalism," but have tended to respond by arguing not for minority rights, but rather for the critical enlargement and reshaping of human rights (Woods 2014).

Of course, this change *could* involve multicultural minority rights, and this is a neutralizing option. But while neutrality can involve minority rights, it does not need to. If an institution can still meet its purpose with multicultural minority rights, then it likely can meet its purpose if these accommodations are simply generalized. That is, the institution simply broadens its range of possible options rather than provides particular rights to certain individuals. As I have argued, institutions are at their most accommodating of minority ways of life when they do not provide multicultural minority rights at all.

So while Nieguth may argue that "there are only two approaches for the state to address cultural diversity: privilege and recognition," there is a third, neutrality, which is not "a myth" at all. It is both very real and very accommodating of cultural diversity. But this is not quite accurate: the recognition and multicultural minority rights he favors are a form of neutrality. Unless we want to support majority privilege, we do have two choices to accommodate cultural diversity, both of which are neutralizing multicultural minority rights and active indifference.

Multicultural minority rights do allow some minorities to do and be things that they would have difficulty doing otherwise. In this sense, they are better than continuing with institutions that favor the majority. Multicultural minority rights have allowed Jews and Muslims to eat meat according to their dietary traditions, and for Sikhs to join the police and the military, among many other things. But multicultural minority rights are not without serious risks—risks that are acknowledged even by those who advocate for them. Multicultural minority rights require recognition. This leads to the issue of working out who exactly is a member of a group as well as which type of groups actually count. The recognition of particular groups is known to help construct the identity of that group—the group's identity and makeup respond to and are shaped by this granting of recognition and minority rights. This recognition can reify and essentialize an identity, pushing against the usual fluidity and variability of identity. One key problem here is that minorities within minorities— such as women or those with progressive or divergent views from the group's authorities—can be left more vulnerable, as the more conservative authorities are further empowered. So while multicultural minority rights do lead to minority accommodation, they are not without costs and risks, costs and risks accepted by both their advocates and their critics.

Multicultural minority rights are by their nature targeted at specific groups. But multicultural accommodation does not need to be targeted at all. Our institutions already change and adapt to accommodate our needs without targeting specific groups. What I have called active indifference is not only possible, but we see it in practice right now. Our institutions can, and have, adapted and changed to accommodate new needs and desires and to continue to properly serve their purpose.

When institutions change and adapt without recognizing any particular ways of life or providing minority rights, then not only are the agreed problems of multicultural minority rights avoided, but they offer greater freedom to all of us. Those who would have been accommodated by minority rights are still accommodated, and everyone else is also given greater freedom. We now not only have fewer restrictions, but more options to choose from. Active indifference should appeal to classically minded liberals who are concerned with restrictions and too much state involvement. They will see multicultural minority rights as adding new restrictions and complicating and growing state institutions. But it should also appeal to autonomy-focused liberals, who are concerned that individuals have a sufficient number of meaningful options to choose from and that they are not constrained by their circumstance. Active indifference is consistent with the broad range of liberal views.

While multicultural minority rights and active indifference are both neutralizing of majority privilege, these two forms of neutrality are not equal. If the problem is majority privilege, the solution should be removing that privilege rather than adding new forms of privilege.

My argument has explicitly been against *multicultural* minority rights, and I have been careful to distinguish these from other forms of minority rights. I have argued that when the problem is relative institutional disadvantage, then multicultural minority rights should not be the solution. But there are other cases where the problem is more than relative institutional disadvantage. Histories of gender and race discrimination, colonization, and other historical injustices provide a different set of justifications for minority rights. In the case of Indigenous peoples, for example, a lack of ceded sovereignty and issues of both contemporary and historic injustice may justify minority rights. These justifications are not present in multicultural contexts. Though even here, if it is possible to achieve accommodation through active indifference, then this pathway should be preferred—the problems of minority rights exist in this sphere too. But where active indifference will not achieve accommodation, these additional arguments may justify minority rights—arguments that are not present in the multicultural context. The existence of minority rights in this sphere in no way justifies them in the multicultural context.

Finally, multiculturalism and the accommodation of minority ways of life are not just about relative institutional disadvantage—despite many of the more well-known examples. If minorities are to be successfully accommodated in our diverse societies, then it is up to all of us to help this happen. We all have the power to accommodate, or not; whether it be as teacher, bus driver, customer, business owner, or otherwise. Despite the importance of antidiscrimination legislation, it will not be enough to achieve accommodation—we need some sort of multicultural virtue. This realization is not new, and policymakers, educators, and legislators have had this concern for some time. However, in their quest to aid accommodation, some of them have overstepped the mark. In advocating that we should respect and appreciate each other's differences, they have, perhaps unwittingly, pushed against the broad accommodation of diversity. The range of ways of life that can be both respecting and respectable is much narrower than those that can be tolerating and tolerable (Balint 2010). And while a life that involves respecting and appreciating other ways of life may be appealing to liberal-minded individuals, a diverse society is made of more than liberal-minded individuals.

The alternative to respecting and appreciating other ways of life as a multicultural virtue is tolerance of difference. Tolerance does not require a positive attitude, only accommodation. In this way it is much more accommodating than respect and appreciation of difference. Individuals do not have to rid themselves of objections, and therefore change their values. And nor are they pressured to make their ways of life more appealing to the majority. All that matters is their actions.

It is true that many people don't just want to be tolerated. But being tolerated is much better than being subject to intolerance, and in the hard cases that multicultural accommodation should be focused on, it may well be the best that can be hoped for (Horton 2011). Asking those with deep differences to respect and appreciate each other's ways of life is likely a bridge too far. Acknowledging their objections, but asking for accommodation, seems more feasible and more reasonable, and more accommodating of minority ways of life all round. Finally, promoting tolerance of difference is much more neutral toward people's ways of life: they can forebear, be indifferent, or even respect other people's ways of life; all that matters is that they accommodate. And so if we care about the accommodation of minority ways of life, then neutrality matters for both our institutions, and the demands that are placed on us as individuals in diverse societies.

Part III

RESPONSES

13

Response to Balint

Culture, Not Colanders, or Why Neutralism Fails to Respond Effectively to the Challenges of Cultural Diversity

AT THE FOUNDATION OF THE disagreement between Balint and myself is, I believe, the relative importance of cultural membership in the lives of individuals, both privately and politically. Whereas I proceed as though cultural membership is deeply valuable to its members, and shapes how they interact in private and public in profound ways, Balint treats cultural membership as one of many private choices that individuals should be freely permitted to make. For me, but not for Balint, protecting culture requires active political intervention by states—to ensure access to differentiated rights for minority cultures—to protect and support it in multiple ways. This foundational disagreement shapes my response to his neutralist view. Balint's provocative and well-argued view has two main planks. The first plank focuses on articulating the concept of neutrality, as it applies to institutions. Neutral institutions are those that are reasonably acceptable to citizens with a wide range of ways of life; this, Balint says, is neutrality of justification. As well, neutral institutions intend to be neutral among ways of life, that is, in his words, they must not "knowingly and

Debating Multiculturalism. Peter Balint and Patti Tamara Lenard, Oxford University Press. © Oxford University Press 2022. DOI: 10.1093/oso/9780197528372.003.0014

avoidably" ("Neutrality of Intent" in chapter 8) favor some ways of life over others. The second plank focuses on the concept of active indifference, which, says Balint, advises a public policy focus on removing majority privilege from institutions that are aiming at neutrality. This second plank distinguishes his view from mine, since (using his language) mine is in favor of adding minority privilege in the form of protected rights for cultural minorities, and *only* for cultural minorities. In what follows, I shall not argue against the policies that flow from a commitment to active indifference as Balint describes it, except to suggest that these policies will be insufficient to resolve the challenges posed by minority cultures in liberal democratic sates. My disagreements lay elsewhere.

First, I will examine Balint's suggestion that attempts to define "culture" are so riddled with challenges that, together, they count as a reason in favor of looking for alternatives to respecting minority cultural rights. I will of course deny that this conclusion is warranted. Second, and in the course of doing so, I will give some special attention to the domination worry that he raises, in part by examining the political participation of Orthodox Jewish communities in the United States. Finally, I will question Balint's confidence in the role that toleration can play in sustaining solidarity in a diverse political space.

WHO IDENTIFIES MEMBERS OF CULTURES AND WHY IT MATTERS

Culture is very hard to define. In my own contribution, I emphasized the importance of treading carefully, to recognize that a "culture" is typically defined by a wide range of practices, norms, and values, which members recognize and adopt as their own to varying degrees. These practices, norms, and values sometimes have a religious basis, and other times ethnic and racial bases. I noted, as well, that the defining features of a culture shift over time, gaining or weakening in resonance for members, in response to a wide range of factors, some internal and some external. Cultures can collectively make choices to abandon certain practices which become recognized as harmful, and they can feel pressure from external forces to abandon others that are inconsistent with the wider political or moral values of the society in which they live. As I have described it, the defining features of a culture are always in flux and, correspondingly, its boundaries are inevitably fuzzy. I believe that Balint and I are in agreement about this way of understanding culture.

But, worries Balint, if this way of understanding culture is accepted, it raises a number of difficult—for him possibly irresolvable—questions about how, thereby, to identify who is a member of a particular cultural group, especially when political privileges are awarded on that basis. He wonders, "So should membership of a group and entitlement to a right simply be given to all those who self-identify as members? Or do they need to be recognized by an authority from that particular group? Or is there some objective criterion on which genuine membership lies?" ("Avoiding the Costs and Risks of Recognition" in chapter 9). Balint sees challenges with answering yes to any of these: if individuals can simply choose to be a member, then there is room for opportunism—an individual might disingenuously claim connection to a minority group in order to gain access to a particular minority right. But if members are identified by a group authority, which may seem more authentic—it offers a way to protect cultures from fraudsters, who set their sight on accessing coveted minority rights—individuals who do not obviously meet the requirements set out by the group authority are excluded from the culture and its benefits. Moreover, any attempt to set up a list of objective criteria for cultural membership will be inevitably contested, and would only operate to essentialize the culture, artificially halting the natural process of change to which it would have been subject otherwise. So, Balint says, it can't work to allow individuals to self-identify as members, and it also cannot work to allow group authorities to identify members. This, he says, is a problem of normative vagueness: the challenge of picking out cultural minority groups, and then of identifying their members, feels hard enough to him that we ought to search for an alternative way to engage with minority cultural claims.

I think the first of Balint's worries is overstated. It is, in effect, a worry about fraudulent claims—someone fraudulently claims an identity, and crucially the benefits from doing so, to which she is not entitled. It is of course the case that individuals claim new and distinct identifies, often over the course of their lives. And it is also true that there are cases where it seems right to say that someone has claimed an identity to which she is not entitled. Here is an example: Associate Professor of History Jessica Krug appears to have assumed a range of racial identities over the course of her adult life, and benefited from a number of academic opportunities as a result. She said of herself, in a widely circulated apology letter: "To an escalating degree over my adult life, I have eschewed my lived experience as a white Jewish child in suburban Kansas City under various assumed identities within a Blackness that I had no right to claim: first North African Blackness, then US rooted Blackness, then Caribbean rooted Bronx Blackness" (Al Jazeera 2020). I believe, however, that such cases are likely to be so rare that they do not outweigh the benefits of a self-identification view, nor justify abandoning it, as I will describe later.

One reason to defend, broadly, an account of culture that permits and reinforces self-identification is that it is freedom-preserving, and this is why I believe Balint supports this strategy for identifying members of cultural minorities, in spite of the objections he mounts against it. Of course, most individuals who are members of cultural groups do not entirely experience the membership, and the ensuing identity, as chosen, in the same way as one chooses an occupation or a life partner. Additionally, individuals can and do shift their identities in response to a range of factors: individuals can change religions, for example, and they can claim attachment to cultural and ethnic practices with more or less vigor over the course of their lives (Eisenberg 2009). These are shifts that are permissible, and even welcome, in liberal political theory. Crucially, although individuals do not typically treat their cultural membership as chosen, the liberal state *does*, and so is on guard for cases where cultural groups claim members as their own against their will.

Balint's worry is not that individuals will, if the self-identification view is accepted, experiment with cultural identities over the course of their lives, abandoning some and adopting others with various levels of strength and commitment. His worry is that, in doing so, they will claim a "privilege" that is widely desired, but must be protected for genuine cultural minorities only. In a pure self-identification model, the danger is that the state announces benefits for minorities, allows individuals to self-identify as those minorities, and uncritically dispenses benefits on that basis. It is a system ripe for abuse of the type that Krug perpetuated.

How many minority cultural rights are benefits of a kind such that it is critical they be protected for only real minorities, however? Should we worry that fraudsters claiming Jewish identity will demand kosher food in a cafeteria? Or that fraudsters claiming Sikh identity will request to wear a turban as part of their uniform? In order for the worry about fraud to be pressing, it must focus on goods that are of value to minorities and noncultural minorities alike, so valuable that it would prompt the fraudulent claiming of identities. There are cases where fraud could be a worry—educational, for example, as Krug's case demonstrated—where there are spaces explicitly reserved for minorities on the grounds of historical discrimination against them. But that there are a limited number of cases where benefits that are reserved for minorities are widely recognized as valuable is not necessarily a reason to abandon, entirely, a self-identification model which retains the benefits I have described. Rather, it is a reason to adopt—for some limited cases—a system of verifying identity-based claims where benefits are claimed as a result.

The procedures for identity-verification are undoubtedly tricky—one option is to rely on a system in which the sincerity of the relevant identity is assessed using a range of criteria, including evidence of past behaviors and ethnic or racial background (Golemboski 2019; Martin 2020). Since Balint already believes that affirmative action policies may serve as an appropriate mechanism by which to remedy past injustices, and since nearly all of the widely valuable goods reserved for minorities will be distributed for those reasons, he should not have any reason to challenge this way of proceeding. I think this is the right strategy to pursue overall, that is, to permit self-identification in general, and to require verification where access to highly valuable goods is on the line.

On the other hand, and in response to Balint's second stated worry with respect to cultural membership, I am in agreement about the dangers associated with giving license to group authorities to identify and exclude members. The dangers are well acknowledged: in many minority cultural groups, group authorities are older men, often with rigid interpretations of often burdensome cultural norms and practices that are largely borne by women, sometimes against their will. This is the problem, as Balint says, of "minorities within minorities"—if groups are permitted to define the parameters of membership, including which norms must be adhered to as a condition of membership, there will be minorities who are forced into making difficult choices, to conform to norms they reject or wish to reject, or to risk excommunication from the culture, thereby losing much of what is valuable to them, including access to their families and, especially, their children (Eisenberg and Spinner-Halev 2005).

Later I will say more about how to respond to groups where dominant members have, or take, authority to define membership, but there are two important preliminary observations to make first. First, in shifting from raising the challenges associated with self-identification to the challenges of group authority mechanisms for identifying members, the discussion has shifted from the challenges posed by one form of cultural minority to those posed by another. Where the worry is cultural fraudsters, the fear is about access to highly valuable state-provided goods reserved for cultural minorities. When we shift to the challenges associated with group authority identification, the worry is domination of vulnerable minorities by group authorities. But notice that in the first case, at issue are individuals claiming specific rights that are intended to support the political inclusion I considered in chapter 2, whereas in the latter, the focus is on the culturally isolationist groups I considered in my chapter 5. I do not say the following to diminish their importance as moral questions, but it is valuable to note that while the latter kinds of cases are the most troubling for liberals, they are also the *significant minority* of cases that liberal democratic states must confront. It is clear, however, from Balint's language that he has misunderstood this fact—his choice to, persistently, refer to cultural minority "ways of life," rather than simply a practice or norm in need of accommodation, tells readers that he is focused mainly on this relatively small number of multicultural claims. Rather, most requests for cultural rights protection are not about protecting "ways of life;" they are instead mainly focused on ensuring that key cultural norms and practices do not bar minority citizens from accessing the goods that are meant to be widely available.

A second observation is that, in the case of illiberal groups, there are two separate benefits that are made available on the basis of group membership. One benefit is the state-provided benefit, in the form of exemptions from certain mandatory laws, including education. But another, and arguably more important one, is the good of membership itself. In other words, in the vast majority of cases where group authorities claim control over the contours of membership, the valuable benefits at stake are not offered by the state, but rather by the group itself. So, the question is whether, if a group authority is permitted to define the contours of membership, individual members will be forced into accepting conditions they would otherwise reject, in order to access the goods over which the group authorities have control. This problem is real, but it is not so clear that denying the right of group authorities to define the parameters of membership is an appropriate strategy in these minority of cases. It is hard, moreover, to know what this denial would look like in practice.

Readers might reasonably wonder, though, whether a political inclusion model really does better than Balint's neutralist view, especially in hard cases. What I said in chapter 6 is that a focus on political inclusion guides us toward accepting exemptions where exit is protected, and it guides us to accepting internal conflict resolution mechanisms so long as those who are subject to them can also, if they need or desire, access the support of the larger state. These were, I said, imperfect compromises, intended to protect the trust on which democratic states rely. However, a critical reader might point out that a political inclusion framework can deliver problematic or at least confusing responses, in at least the following kind of case.

In chapter 5, I described two Orthodox Jewish communities in the United States, and suggested that in one, the wider state reneged on an agreed compromise by failing to respect the religious convictions of Jewish students, and that in another, the failure to respond to the community's needs in a culturally sensitive way undermined trust, thereby hampering the cooperation required to reduce the transmission of Covid-19. One feature that I did not consider there is that, in fact, along some dimensions, these communities are—as are Orthodox Jewish communities in Israel—politically included, and indeed, politically powerful.

In New York State, it is conventionally understood that members of Orthodox Jewish communities reliably vote in blocs, according to the dictates of their political leaders— and so, political leaders in New York State have political incentives to accede to their demands. In turn, minority cultural groups have an incentive to ramp up internal domination—if the power of group authorities to secure political concessions from state leaders rests on their capacity to deliver large numbers of votes, then these authorities have incentives to act aggressively to coerce their members to remain members; they do so by threatening would-be leavers, or even would-be internal campaigners for change, with harsh penalties, including exclusion from the community and its many benefits.[1] I do not wish to deny the potential of this dynamic, although I believe the worry is overstated. For one thing, the objection gains some of its strength from the belief (which remains implied rather than stated) that, ultimately, most (women) members of these groups are coerced at some level to remain and that many more would leave if they could. I think this

---

1. I would like to thank Alasia Nuti and Alice Pinheiro Walla for pressing this point.

assumption is wrong, however, and on the contrary believe that the success of these communities lies precisely in their members' deep comfort and enjoyment of membership and its benefits. That is, while I would not deny that these communities exercise power over their members, sometimes in ways that are problematic, I believe on the contrary that membership in them provides considerable value to their members. For another, it is at least equivalently plausible to propose that, because group leaders of these communities want to ensure that their group's power is sustained over time, they work hard to ensure that membership remains valuable to members (and therefore that members do not desire to leave). Ultimately, however, the political engagement of the group's members, following the dictates of group leaders, does not tell against the lesson I derived from the political inclusion model, namely, that there are reasons to work to sustain trust relations between minority communities and the larger state, so that where shared political objectives require collaboration to achieve, the trust needed to do so is available.

Moreover, it would also not do to say because a group has political power, the state should intervene to undermine the group's authority to define the contours of membership. A better strategy is to support insiders in their quests for achieving rights protection for members whose rights are constrained in ways that they wish to resist. Recall that for many women members, whose rights are constrained in problematic ways, they do *not* desire to cut ties, but rather to reform problematic norms and practices from within (Deveaux 2006). To consider just one example, there are nongovernmental organizations *run by members* that aim to secure, for Orthodox Jewish women, a fair "get," the traditional name for a Jewish divorce (ORA 2020). Their objective is to support Orthodox women who are victims of domestic abuse, who do not wish to leave the community, to divorce in a culturally appropriate way. The lawyers who support women through these processes, by and large, have secular legal educations that enable them to navigate both state and community law, and thereby to ensure that the rights of such women are protected from abuse by members.

So, the political inclusion model I have defended is robust against a range of criticisms: it accepts the possibility of cultural fraudsters in exchange for giving individuals the agency they need in matters of culture, and it does not simply dismiss the reality that the state will be forced to engage with insular cultural minorities. It invites a careful look at how best to proceed, knowing that at multiple levels, what the right goal is, in a democratic society, is political inclusion on trusting terms. It is fundamentally a political, action-guiding model, rather than an ideal at which to aim. It guides us in the present to engage with challenges posed by cultural minorities in liberal democratic states, and it allows us to treat comparable cases alike and also to recognize that contextual considerations will always be relevant in particular cases. It is, to borrow Joseph Carens's term, an even-handed approach to the challenges posed by diversity in liberal democratic states (Carens 2000).

But, Balint might say, so is the neutralist model he advocates—his model guides states to select policy options that come closest to treating citizens neutrally whatever their background. It also directs states to select policy options that expand freedom. So, he tells us, there may be many reasons to desire to wear a turban or a headscarf—one might be a religious conviction and one might be fashion consciousness. Permitting anyone with a sincerely stated reason to modify uniform requirements has the advantage, as well, of being freedom expanding: "New opportunities created are not limited to particular people. So if an institution now allows the wearing of headscarves as part of its uniform, this would allow anyone to wear a headscarf—whether they be orthodox Muslim, fashion conscious, having a bad hair day, or just trying it out" ("Objections to Active Indifference" in chapter 9). Cultural minorities standing by as others choose to experiment with turbans, or headscarves, ought not to feel offended—they have what they need, and want, in the form of a rule that permits them to carry out their religious obligations.

I agree with Balint that in this case the result is relatively congenial, though I think he downplays the hurtful experience of being a cultural minority member and watching others experiment with the practices and traditions that the minority group holds dear.[2] But it is important to see that he has selected the example so that there is no significant cost associated with accommodating the request, and expanding it to everyone regardless of their reason. What if there are costs, however, as there are in cases where individuals require breaks to pray, or specially prepared food to be made available, or material support to sustain a minority language, to establish a culturally separate school, or to sustain self-governance institutions? He may well stick to his guns, explaining that if the case

---

2. This hurt, associated with watching "outsiders" experiment with cultural practices and traditions, is one of the harms of cultural appropriation. See Lenard and Balint 2020.

can be made for a cultural minority individual or group to gain access to material support in support of any of these, it must be made available for all, regardless of expense. If the material resources to support this right extension for all are not available, however, it is not so clear how Balint recommends proceeding. One ordinary mechanism would be to ask for priority rules, but noting that the fashionable really value their fashionable clothing, Balint says, the state does not have adequate reason to treat culture as though it were special. If no particular value sets are recognized as more valuable in general, such priority rules are impossible to implement. We might even ask, how can a neutrality approach defend standard uniform requirements at all, since in principle and indeed in practice, anyone can exempt themselves from them on the basis of a sincerely held commitment (including, apparently, that the uniform isn't flattering)? Members of cultural minority groups would, in my view, be entitled to understand this equivalence as a form of misrecognition.

In the final chapter of his defense of neutrality, Balint considers the attitudinal orientations a citizenry requires in order to sustain a commitment to neutrality, toward cultural and all other forms of difference. He says that it is of course true that a diverse society requires more than merely appropriate institutions in order to run well; it requires that its citizenry demonstrate tolerance toward others. Although Balint refers to tolerance as a behavior, it is also an attitude. Indeed, a tolerant attitude is generally required to support consistently tolerant behaviors. Tolerance is an attitude that is marked by the willingness to accept that others have values with which one does not agree, and also that they engage in practices that one finds silly or boring or even anathema, and to leave them be. Antidiscrimination legislation can get us part of the way there—such legislation nominally protects minorities from being unfairly excluded from valuable educational and employment opportunities, for example. But fundamentally, this legislation is effective only if, as well, those who are subject to it operate it with an attitude of tolerance. Tolerance is contrasted with the more demanding requirements allegedly defended by advocates of minority cultural rights, namely, "deep understanding and respect for," as well as "appreciation of," cultural diversity. All of these attitudes preclude finding the practices of others "objectionable" and so can be quite demanding on citizens; it takes work to "understand people's uniqueness in order to properly accommodate them" ("Tolerance and Respect" in chapter 11).

Although I concede that Balint can find quotations from early multicultural theorists, advocating what seem to be robust accounts of what is demanded of citizens in diverse states, and although I agree with Balint that a diverse state requires not only robust institutions but also citizens with the right attitudes to operate them, as well as to enact their spirit in their everyday interactions with others, I believe Balint has mischaracterized what multicultural theorists are aiming to communicate by advocating for respect rather than mere tolerance. Tolerance, mind you, is not as easy a stance to adopt as Balint suggests, since it requires overcoming a dislike of others and their practices in order to treat them fairly and equally—it does not recommend indifference or ignoring difference, but rather confronting it, disliking it, and putting that dislike aside in the name of treating others equally. I of course agree that we ought to do that, but it is a hard ask, and there is no value in refusing to confront that, as Balint seems to do. Leaving that aside, however, I think it is crucial to reconceptualize the respect that is being asked of citizens in a diverse state. Balint suggests that the respect that is being asked for must be directed toward certain practices and norms valued by others. We are—though he does not offer this as an example—asked to respect the gender inequality that is central to some orthodox religions, or the rejection of modern medicine that is valued by others. But that is incorrect.

The respect we are asked to demonstrate is toward fellow citizens themselves, and their entitlement to the full complement of democratic rights to which each of us is entitled. The respect is for the ways in which some citizens, in the cases at issue here, and in virtue of cultural values that they hold dear, fail to achieve substantive political inclusion. Respect for them *as persons*, who hold cultures dear, demands that we work collaboratively to ensure their full political inclusion. It demands taking their attachments to their culture seriously, and recognizing that these attachments may impede access to some of the main dimensions of political inclusion, and attempting to identify where cultural rights protection can erase or mitigate these challenges. The motivation to do this work stems from the respect we have for each other as fellow citizens, not from the respect we have for the values that they hold and the practices that define them. Tolerance cannot motivate us to do that work; it can only motivate us to live and let live, but that is not sufficient in a diverse state where our cultural differences often shape the way in which we are treated by others, and whether or not we can access the rights and privileges of citizenship.

In the early 2000s, a Danish newspaper published caricatures of the Islamic prophet Muhammad—the most well-known of which was a cartoon of Muhammad with a bomb on his head in the place of a turban—knowing full well that the depiction of the Prophet is considered blasphemous. The French magazine *Charlie Hebdo* similarly published cartoons of Muhammad in 2012. In all of these cases, violent controversy erupted, in many cases fueled by religious leaders who had much to gain by fomenting violence in liberal democratic countries. In the fall of 2020, a French teacher was stabbed to death by a religious militant claiming to avenge Muslims for the teacher's choice, in class, to display the infamous cartoons (published in *Charlie Hebdo*), as part of a lesson on offensive speech's place in democratic society. The publication of these cartoons, and the choice to show them as part of a school lesson, ought never to lead to violence, and they are never justifications for murder. This conclusion is unambiguous. Balint's view of tolerance explains why: even if we hate what others do or believe, we must simply leave them be.

But what a view of tolerance cannot do is explain how the teacher, or the media, *ought* to act in these kinds of cases. The media outlets are absolutely protected by the right to free expression that is essential in democratic states and deservedly protected as a result. What explains why they should nevertheless refrain from publishing this knowingly offensive material? The duty of civility explains why, and it is my contention that the duty of civility is motivated by a commitment to the respect of others in a diverse democratic state. The duty of civility—a moral and not a legal duty—directs us to treat others civilly, one component of which is to avoid knowingly and intentionally offending others where we can do so, and where the gain associated from offending others is minimal (Carens 2006). Some defenders of the media outlets, and even the teacher, suggested that it is important in a democratic society that we be permitted to ridicule others, and that we must be tough enough to accept being the subject of ridicule (Dworkin 2006). We can agree with this statement, and the normative commitment that underpins it, however, and still recommend against doing so where we know that doing so will cause offense and hurt. Such a recommendation is especially strong where the subject of ridicule is a minority culture that is the victim of discrimination and often hate, manifest in the vast empirical evidence suggesting that they struggle to access political inclusion across all four of its dimensions (Modood 2006). It is respect for others—not their cultural practices or their values—and the importance of their being included politically, fully, that is required to support a robust democratic society.

CONCLUSION

Cultures are deeply valued by their members. The cultures that we form a part of shape the norms and practices that we hold dear. As well, they impact how we relate to others, privately and politically. It has been my contention that a genuinely politically inclusive state will need to protect a wide range of cultural minority rights. Such a conviction does not deny the challenges that the defining of cultures, and their members, faces; nor does it avoid confronting the fact that groups will engage in practices that are problematic from a liberal point of view. A politically inclusive state's job is, I have argued, to protect minority rights in many cases, and in others, to engage with minority groups respectfully so as to protect trust between them and the larger state. This latter requirement does not mean that a politically inclusive state permits group authorities to violate and undermine the rights of internal minorities; it means that a politically inclusive state interacts with cultural minorities to protect the rights of minority cultural groups in a culturally sensitive way. A neutralist orientation toward minority rights generates some benefits, as I have conceded, but it ultimately fails to take seriously the role of culture in the lives of individuals, and therefore cannot offer a robust way forward in diverse and increasingly diversifying states. A focus on political inclusion, as I have argued, offers a principled, concrete, action-guiding way in which to resolve the cultural conflicts that diverse democracies face.

14

Response to Lenard

Multiculturalism without Minority (or Majority) Rights

LET ME BEGIN MY RESPONSE to Lenard in this final chapter of the book with an example that helps highlight our different views. In 2015, a Muslim man, who had signed a declaration of loyalty to the German constitution and against extremism, passed his citizenship test with the best possible score. But he was still denied German citizenship. Why? Because, for religious reasons, he had refused to shake hands with the responsible official, a woman, when she handed him the naturalization certificate. She withheld the certificate and rejected the application. This decision was upheld by the Administrative Court of Baden-Württemberg in 2020, where it was ruled that someone who rejects a handshake due to a "fundamentalist conception of culture and values" was thereby rejecting "integration into German living conditions" (DW 2020).

What should have happened in this case? Here I think Lenard and I would differ markedly. Lenard argues for the importance of having a shared public culture. This, she argues, is necessary to sustain the trust between citizens for welfare redistribution and other cooperative social enterprises. Her shared public culture explicitly includes

Debating Multiculturalism. Peter Balint and Patti Tamara Lenard, Oxford University Press. © Oxford University Press 2022. DOI: 10.1093/oso/9780197528372.003.0015

forms of greeting, and so would include the norm of shaking hands. Shared public cultures need support, and so handshaking should be supported. But Lenard also argues for the importance of political inclusion, that everyone is fully included in the democratic politics of a society. The value of political inclusion means granting minority rights so that minorities can be fully included and have sufficient political voice. Lenard's argument for political inclusion should mean granting this man (and other Muslims) an exemption from this general rule so that they can interact with public officials without shaking hands. In other words, on Lenard's argument, this case merits a minority right.

I, on the other hand, would argue that there is nothing neutral in requiring shaking hands. Handshaking as a form of greeting is particular to only some ways of life. The barrier of requiring handshakes with public officials is not just an issue for many Muslims, but also for Orthodox Jews, as well as germaphobes, among others. Moreover, the institution of granting citizenship can clearly be done without shaking hands. The man had already sworn an oath of allegiance, and so handshaking should not be necessary. To insist on the need to shake hands is to insist on unnecessarily privileging the majority way of life. If some people still want to shake hands, they can, but it should not be an essential part of a citizenship ceremony. Cooperative social enterprises do not require shared cultural norms such as shaking hands. They can be achieved through other less cultural means. So, in stark contrast to Lenard, I would argue that this case merits changing the institution to remove unjustified majority privilege, and not granting any minority rights.

But note a key similarity here. Both Lenard and I think this man should be granted citizenship—*we both take minority claims seriously*. While Lenard wishes to both support shared public cultures and grant minority rights for those whose ways of life make fitting in harder, I simply argue for a change in our shared institutions so that they can accommodate as broad a range of ways of life as possible. In her section of this book, Lenard argues in favor of minority rights in almost all cases. She justifies granting minority rights through the importance of political inclusion. Hers is a democratic argument. A society is a cooperative enterprise that requires all citizens to feel equally involved in its institutions and decision-making. It is also, in her words, a "maximalist" argument, in that there are very few cases—including ones where minorities appear to seek political exclusion rather than inclusion—in which she thinks minorities should not be granted the differentiated rights they seek.

In my response to Lenard I focus on three issues. The first is the stretching of "political inclusion" to fit all cases, as well as the risks of relying too heavily upon it. I suggest it may actually push against minority accommodation instead of leading to it. The second is Lenard's argument for a shared public culture, which she thinks will counteract the potential fragmenting that may occur because of multicultural accommodation. Here I suggest not only that she takes this concern too seriously and seems to forget about the state, but there are nonidentity ways of achieving social cooperation. The third is the fact that many of Lenard's examples seem to involve no minority rights at all, and so seem to actually support my argument for neutrality as active indifference as the best way of gaining minority accommodation.

POLITICAL INCLUSION

Lenard uses the importance of political inclusion, with a focus on "voice," as the justification that will cover all minority accommodations. This does not just involve formal political rights, but she argues that citizens need to have a genuine and equal say in the laws that govern their lives. In her words, it "is not simply about voting . . . it is also about the conditions in which people raise their voices and that shape how they are heard, if at all" ("Inclusion and Voice in the Public Sphere" in chapter 2). Citizens require both formal and substantive access to the political sphere and effective representation, but they also need to be recognized as valid speakers and makers of claims. Too often minorities are denied voice; this is especially, but not only, when they are not recognized as legitimate interlocutors in political discussion. Lenard argues that the cultural claims that minorities make almost always target a barrier to achieving an equal say, and if one cares about full political inclusion, then these claims should be granted. Even the strongest claims for separation and isolation—such as those of the Amish, Hutterites, and Mennonites—should still be granted on grounds of political inclusion. She explains that their separation is always incomplete, trust needs to be maintained, members may still move between these groups and the broader society, and exemptions can serve to keep the dialogue open.

This is a significant and unique contribution, and one that provides a different way of justifying minority rights. Other minority rights theorists have focused on identity recognition, integration, fairness, welfare, and autonomy as justifications for granting minority rights, and Lenard offers a novel alternative. Substantive political inclusion certainly tracks key problems in multicultural societies— too often minorities are excluded from full participation in the democratic process. For democracies to function they need to represent all those who are affected by political power, and political exclusion certainly works against this good.

Yet despite its importance, *political inclusion as the basis for adjudicating minority claims seems to offer dual risks.* On the one hand, it does not seem able to do all the work Lenard wants it to. She is clearly sympathetic to minority claims, but I am not sure "political inclusion" always gets us there. On the other hand, using the value of "political inclusion" may risk doing too much work and actually push against minority accommodation rather than help achieve it. I will take these two opposed problems in turn.

The first problem is that *political inclusion seems stretched to fit at times,* rather than always offering the obvious justification for granting minority claims. Political inclusion clearly works for what Lenard calls "representation rights." These may involve reserved seats in parliaments, party lists that put minorities at the top of winnable seats, and so on. The aim here is certainly to politically include. But many of the other cases Lenard describes seem tenuously, at best, connected to political inclusion. Let me run through six of her examples which do not seem connected to political inclusion:

- Lenard talks about the importance of healthcare providers, community centers, and businesses adapting to meet their customer's needs. This is clearly important—people need to be able to access services, and providers need to meet their customer's needs to survive. But this can only be understood as "political" in the broadest of possible terms. It seems much more about welfare and needs.

- Affirmative action is described by Lenard as an "indirect route" to political inclusion as it provides the grounds for securing "high-quality employment and educational opportunities," which she argues means minorities are better positioned to engage politically. While one might wonder the extent that well-off members of minorities really do advocate for the needs of the rest of their "group," it also seems, particularly given Lenard's examples, that this is not about political inclusion at all. The main example Lenard provides is about the importance of culturally appropriate medical care for Indigenous Canadians, using the case of reserving medical school spaces for Indigenous students so that Indigenous patients can have access to qualified, competent, and culturally sensitive doctors. While not denying the importance of such access, especially given the dire health outcomes for Indigenous peoples around the world, how is this political inclusion? Once more, it looks much more like welfare and need.

- Lenard's "self-determination rights" seem to be more about political *exclusion* than about inclusion. Yes, minorities seeking self-determination usually do so within an existing overarching political structure, but to see them asking for greater inclusion seems to misunderstand their demand. The examples Lenard provides of cultural separation and isolation, such as the Amish and ultra-Orthodox Jews, are clearly moves for exclusion. Yes, members of these groups may come back and the separation is not complete, but the nature of the claims is not focused on inclusion, even if Lenard thinks it is why the claims are ultimately justified.

- Her support for Indigenous groups to decide for themselves which individuals should be excluded from land or membership benefits also seem about political exclusion, not inclusion. The fact that she suggests claims should be granted for "reasons of 'corrective' or 'reparative' justice" ("Indigenous Self-Determination" in chapter 4) immediately suggests something else is actually going on here. Her support for recognition of Indigenous people in the Australian constitution is because it offers "more substantive inclusion in political space," but crucially she also argues that it is justified by "protection from past and ongoing discrimination" ("Recognition Claims" in chapter 3). These two Indigenous examples seem much better explained by historic injustice and contemporary socioeconomic disadvantage, something that Lenard directly draws upon.

- Lenard argues for state support for ethnic media on grounds of political inclusion. This is because it allows those whose first language is not the majority language an opportunity to participate in democratic politics, and it can be called on in times of crisis to communicate key messages to all communities. I do not deny its importance in times of crisis—and ethnic media played an important role during the Covid-19 pandemic—but a large amount of ethnic media involves playing news and cultural items from the "homeland" rather than items about local issues.

- Support for minority schools is justified, as a "a culturally appropriate environment can better support minority students to gain the skills they need" ("Culturally Separate Schools" in chapter 4). In other words, without this environment, minorities would fall behind. There are two things to note here. First, this also looks more straightforwardly like a welfare and need claim. And second, this way of couching the claim would seem to fail to provide the full suite of minority schools, which I assume Lenard would support. It is hard to see how many Catholic, Jewish, and Quaker schools today, for example, could be seen as necessary for minority students to gain "the skills and confidence they need to engage in the larger economic and political spaces that, unfortunately, continue to stigmatize them" ("Culturally Separate Schools" in chapter 4). They seem much more straightforwardly justified through schooling choice.

So while political inclusion can do some important work in gaining minority accommodation, it seems a little too stretched to cover the cases Lenard wants included—some of which involve more exclusion than inclusion. Other principles seem much more motivating in many of the cases she describes. If *everything* involved political inclusion, the concept would lose its useful specificity.

The second problem with using political inclusion as the main justificatory strategy in dealing with minority claims is that *political inclusion may actually resist minority claims*, at least without other values in play. According to Lenard, the key question when deciding on minority cultural rights is whether granting the minority right will "produce more and better political inclusion" (chapter 3). If it does, then the right should be granted. But as Lenard is aware, substantive political equality is no minor thing. Small differences between groups of citizens can quickly see one group discount the legitimacy of the claims and interests of the other. As she argues, political inclusion goes beyond resources and access, and takes in the view others have of you. Your fellow citizens must see you as worthy of making claims, and your claims worthy of consideration. In diverse political communities this is a serious challenge. To see why, we simply need to reflect on partisan politics—and one does not necessarily even have to include the current US split to see how other voices are quickly discounted as nonlegitimate.

The challenges of substantive political equality are why the patron saint of democratic equality, Jean-Jacques Rousseau, was so concerned about divergent interests among the citizenry. In response, he suggested outlawing factions and political parties, and doing whatever can be done to make citizens interests align, including, as I discussed, sharing a common civil religion. He thought equality and full inclusion in the democratic process could only occur if all our interests are properly aligned, including a large part of our identities.

It is here that Lenard's justification—albeit with very different ends—sails close to the ideals of the public sphere that have led French regimes to be hostile to many visible forms of diversity, most notably, but not only, those of Islam. Cécile Laborde, for example, writes that the French ideal of *laïcité* has been "understood as the privatisation of religious matters . . . as a guarantee of inclusiveness. All citizens . . . could identify equally with a shared, non-discriminatory public space where religious beliefs and allegiances were 'bracketed off' . . . [this] has become a blueprint for the contemporary management of multiculturalism in France" (Laborde 2003, 163–64; see also Guérard de Latour 2013).

If we need to all be seen by each other as substantively equal in the political and public arenas, then a removal of diversity is a logical step. This step ensures substantive political inclusion too. The easiest way to see each other as equals is to be as similar as possible. And while Lenard's use of substantive political inclusion is supposed to make space for diversity, the logic of this justification can easily pull in very much the other direction.

Perhaps here Lenard might be able offer limits or other principles to help ensure that political inclusion pulls toward, and not away from, minority accommodation. But Lenard does not draw on any principles or limits outside of political inclusion. It does, however, seem there are other principles at play, especially in the way almost all her cases—despite the sometimes tenuous links to political inclusion—end up with minority accommodation.

Let me suggest that the silent background justification in Lenard's examples that points political inclusion in the continued direction of minority accommodation,

rather than assimilation, is a much more traditional liberalism. That is, why shouldn't these minorities be able to do
the things they want? They aren't harming anyone, so we
are not justified in denying their requests. As a result, we
need to modify our institutions in order to accommodate
them. This is a traditional liberal justification for minority
accommodation.

And to push further, it would seem that this traditional
liberalism does not need the scaffold of political inclusion
at all if the concern is minority accommodation. So rather
than trying to squeeze all cases of concern into "political inclusion," we could just focus on individual freedom
and the need to justify restrictions, rather than their lack.
Liberalism, rather than a democratic concern for political
inclusion, is both a more direct and reliable route to minority accommodation.

Of course, how this traditional liberalism is interpreted
is an issue. We know that it is a version of this that multiculturalists are arguing against—this is the problem of a
"false neutrality" shaped in the majority's image. But the
"false" here is a giveaway. These are not the principles of
traditional liberalism, but a perverted practice. When neutrality is properly applied, minorities are accommodated.

Traditional liberalism was about less, rather than
more, state interference. And the minority rights favored
by multiculturalists involve increasing state power and
interference. And so while multicultural minority rights
are a form of neutrality, they come with all the risks to
freedom that traditional liberals are concerned about from
state interference. A neutrality that is about less, rather
than more, state power is not only in line with traditional
liberal ideals, but is more accommodating of diversity. This

is the neutrality that I have called *active indifference*, which broadens and removes unnecessary and unjustified institutional barriers. If somebody wants to do or be something and is stopped by an institutional barrier, then the question is simply whether that barrier is neutrally justified and whether it is neutral in intent. If not (and there are no outweighing considerations), then the barrier should be removed.

Note here how this is no longer a "cultural" argument. *Unjustified barriers are bad.* Yes, they are likely worse for those with deeply held beliefs, but they are wrong regardless. We no longer need culture or religion or some other criterion to make this case—and so can avoid the problem of which groups count. We should all be able to do what we want or be within the confines of properly justified barriers. When these barriers are too narrow and our freedom is constrained, we all lose out. Looking at minority claims through the lens of avoiding unjustified restrictions on people's freedom goes a long way toward minority accommodation, without minority rights.

So despite the originality of political inclusion in assessing minority claims, it does not seem to cover all relevant cases, it may actually stifle minority accommodation, and it seems better replaced with a freedom-based liberalism (cf. Ceva 2020).

THE SOLIDARITY CHALLENGE

Both Lenard and I are likely to be criticized by those concerned about social cohesion and a shared national identity. Lenard's argument involves continually accepting minority claims, and mine involves continually removing majority privilege. On the face of it, those concerned with the importance of national identity and shared social glue may think both our arguments are likely to lead to fragmented and nonfunctioning polities with nothing to hold us together. Lenard accepts much of the premise of this criticism. I do not.

For Lenard, solidarity is essential for a democratic polity because, she argues, the cooperation that is required to deliver its benefits is substantial. Lenard argues that a *shared public culture* can be the glue that holds a polity together. She suggests that it can solve "the particularity problem." That is, if we all follow liberal democratic values, and our ethnicity should not count in our national identity, then why should we be tied to our particular polity and not someone else's? After all, we should all be loyal to the same values, and so any polity is as good as another. To show how a shared public culture would solve the particularity problem, Lenard takes up the importance of welfare redistribution. She argues that this is a cooperative scheme that requires sufficient trust between people who do not know each other for it succeed. A shared public culture, she argues, can deliver the necessary trust to support welfare redistribution including welfare payments, public education, and public health. In this section I outline four problems with Lenard's response to this challenge.

The first problem is *the almost complete lack of state power in her discussion*. Almost all the things Lenard describes as parts of a shared public culture are true. Different countries do have different ways of doing things. But this is not a remarkable claim. The concern of both those who worry about not enough national identification and those that worry about too much is not that different places have different ways of doing things. It is about state power. And state power is almost entirely missing from her analysis. I am someone who is concerned about the assimilatory and exclusionary pressures of national identification, and I have little problem with Lenard's argument. No antinationalists argue against what might be called "organic particularism" (within a framework of nondiscrimination), from which local cultures and ways of doing things emerge. What Lenard describes in her account of shared public culture is mostly a series of benign things that are developed organically and almost always without the state's intentional power. So her observation that Australia apparently has lots of cafes (don't Italy and many other European countries too?) is simply the product of free market forces. Cafes are not subsidized by the state. Likewise, there is no state power in her invocation of the Australian bushfire crisis of 2019–2020, which was a natural disaster. She also points to the fact that certain artists or athletes are treated as representative of a country and its culture. But this too is usually the product of a combination of market forces, the popularity of certain sports, and the media covering some things and not others. Yes, governments do align themselves with sport stars and artists, but this is usually after the fact. The same can be said of her example of the beaver on Canadian clothing and the koala in the rest of the world's view of Australia. There is no intentional state power here.

If Lenard's argument is "Don't worry about constructing a particular national identity, one will form organically in liberal democratic states," then she is not arguing against those who think the state should stay out of the cultural national identification game (for example, Abizadeh 2002, 2004). She is entirely agreeing with them. The concern from those of us who dislike the construction and maintenance of national identity is the use of state power. There are long histories of often violently excluding and assimilating minorities, and there is the continued, less violent, yet pernicious, ways it shapes national identity to meet its needs.

To be fair, Lenard is aware of the concern about the history of state power in national identification. But when Lenard does mention the state, this seems to confuse rather than clarify. She suggests a "noncoercive" role for the state in "informing" newcomers about cultural norms, and one which involves citizenship tests. But if migration controls are not coercive, then what is? And the example that is given of Lenard explaining the importance of the Canadian ice hockey player Paul Henderson to her American partner has nothing to do with the state at all.

The second issue with Lenard's shared public culture is *her claim that a shared public culture can be fully inclusive of minorities.* As she writes, "A shared public culture is accessible if its central features can be adopted by cultural minorities *without* requiring them to sacrifice norms, values, and practices that are particular to their own culture" ("Solidarity in Multicultural States" in chapter 6). But once again, her examples suggest otherwise. Lenard insists on the importance of liberal democratic values, but allows local "cultural inflection" so that each public culture has its own particular version of liberal democratic values. The example we are given is the contrasting laws and culture regarding freedom of speech in Canada and the United States. Apparently, some US political scientists were not willing to go a conference in Canada because it has much more restrictive freedom of speech laws. But this example actually demonstrates how local "cultural inflection" of liberal democratic values may not always be so inclusive, and may actually "sacrifice norms, values, and practices." This is not just an issue for privileged academics, but many minority groups have strong and offensive-to-most beliefs. It would seem that local "cultural inflection" of liberal democratic values may not include their particular beliefs and practices. My worry is that a shared public culture as described may claim to be inclusive, but would only suit left-leaning groups, and as such would not be very diverse. As I wrote in my section of this book, liberals need to be able to put up with things they find offensive and wrong— this is the key value of toleration. Without it, there is not really much meaningful diversity. Lenard's response to this objection is that some values are nonnegotiable—that is, liberal democratic ones—but if these are to have "cultural inflection," then we are right back to a not fully inclusive shared public culture.

Lenard's examples of the practices of queuing and greetings seem similarly noninclusive. On queuing, one just has to compare many Middle Eastern countries where queuing is virtually nonexistent with the United Kingdom, where it is almost sacrosanct. Surely migrants between these regions would have to strongly alter their norms and practices. On greetings, the questions of kissing (how many times?) versus hugging versus handshakes versus no contact at all immediately suggests problems of inclusion, especially, as my opening example showed, when some people have deeply held values that mean they want to avoid all physical contact with the opposite sex.

My point is not that there shouldn't be differences in public cultures, but let's not pretend they are inclusive. Lenard's response to cases where public cultures are not deemed inclusive is to argue that when cultural markers are contested by minorities, this "ought to be treated as a presumptive reason to modify or abandon the questionable marker" ("How Does a Shared Public Culture Facilitate Political Inclusion?" in chapter 6). As the number of examples without state power suggests, however, either this is just an issue for the cultural marketplace and a hope that citizens may modify their behavior, or it can be seen as an argument for a neutral state. That is, there is so much actual diversity in a modern multicultural state that *the state should avoid endorsing any cultural markers at all*, as they will always be contested by minorities.

In fact, if one takes the theory behind her "shared public culture"—that is, it should be accessible to all—and not the examples, which often are not—then not only would we end up with a neutral state, but we would negate the need for minority rights altogether. In other words, the most inclusive public culture is the one with minimal state involvement.

The third issue with Lenard's argument for a shared public culture is *her acceptance of the premise that a shared identity is necessary for the trust* which is necessary for cooperative enterprises. That is, a shared public culture leads to trust, and trust leads to support for cooperative enterprises. She frames her argument in opposition to the claim that "collaboration stems from shared commitment to abstract liberal democratic ideals" ("Conclusion" in chapter 6). I too think collaboration is unlikely to come from a "shared commitment to abstract liberal democratic ideals." The real story of social cooperation is significantly more complex than either of these views. It will involve self-interest, history, and a sense of fairness, among other motivations. As I argue subsequently, identity and culture seem very much beside the point in this regard.

Let me start with Lenard's concern over welfare redistribution. Her claim that a shared public culture will support "the willing cooperation of citizens in redistributive programs that protect the equality of all citizens" ("How Does a Shared Public Culture Facilitate Political Inclusion?" in chapter 6) seems entirely speculative. As she shows, all countries have shared public cultures—and often very strong ones—but certainly not all countries have redistributive programs "that protect the equality of all citizens." In fact, such programs are rare. She accepts her shared public culture is ideal, not real. In fact, actual states often have much stronger, and often ethnic, public cultures. But these cultures do not lead to redistribution of the type she desires, so why should this weaker ideal type? South Korea and Hungary, for example, would seem to have strong public cultures, but usually rank very low among OECD countries when it comes to welfare spending (OECD n.d.). Instead, the social science on this seems to point to welfare redistribution succeeding when there is a history of it and when there is a sense of it being fair.[1]

The sort of trust that Lenard hopes will lead to support for welfare redistribution is particular in nature. That is, somebody will trust / not trust somebody as an X to do / not do something (Weinstock 1999), the X here being "one

---

1. The following discussion draws on some material from Balint 2014, 2017.

of us" or someone who shares our culture/identity. But there is another form of trust that is much more general (Uslaner 2002). Generalized trust is much less contingent on particular experiences and characteristics, and is more like a moral disposition in which a person is either likely to trust or not. This means, unlike the particular form of trust, generalized trusters are more likely to trust those not in their in-group. Rather than A trusts B as an X, generalized trusters are better described simply as "A trusts" (Uslaner 2002). Citizens who are generalized trusters have many positive social characteristics; they tend to be more tolerant of minorities, be more active in both politics and civic organizations, give more to charities, have a more positive view of their democratic institutions, and be more optimistic in general (Rothstein and Uslaner 2005, 41). They are also more likely to support welfare redistribution.

What is most interesting is that generalized trust "depends upon a foundation of economic and social equality and contributes to the development of a more egalitarian society" (Rothstein and Uslaner 2005, 45). The more economically and socially equal a society is, in both outcomes and opportunities, the more generalized trust that exists, and with it the more likelihood for support of policies to maintain this equality. According to Eric Uslaner and Bo Rothstein, inequality, of either incomes or opportunities, undermines generalized trust, and conversely, equality supports this type of trust—this correlation can be demonstrated across a range of countries (Rothstein and Uslaner 2005). It seems countries that have a high number of universal welfare programs, for example those of Scandinavia, usually have much greater generalized trust (and less economic inequality) than countries that have a proportionally higher number of targeted welfare programs (Rothstein 1998, chapter 6). In universal welfare programs, everyone gets the same benefits, while targeted programs target only those in need. From this we might surmise that if almost all members of society *feel* they are benefiting from a welfare program, then it is more likely to have broad support. It seems that universal welfare programs result in a greater redistribution of wealth than targeted programs, especially, but not only, with a system of progressive taxation (Rothstein 1998; Kumlin and Rothstein 2005). We should also not discount the view people have of their institutions (not necessarily each other), which need to be seen as trustworthy, impartial, and noncorrupt to help maintain support for the welfare state (Daniele and Geys 2015; Rothstein, Samanni, and Teorell 2012).

We may also wish to look here at the social psychology of why people do things. We might think that people need a particular *attitude*, in this case trust, in order to *behave* in the right way (for example, keep paying taxes or do some civic duty). But the social psychology on this is pretty clear: when people behave in a particular way, their attitude is likely to become consistent with this behavior in order to avoid cognitive dissonance (Myers 2014). That is, *attitude follows behavior*, perhaps more so than the other way around (Pederson, Walker, and Wise 2005). For example, wherever seatbelts have been made compulsory, there is usually resistance, but after a period of time most people internalize the rightness of wearing them (Steptoe et al. 2002). Or take the example of compulsory voting. Over 75% of Australians support this institution (Hill and Young 2007). But this is not because of either their trust in one another or because of the coercive force of the state (it is a small fine that is rarely enforced), but because they've been socialized into voting and have internalized its rightness. This may help explain why states with strong welfare programs have large public support for them. An example here would the very high esteem held for the National Health Service in the UK (Burkitt et al. 2018). We should not discount initial coercion and then the role of tradition in keeping these institutions going. This seems a more plausible explanation than an untested inclusive shared public culture, especially when stronger shared public cultures have not achieved these social goods.

While generating sufficient support for welfare redistribution is a key concern for left-liberals worrying about national identification, defense of the state is a concern for those more to the right politically. To put it bluntly, they are worried about how we will recruit soldiers to defend and die for the nation without a strong national identity (Balint and Dobos 2015). While Lenard's motivation for her shared public culture was welfare related, I want to show how those with very different political convictions should also not worry about this problem. In other words, regardless of our political convictions, *the worry about national identification and support for cooperative projects is overstated.*

If we look at the problem of military recruitment, soldiers have a range of motivations for joining the military, many of which have little to do with national identification. US studies have consistently shown that occupational reasons such as pay and conditions, educational expenses and opportunities, and vocational training motivate the voluntary enlistment of a large proportion of soldiers (Gorman and Thomas 1991; Griffith and Perry 1993; Lakhani and Fugita 1993; Eighmey 2006; Woodruff, Kelty, and Segal 2006; Griffith 2008). This is not lost on recruiters, whose advertising has played on these occupational motivations (Eighmey 2006; Griffith 2008). Moreover, militaries from Ireland, Great Britain, France, and Belgium, among others, actively recruit nonnationals. Historically, and with a highly exclusionary (and legally enforced) national identity in place—the "white Australia" policy—the Australian volunteer military in World War I had a significant number of non-British and non-Australian-born men, even when expressed as a percentage of the general population. Several of these soldiers even came from countries which were considered "nonwhite," and many went on to win important medals of valor (Connor 2002; Gilchrist 1997).

Nor is national identification necessary for military capability. Indeed, the success of private military companies in recent years shows how using people who treat this work like a job and are motivated by material self-interest has not made them militarily ineffective. Private contractors have been behind some of the most decisive military victories in recent memory. Take, for example, the success of Executive Outcomes, a South African private military firm, in Sierra Leone. The civil war in that country had been raging for four years with no end in sight, and the Revolutionary United Front had gained the upper hand against the national armed forces. This changed after the government enlisted the help of Executive Outcomes. In less than two years they managed to secure Freetown, oust the rebels from the capital's periphery, and destroy their headquarters. Before long a peace agreement was signed and democratic elections followed (Hough 2007, 9). In the course of the operation, Executive Outcomes employees took risks and made sacrifices comparable to those that earn national soldiers medals of honor (Fitzsimmons 2013, 262). So while governments, elites, and the more politically conservative will often justify state support for national identity building through and on military and defense grounds, it seems militaries can recruit and function effectively without it.

A fourth and final point can be made about Lenard's defense of a shared public culture, and this is "the problem of segregation." But *why should we accept the premise that segregation is a problem*? (Lenard also accepts this as an issue when dealing with cultural preservation rights, and the fact that they help manifest separation rather than inclusion and integration). In challenging the "problem of segregation," I am not saying communities segregating is never a problem—clearly this would be false. But there is too often a peculiar focus in multicultural societies on *cultural* separation, with a deep worry about high concentrations of ethnic, immigrant, and cultural groups living together in one place. What almost always seems to be missing here is any concern over socioeconomic segregation. Government policies on taxation, employment, housing, welfare, and education all impact socioeconomic segregation. But somehow the fact that the poor are concentrated in one part of town and the rich in another does not seem to raise the same level of handwringing as ethnic and cultural segregation. We also know that people like to be with people who have similar backgrounds, interests, and identities, so it should be no surprise that ethnic and cultural groups settle in clumps. Of course, when ethnic and cultural identities coincide with socioeconomic disadvantage, there is a reason for concern, but we should not be tricked into thinking it requires an ethnic and cultural fix and not a socioeconomic one.

MINORITY RIGHTS OR ACTIVE INDIFFERENCE?

Lenard promises us in her introduction (chapter 1) "a defense of multiculturalism, that is, a defense of differentiated rights based on minority cultural identities." In my section of the book I argued directly against such rights. But reading Lenard's section, something odd starts to happen. In many of her examples, instead of a defense of minority rights, we often seem to get a defense of minority accommodation *without* differentiated rights. On this, I am obviously in full agreement. Minorities should be accommodated without granting differentiated rights. When *a neutrally justified institution* can meet its purpose by doing things differently and accommodate more ways of life, it should. That is my argument *against* multicultural minority rights. Large parts of Lenard's section seem justify my argument.

The following of Lenard's examples do not seem to involve any minority rights at all:

- Global aviation standards changing to allow daggers shorter than six centimeters. This may not be the right thing to do, but there is no mention of having to be a Sikh to wear such a dagger.
- Not banning headscarves and face coverings in public, or while receiving public services. This is not a

differentiated right for Muslims, but simply the overturning or resisting of a ban on all of us.

- Healthcare providers, community centers, and many businesses adapting to meet their customer's needs. This seems to be just broadening rather than any granting of rights.

- The 1991 Arbitration Act in Ontario, where parties to a dispute were asked to agree on an arbiter, whose decision would be binding as long as it was consistent with Ontario and Canadian law. Yes, this was taken up by religious groups, but on Lenard's depiction it did not have to be—it was open to anyone. I am not saying it is a good idea, just that it is not a minority right, but a broad accommodation clearly in line with active indifference.

- Culturally separate schools. Lenard's main example, the Africentric Alternative School in Toronto, is actually open to anyone to attend without restriction.

- Ethnic organizations being catered to and recruited into political campaigns. This just looks like freedom of association. Lenard does argue that the state should "actively support" such organizations. But as we see in many multicultural polities, state interference is not necessary. Ethnic organizations are commonly recruited into the party political process, as their numbers and voting blocs are very attractive to party operatives.

My point here is that for those who care about minority accommodation, rights are not necessary. Much better is to simply *reform the institution*. And despite Lenard's claim that she will offer a "defense of differentiated rights," she seems quite happy to argue for minority accommodation without multicultural minority rights—as she should. Indeed, it seems *neutrality as active indifference* is significantly more accommodating of diversity than political inclusion against a background of a shared public culture.

Neither Lenard nor I think minorities should always be accommodated. To use a recent example where I think accommodation should not be granted, we can turn to the US Supreme Court decision that blocked New York from enforcing attendance limits at places of worship in areas hit hard by Covid-19. The caps on attendance limits in places of worship (which were more generous than for other indoor places) were deemed to violate the Free Exercise Clause of the First Amendment (*Roman Catholic Diocese of Brooklyn, New York, v. Andrew M. Cuomo, Governor of New York* 2020). Here, I think, the importance of broader public health should have outweighed accommodation. Minority claims should not always be met.

Lenard makes many interesting and original points— her focus on political inclusion is highly novel and brings an important new dimension to the debate over multiculturalism and minority rights. But it is unnecessary and carries the risk of not doing what it sets out to do, perhaps even helping those who resist minority accommodation. Much simpler and safer is neutrality as active indifference supported by traditional liberal values. Restrictions on freedom need to be justified, rather than our reasons for removing such barriers. Neutrality as active indifference not only avoids the risk of multicultural minority rights, but offers benefits in the form of increased freedom. Lenard's solution to the "glue" that binds us introduces new problems—and problems that cut against minority accommodation. While support for cooperative projects is important, we should not assume that shared culture is either necessary or sufficient to gain this support. There will be several nonidentity motivations that sustain such projects. Finally, despite Lenard's promise of a robust defense of minority rights, too often her examples point toward liberal neutrality and an avoidance of recognition of identity and culture. Many of our current problems of minority accommodation have been, and should be, solved by removing barriers for minority accommodation and majority privilege, rather than adding news forms of privilege in the form of multicultural minority rights.

REFERENCES

Abizadeh, Arash. 2002. "Does Liberal Democracy Presuppose a Cultural Nation? Four Arguments." *American Political Science Review* 96 (3): 495–509.

Abizadeh, Arash. 2004. "Historical Truth, National Myths and Liberal Democracy: On the Coherence of Liberal Nationalism." *Journal of Political Philosophy* 12 (3): 291–313.

Addis, Adeno. 1996. "On Human Diversity and the Limits of Toleration." In *Nomos 39: Ethnicity and Group Rights*, edited by Ian Shapiro and Will Kymlicka, 112–53. New York: New York University Press.

Adrian, Melanie. 2009. "France, the Veil and Religious Freedom." *Religion, State and Society* 37 (4): 345–74.

Al Jazeera. 2020. "White Professor Who Pretended to Be Black Admits Faking Identity." *Al Jazeera News*, September 4, 2020. https://www.aljazeera.com/news/2020/9/4/white-profes sor-who-pretended-to-be-black-admits-faking-identity.

Albeck-Ripka, Livia. 2019. "Australia Will Hold Referendum on Indigenous Recognition." *New York Times*, July 10, 2019, sec. World. https://www.nytimes.com/2019/07/10/world/austra lia/indigenous-recognition-referendum.html.

Anderson, Elizabeth. 1999. "What Is the Point of Equality?" *Ethics* 109 (2): 287–337.

Anderson, Elizabeth. 2010. *The Imperative of Integration*. Princeton, NJ: Princeton University Press.

Appleby, Gabrielle, and Eddie Synot. 2020. "A First Nations Voice: Institutionalising Political Listening." *Federal Law Review* 48 (4): 529–42. https://doi.org/10.1177/0067205X20955068.

Arneson, Richard J. 2003. "Liberal Neutrality on the Good: An Autopsy." In *Perfectionism and Neutrality: Essays in Liberal Theory*, edited by George Klosko and Steven Wall, 191–18. Lanham, MD: Rowman & Littlefield.

Arneson, Richard J., and Ian Shapiro. 1996. In *Nomos 38: Democratic Autonomy and Religious Freedom: A Critique of Wisconsin v Yoder*, edited by Ian Shapiro and Russell Hardin, 365–411. Washington, DC: American Society for Political and Legal Philosophy. https://www.jstor.org/stable/24219558.

Australian Government. 2019. "Diversity: Defence Diversity & Inclusion Strategy." https://www.defence.gov.au/Diversity/strategy/priorities.asp.

Australian Human Rights Commission. n.d. "About Constitutional Recognition." Accessed September 11, 2020. https://humanrights.gov.au/our-work/about-constitutional-recognition.

Australian Law Reform Commission. 2017. "Incarceration Rates of Aboriginal and Torres Strait Islander Peoples: Discussion Paper." Australian Government.

Baier, Annette. 1994. *Moral Prejudices: Essays on Ethics*. Cambridge, MA: Harvard University Press.

Bakht, Natasha. 2009. "Objection, Your Honour! Accommodating Niqab-Wearing Women in Courtrooms." In *Legal Practice and Cultural Diversity*, edited by Ralph Grillo, 115–33. Surrey: Ashgate Publishing.

Balint, Peter. 2010. "Avoiding an Intolerant Society: Why Respect of Difference May Not Be the Best Approach." *Educational Philosophy and Theory* 42 (1): 129–41.

Balint, Peter. 2011. "Education for Tolerance: Respecting Sameness, Not Difference." In *Religious Tolerance, Education and the Curriculum*, edited by Elizabeth Burns Coleman and Kevin White, 41–52. Rotterdam: Sense Publishers.

Balint, Peter. 2013. "Against Respecting Each Others' Differences." *Journal of Applied Philosophy* 30 (3): 254–67.

Balint, Peter. 2014. "Diversity, National Identity and Social Cohesion: Welfare Redistribution and National Defence." In *Allegiance and Identity in a Globalised World*, edited by Jenkins Rubenstein and Mark Nolan, 426–61. Cambridge: Cambridge University Press.

Balint, Peter. 2015. "Identity Claims: Why Liberal Neutrality Is the Solution, Not the Problem." *Political Studies* 63 (2): 495–509.

Balint, Peter. 2017. *Respecting Toleration: Traditional Liberalism and Contemporary Diversity*. Oxford: Oxford University Press.

Balint, Peter, and Ned Dobos. 2015. "Perpetuating the Military Myth: Why the Psychology of the 2014 Australian Defence Pay Deal Is Irrelevant." *Australian Journal of Public Administration* 74 (3): 359–63.

Balint, Peter, Lina Eriksson, and Tiziana Torresi. 2018. "State Power and Breastfeeding Promotion: A Critique." *Contemporary Political Theory* 17 (3): 306–30.

Banducci, Susan A., Todd Donovan, and Jeffrey A. Karp. 2004. "Minority Representation, Empowerment, and Participation." *Journal of Politics* 66 (2): 534–56. https://doi.org/10.1111/j.1468-2508.2004.00163.x.

Barry, Brian. 2001. *Culture and Equality: An Egalitarian Critique of Multiculturalism*. Cambridge, MA: Harvard University Press.

Bassel, Leah. 2017. *The Politics of Listening: Possibilities and Challenges for Democratic Life*. London: Palgrave Macmillan.

BBC News. 2019. "Leicester Islamic Faith School Told to Stop Separating Girls and Boys." *BBC News*, May 29, 2019, sec. Leicester. https://www.bbc.com/news/uk-england-leicestershire-48446674.

Bellafante, Ginia. 2020. "When Covid Flared Again in Orthodox Jewish New York." *New York Times*, October 5, 2020, sec. New York. https://www.nytimes.com/2020/10/05/nyregion/orthodox-jewish-nyc-coronavirus.html.

Benhabib, Seyla. 2002. *The Claims of Culture: Equality and Diversity in the Global Era*. Princeton, NJ: Princeton University Press.

Bessone, Magali. 2012. "Beyond Liberal Multicultural Toleration: A Critical Approach to Groups' Essentialism." *European Journal of Political Theory* 12 (3): 271–87.

Bilodeau, Antoine. 2014. "Is Democracy the Only Game in Town? Tension between Immigrants' Democratic Desires and Authoritarian Imprints." *Democratization* 21 (2): 359–81. https://doi.org/10.1080/13510347.2012.712515.

Boran, Idil. 2001. "Contra Moore: The Dependency of Identity on Culture." *Critical Review of International Social and Political Philosophy* 4 (2): 26–44.

Borrows, John. 2016. *Freedom and Indigenous Constitutionalism.* Toronto: University of Toronto Press. https://utorontopress.com/ca/freedom-and-indigenous-constitutionalism-4.

Boyd, Marion. 2004. *Dispute Resolution in Family Law: Protecting Choice, Promoting Inclusion.* Toronto: Ministry of the Attorney General.

Bradley, Chief Magistrate H. B. 2005. "Darwin Community Court: Guidelines." www.nt.gov.au.

Brock, Gillian. 2002. "Are There Any Defensible Indigenous Rights?" *Contemporary Political Theory* 1 (3): 285–305.

Brock, Gillian. 2020. *Justice for People on the Move: Migration in Challenging Times.* Cambridge: Cambridge University Press.

Brown, Étienne. 2020. "Political Liberalism and the False Neutrality Objection." *Critical Review of International Social and Political Philosophy* 23 (7): 874–93. https://doi.org/10.1080/13698230.2018.1511171.

Burkitt, Rachel, Kate Duxbury, Harry Evans, Leo Ewbank, Freddie Gregory, Suzanne Hall, Dan Wellings, and Lillie Wenzel. 2018. "The Public and the NHS: What's the Deal? The King's Fund." https://www.kingsfund.org.uk/sites/default/files/2018-06/The_public_and_the_NHS_report_0.pdf.

Burnett, Jonathan. 2004. "Community, Cohesion and the State." *Race and Class* 45 (3): 1–18.

Burns, John F. 2011. "Cameron Criticizes 'Multiculturalism' in Britain." *New York Times*, February 5, 2011. https://www.nytimes.com/2011/02/06/world/europe/06britain.html.

Burtt, Shelley. 1994. "Religious Parents, Secular Schools: A Liberal Defense of an Illiberal Education." *Review of Politics* 56 (1): 51–70.

Caffrey, Susan, and Gary Mundy. 1997. "Informal Systems of Justice: The Formation of Law within Gypsy Communities."

American Journal of Comparative Law 45 (2): 251–67. https:// doi.org/10.2307/840849.

Callan, Eamonn. 2006. "Galston's Dilemmas and Wisconsin v. Yoder." *Theory and Research in Education* 4 (3): 261–73.

Carens, Joseph. 2000. *Culture, Community and Citizenship: A Contextual Exploration of Justice as Evenhandedness.* Oxford: Oxford University Press.

Carens, Joseph. 2005. "The Integration of Immigrants." *Journal of Moral Philosophy* 2 (1): 29–46.

Carens, Joseph. 2006. "Free Speech and Democratic Norms in the Danish Cartoons Controversy." *International Migration* 44 (5): 33–42.

Casals, Neus Torbisco. 2006. *Group Rights as Human Rights: A Liberal Approach to Multiculturalism.* Dordrecht: Springer Netherlands. https://www.springer.com/gp/book/ 9781402042089.

Cassidy, Katie. 2010. "Merkel: Multiculturalism Has Failed in Germany." *Sky News Online*, October 17, 2010. http://news. sky.com/home/world-news/article/15759757.

CBC. 2017. "The Turban That Rocked the RCMP: How Baltej Singh Dhillon Challenged the RCMP—and Won." May 11, 2017. https://www.cbc.ca/2.7331/canadathestoryofus/the- turban-that-rocked-the-rcmp-how-baltej-singh-dhillon-cha llenged-the-rcmp-and-won-1.4110271.

CBC News. 2014. "'I Wish I Could Live Here': Reserve Removes Those Who Marry Non-Mohawks." *CBC News*, August 14, 2014. https://www.cbc.ca/news/canada/montreal/mohawks- seek-to-remove-non-natives-from-kahnawake-1.2736555.

CBC Radio. 2017. "World Sikh Organization Welcomes Canadian Decision to Allow Small Kirpans on Flights." *CBC.Ca*, November 8, 2017. https://www.cbc.ca/radio/asithappens/ as-it-happens-tuesday-edition-1.4391247/world-sikh-organ ization-welcomes-canadian-decision-to-allow-small-kirp ans-on-flights-1.4391256.

Ceva, Emanuela. 2020. "The Good of Toleration: Changing Social Relations or Maximising Individual Freedom?" *Critical Review of International Social and Political Philosophy* 23 (2): 197–202.

Ceva, Emanuela, and Federico Zuolo. 2013. "A Matter of Respect: On Majority-Minority Relations in a Liberal Democracy." *Journal of Applied Philosophy* 30 (3): 239–53.

Chin, Clayton. 2019. "The Concept of Belonging: Critical, Normative and Multicultural." *Ethnicities* 19 (5): 715–39.

Christiano, Thomas. 2004. "The Authority of Democracy." *Journal of Political Philosophy* 12 (3): 266–90.

Citizenship and Immigration Canada. 2001. "Immigrant Integration in Canada: Policy Objectives, Program Delivery and Challenges." http://atwork.settlement.org/downloads/atwork/Immigrant_Integration_in_Canada_discussion_paper_Hauck_May01.pdf.

Clarke, Simon. 2014. "Consequential Neutrality Revivified." In *Political Neutrality: A Re-Evaluation*, edited by Roberto Merrill and Daniel Weinstock, 109–21. Berlin: Springer.

Cohen, Andrew Jason. 2014. *Toleration*. Cambridge: Polity Press.

College of Policing. n.d. "Appearance Standards National Guidance." https://recruit.college.police.uk/Officer/Documents/Appearance_Standards_GuidanceDocument.docx.

Community Services (Aborigines) Act. 1984. Queensland.

Connolly, Kate. 2010. "Angela Merkel Declares Death of German Multiculturalism." *The Guardian*, October 17, 2010.

Connor, John. 2002. "Friendly, Neutral and Enemy Aliens: The Enlistment of Non-British Subjects in the Australian Imperial Force, 1914–18." Conference presentation at "The Frontlines: Gender, Identity and War." Monash University, July.

Coulthard, Glen Sean. 2014. *Red Skin, White Masks: Rejecting the Colonial Politics of Recognition*. Minneapolis: University of Minnesota Press.

Cranston, Maurice. 1987. "John Locke and the Case for Toleration." In *On Toleration*, edited by Susan Mendus and David Edwards, 99–121. Oxford: Oxford University Press.

Crouch, Gregory. 2006. "A Candid Dutch Film May Be Too Scary for Immigrants." *New York Times*, March 16, 2006. https://www.nytimes.com/2006/03/16/world/europe/a-candid-dutch-film-may-be-too-scary-for-immigrants.html.

Crowder, George. 2013. *Theories of Multiculturalism: An Introduction*. Cambridge: Polity Press.

Dalhousie University. n.d. "Affirmative Action Statement." Dalhousie University. Accessed September 11, 2020. https://medicine.dal.ca/departments/core-units/admissions/about/affirmative-action-policy.html.

Daniele, Gianmarco, and Benny Geys. 2015. "Interpersonal Trust and Welfare State Support." *European Journal of Political Economy* 39: 1–12.

Darwall, Stephen. 1977. "Two Kinds of Respect." *Ethics* 88 (1): 36–49.

De Marneffe, Peter. 1990. "Liberalism, Liberty, and Neutrality." *Philosophy & Public Affairs* 19 (3): 253–74.

De Vries, Bouke. 2020. "Against Hands-On Neutrality." *Politics, Philosophy & Economics* 19 (4): 424–46.

Deveaux, Monique. 2006. *Gender and Justice in Multicultural Liberal States*. Oxford: Oxford University Press.

Dewar, Helen. 1993. "Senate Bows to Braun on Symbol of Confederacy." *Washington Post*, July 23, 1993. https://www.washingtonpost.com/archive/politics/1993/07/23/senate-bows-to-braun-on-symbol-of-confederacy/3f88095a-2253-4fb9-b410-8ce75dbb308c/.

Dhamoon, Rita Kaur. 2013. "Exclusion and Regulated Inclusion." *Sikh Formations* 9 (1): 7–28. https://doi.org/10.1080/17448727.2013.774709.

Dovi, Suzanne. 2018. "Political Representation," The Stanford Encyclopedia of Philosophy, edited by Edward N. Zalta, https://plato.stanford.edu/archives/fall2018/entries/political-representation/.

Dragnea, Carmen, and Sally Erling. 2008. "The Effectiveness of Africentric (Black-Focused) Schools in Closing Student Success and Achievement Gaps: A Review of the Literature." https://www.tdsb.on.ca/Portals/research/docs/reports/EffectivenessOfAfricentricSchoolsInClosing Student Success Achievement Gaps.pdf.

Drerup, Johannes. 2018. "Education for Democratic Tolerance, Respect and the Limits of Political Liberalism." *Journal of Philosophy of Education* 52 (3): 515–32.

Drerup, Johannes. 2019. "Education, Epistemic Virtues, and the Power of Toleration." *Critical Review of International Social and*

Political Philosophy 24 (1): 108–31. https://doi.org/10.1080/13698230.2019.1616883.

DU Correspondent. 2018. "Ethnic Minorities Demand Constitutional Recognition." *New Age*, June 30, 2018. https://www.newagebd.net/article/44850/ethnic-minorities-demand-constitutional-recognition.

DW. 2020. "Man Denied German Citizenship for Refusing to Shake Woman's Hand." *DW*, October 17, 2020. https://www.dw.com/en/man-denied-german-citizenship-for-refusing-to-shake-womans-hand/a-55311947.

Dworkin, Ronald. 2006. "The Right to Ridicule." *New York Review of Books* 53 (5).

Eighmey, John. 2006. "Why Do Youth Enlist?' Identification of Underlying Themes." *Armed Forces and Society* 32 (2): 307–28.

Eisenberg, Avigail. 2007. "Identity, Multiculturalism and Religious Arbitration: The Debate over Shari'a Law in Canada." In *Sexual Justice / Cultural Justice*, edited by Barbara Arneil, Monique Deveaux, Rita Dhamoon, and Avigail Eisenberg, 211–30. London: Routledge.

Eisenberg, Avigail. 2009. *Reasons of Identity: A Normative Guide to the Political and Legal Assessment of Identity Claims*. Oxford: Oxford University Press.

Eisenberg, Avigail. 2013. "The Rights of National Majorities: Toxic Discourse or Democratic Catharsis?" In *Liberal Multiculturalism and the Fair Terms of Integration*, edited by Peter Balint and Sophie Guérard de Latour, 159–76. Basingstoke: Palgrave Macmillan.

Eisenberg, Avigail. 2020a. "The Rights of National Majorities: Toxic Discourse or Democratic Catharsis?" *Ethnicities* 20 (2): 312–30.

Eisenberg, Avigail. 2020b. "Consent, Resistance and the Duty to Consult." *International Journal on Minority and Group Rights* 27 (2): 270–90. https://doi.org/10.1163/15718115-02702012.

Eisenberg, Avigail, and Jeff Spinner-Halev, eds. 2005. *Minorities within Minorities: Equality, Rights and Diversity*. Cambridge: Cambridge University Press. https://www-cambridge-org.proxy.bib.uottawa.ca/core/books/minorities-within-minorities/25E59FB4077A794D5BA731A0EDBD31E3.

Embury-Dennis, Tom. 2020. "Man Denied German Citizenship for Refusing to Shake Woman's Hand at Naturalisation Ceremony." *The Independent*, October 19, 2020. https://www.independent.co.uk/news/world/europe/handshake-german-citizenship-doctor-court-baden-wurttemberg-b1152776.html.

Ercan, Selen A. 2015. "Creating and Sustaining Evidence for 'Failed Multiculturalism': The Case of 'Honour Killing' in Germany." *American Behavioral Scientist* 29 (6): 658–78.

Ercan, Selen A. 2017. "From Polarisation to Pluralisation: A Deliberative Democratic Approach to Illiberal Cultures." *International Political Science Review* 38 (1): 114–27.

Favell,Adrian.1998.*PhilosophiesofIntegration:Immigrationandthe Idea of Citizenship in France and Britain*. Basingstoke: Palgrave.

Ferretti, Maria Paola. 2009. "Exemptions for Whom? On the Relevant Focus of Egalitarian Concern." *Res Publica* 15 (3): 269. https://doi.org/10.1007/s11158-009-9095-1.

Ferretti, Maria Paola. 2018. *The Public Perspective: Public Justification and the Ethics of Belief*. London: Rowman & Littlefield.

Festenstein, Matthew. 2005. *Negotiating Diversity: Culture, Deliberation, Trust*. Cambridge: Polity Press.

Fitzsimmons, Scott. 2013. "When Few Stood against Many: Explaining Executive Outcomes' Victory in the Sierra Leonean Civil War." *Defence Studies* 13 (2): 245–69.

Fleras, Augie. 1985. "From Social Control towards Political Self-Determination? Maori Seats and the Politics of Separate Maori Representation in New Zealand." *Canadian Journal of Political Science / Revue Canadienne de Science Politique* 18 (3): 551–76.

Forbes, Hugh Donald. 2009. "Is Bridging Not Bonding? Social Capital and Ethnic Conflict." Paper presented to the European Research Centre on Migration and Ethnic Relations, Utrecht University.

Fraga, Bernard L., and Julie Lee Merseth. 2016. "Examining the Causal Impact of the Voting Rights Act Language Minority Provisions." *Journal of Race, Ethnicity, and Politics* 1 (1): 31–59.

Fraser, Nancy. 1995. "Recognition or Redistribution? A Critical Reading of Iris Young's Justice and the Politics of Difference." *Journal of Political Philosophy* 3 (2): 166–80.

Galandini, Silvia. 2013. "Residential Concentration, Ethnic Social Networks and Political Participation: A Mixed Methods Study of Black Africans in Britain." PhD Thesis. Manchester: University of Manchester. https://www.research.manchester.ac.uk/por tal/files/54549410/FULL_TEXT.PDF.

Galeotti, Anna Elisabetta. 1998. "Neutrality and Recognition." *Critical Review of International Social and Political Philosophy* 1 (3): 37–53.

Galeotti, Anna Elisabetta. 2015. "The Range of Toleration: From Toleration as Recognition Back to Disrespectful Tolerance." *Philosophy & Social Criticism* 41 (2): 93–110. https://doi.org/ 10.1177/0191453714559424.

Galston, William. 2002. *Liberal Pluralism: The Implications of Value Pluralism for Political Theory and Practice*. Cambridge: Cambridge University Press.

Gambetta, Diego, ed. 1988. *Trust: Making and Breaking Cooperative Relations*. Oxford: Blackwell.

Garsten, Bryan. 2009. "Representative Government and Popular Sovereignty." In *Political Representation*, edited by Ian Shapiro, Susan C. Stokes, Elisabeth Jean Wood, and Alexander S. Kirshner, 90–110. Cambridge: Cambridge University Press.

Geertz, Clifford. 1973. *The Interpretation of Cultures*. New York: Basic Books.

Gentile, Valentina. 2020. "The Scope of Religious Freedom in Europe: Tolerance, Democratic Equality and Political Autonomy." In *Spaces of Tolerance: Changing Geographies and Philosophies of Religion in Today's Europe*, edited by Luiza Bialasiewicz and Valentina Gentile, 23–42. New York: Routledge.

Gilchrist, Hugh. 1997. *Australians and Greeks*. 2 vols. Sydney: Halstead Press.

Glazer, Nathan. 1998. *We Are All Multiculturalists Now*. Cambridge, MA: Harvard University Press.

Golemboski, David. 2019. "Religious Sincerity and the Reasons for Religious Freedom." *Political Research Quarterly* 73 (4) (July): 866–77. https://doi.org/10.1177/1065912919861150.

Goodin, Robert E. 2006. "Liberal Multiculturalism: Protective and Polyglot." *Political Theory* 34 (3): 289–303. https://doi. org/10.1177/0090591705284131.

Goodman, Sara Wallace. 2010. "Integration Requirements for Integration's Sake? Identifying, Categorising and Comparing Civic Integration Policies." *Journal of Ethnic and Migration Studies* 36 (5): 753–72.

Googoo, Maureen. 2020. "Nova Scotia First Nation Launches Its Own Moderate Livelihood Fishery." *Ku'ku'kwes News,* September 18, 2020. http://kukukwes.com/2020/09/18/nova-scotia-first-nation-launches-its-own-moderate-livelihood-fishery/.

Gorman, Linda, and George Thomas. 1991. "Enlistment Motivations of Army Reservists: Money, Self-Improvement, or Patriotism?" *Armed Forces and Society* 17 (4): 589–99.

Greenhouse, Steven. 2003. "Foes of Idle Hands, Amish Contest a Child Labor Law." *New York Times,* October 18, 2003. https://www.nytimes.com/2003/10/18/us/foes-of-idle-hands-amish-seek-an-exemption-from-a-child-labor-law.html.

Griffith, James. 2008. "Institutional Motives for Serving in the U.S. Army National Guard." *Armed Forces and Society* 34 (2): 230–58.

Griffith, James, and Shelley Perry. 1993. "Wanting to Be a Soldier: Enlistment Motivations of Army Reserve Recruits before and after Operation Desert Storm." *Military Psychology* 5 (2): 127–39.

Grumet, Louis, and John Caher. 2016. *Curious Case of Kiryas Joel: The Rise of a Village Theocracy and the Battle to Defend the Separation of Church and State.* Chicago: Chicago Review Press.

Guérard de Latour, Sophie. 2013. "Is Multiculturalism Un-French? Towards a Neo-republican Model of Multiculturalism." In *Liberal Multiculturalism and the Fair Terms of Integration,* edited by Peter Balint and Sophie Guérard de Latour, 139–58. Basingstoke: Palgrave Macmillan.

Gustavsson, Gina. 2019. "Liberal National Identity: Thinner Than Conservative, Thicker Than Civic?" *Journal of Ethnic and Migration Studies* 19 (4): 693–711.

Gustavsson, Gina, and David Miller. 2020. *Liberal Nationalism and Its Critics: Normative and Empirical Questions.* Oxford: Oxford University Press.

Gutmann, Amy. 1987. *Democratic Education*. Princeton, NJ: Princeton University Press. https://www.amazon.ca/Dem ocratic-Education-Revised-Amy-Gutmann/dp/0691009163.

Hackett, Conrad. 2017. "5 Facts about the Muslim Population in Europe." *Pew Research Center* (blog), November 29, 2017. https://www.pewresearch.org/fact-tank/2017/11/29/5-facts-about-the-muslim-population-in-europe/.

Harris, Kathleen. 2019. "Canada's Military Issues New Policies to Welcome Transgender Troops as Trump Insists on Ban." *CBC News*, March 19, 2019. https://www.cbc.ca/news/polit ics/military-transgender-caf-policy-1.4978669.

Hassan, Adeel. 2019. "Hate-Crime Violence Hits 16-Year High, F.B.I. Reports." *New York Times*, November 12, 2019, sec. U.S. https://www.nytimes.com/2019/11/12/us/hate-crimes-fbi-report.html.

Hayward, Clarissa Rile. 2009. "Making Interest: On Representation and Democratic Legitimacy." In *Political Representation*, edited by Ian Shapiro, Susan C. Stokes, Elisabeth Jean Wood, and Alexander S. Kirshner, 111–35. Cambridge: Cambridge University Press.

Hayward, Clarissa Rile, and Ron Watson. 2010. "Identity and Political Theory." *Washington University Journal of Law and Policy* 33 (1): 9–40.

Heelsum, Anja van. 2005. "Political Participation and Civic Community of Ethnic Minorities in Four Cities in the Netherlands." *Politics* 25 (1): 19–30. https://doi.org/10.1111/j.1467-9256.2005.00225.x.

Hill, Lisa, and Sally Young. 2007. "Protest or Error? Informal Voting and Compulsory Voting." *Australian Journal of Political Science* 42 (3): 515–21.

Holzleithner, Elisabeth. 2012. "Interrogating Exit in Multiculturalist Theorizing: Conditions and Limitations." In *On Exit*, edited by Dagmar Borchers and Annamari Vitikainen, 13–33. Berlin: de Gruyter.

Home Office. 2001. "Community Cohesion: A Report of the Independent Review Team." London: Home Office.

Hooghe, Marc. 2007. "Social Capital and Diversity: Generalized Trust, Social Cohesion and Regimes of Diversity." *Canadian*

Journal of Political Science 40 (03): 709–32. https://doi.org/ 10.1017/S0008423907070722.

Hopkins, Daniel J. 2011. "Translating into Votes: The Electoral Impacts of Spanish-Language Ballots." *American Journal of Political Science* 55 (4): 814–30. https://doi.org/10.1111/ j.1540-5907.2011.00534.x.

Horton, John. 2011. "Why the Traditional Conception of Toleration Still Matters." *Critical Review of International Social and Political Philosophy* 14 (3): 289–305. https://doi.org/ 10.1080/13698230.2011.571874.

Hough, Leslie. 2007. "A Study of Peacekeeping, Peace-Enforcement and Private Military Companies in Sierra Leone." *African Security Review* 16 (4): 8–21.

Houston Police Department. 2020. "General Order 300-15. Subject: Appearance and Grooming Standards." Houston, TX: Houston Police Department.

Howells, Laura. 2020. "Third-Language Media Say They're Left behind by Government Relief Measures." *JSource* (blog), May 27, 2020. https://j-source.ca/article/third-language-media-say-theyre-left-behind-by-government-relief-measures/.

Inglehart, Ronald. 1999. "Trust, Well-Being and Democracy." In *Democracy and Trust*, edited by Mark Warren, 88–120. Cambridge: Cambridge University Press.

Ivison, Duncan. 2008. "Indigenous Rights." In *International Encyclopedia of the Social Sciences*, edited by William A. Darity, 2nd ed., 3:614–17. Farmington Hills, MI: Macmillan Reference USA.

Ivison, Duncan. 2015. "Multiculturalism and Indigenous Peoples." In *Oxford Handbook of Indigenous People's Politics*, edited by José Antonio Lucero, Dale Turner, and Donna Lee Vancott, 1–13. Oxford: Oxford University Press.

Ivison, Duncan, Paul Patton, and Will Saunders, eds. 2000. *Political Theory and the Rights of Indigenous Peoples.* Cambridge: Cambridge University Press.

James, Carl, Philip Howard, Julie Samaroo, Rob Brown, and Gillian Parekh. 2014. "Africentric Alterative School Research Project: Year 3 (2013–2014) Report." York's Centre for Education and Community and TDSB Research &

Information Services. https://www.yumpu.com/en/docum ent/read/54690686/africentric-alternative-school-research-project.

Jones, Peter. 1994. "Bearing the Consequences of Belief." *Journal of Political Philosophy* 2 (1): 24–43.

Joppke, Christian. 2009. *The Veil: Mirror of Identity*. Cambridge: Polity Press.

Joppke, Christian. 2017. *Is Multiculturalism Dead? Crisis and Persistence in the Constitutional State*. Cambridge: Polity Press.

Joppke, Christian, and John Torpey. 2013. *Legal Integration of Islam: A Transatlantic Comparison*. Cambridge, MA: Harvard University Press.

Joseph, Bob. 2018. *21 Things You May Not Know about the Indian Act*. Port Coquitlam, BC: Indigenous Relations Press.

Kaplan, Benjamin J. 2007. *Divided by Faith: Religious Conflict and the Practice of Toleration in Early Modern Europe*. Cambridge, MA: Harvard University Press.

Killmister, Suzy. 2014. "Resolving the Dilemma of Group Membership." In *How Groups Matter: Challenges of Toleration in Pluralistic Societies*, edited by Gideon Calder, Magali Bessone, and Federico Zuolo, 89–108. New York: Routledge.

Klausen, Jytte. 2005. *The Islamic Challenge: Politics and Religion in Western Europe*. Oxford: Oxford University Press.

Koopmans, Ruud. 2018. "Cultural Rights of Native Majorities between Universalism and Minority Rights." Discussion Paper SP VI 2018-106. Berlin: WZB Berlin Social Science Center. https://bibliothek.wzb.eu/pdf/2018/vi18-106.pdf.

Korteweg, Anna C. 2008. "The Sharia Debate in Ontario: Gender, Islam, and Representations of Muslim Women's Agency." *Gender & Society* 22 (4): 434–54. https://doi.org/10.1177/0891243208319768.

KPC News. 2013. "Teen's Arm Cut Off in Saw Accident." *KPCNews*, May 21, 2013. https://www.kpcnews.com/news/latest/eveningstar/article_cd6f381f-a234-5db4-8769-ac221 b4aa1fe.html.

Krishnamurthy, Meena. 2015. "(White) Tyranny and the Democratic Value of Distrust." *The Monist* 98 (4): 391–406.

Kukathas, Chandran. 1992. "Are There Any Cultural Rights?" *Political Theory* 20 (1): 105–39. https://doi.org/10.1177/0090 591792020001006.

Kukathas, Chandran. 2012. "Exit, Freedom, and Gender." In *On Exit*, edited by Dagmar Borchers and Annamari Vitikainen, 34–56. Berlin: de Gruyter.

Kumlin, Staffan, and Bo Rothstein. 2005. "Making and Breaking Social Capital: The Impact of Welfare-State Institutions." *Comparative Political Studies* 38 (4): 339–65.

Kundnani, Arun. 2002. "The Death of Multiculturalism." *Race and Class* 43 (4): 67–72. https://doi.org/10.1177%2F0306396 80204300406.

Kymlicka, Will. 1989a. "Liberal Individualism and Liberal Neutrality." *Ethics* 99 (4): 883–905.

Kymlicka, Will. 1989b. *Liberalism, Community and Culture*. Oxford: Oxford University Press. https://www.amazon.ca/Liberalism-Community-Culture-Will-Kymlicka/dp/0198278713.

Kymlicka, Will. 1995. *Multicultural Citizenship: A Liberal Theory of Minority Rights*. Oxford: Oxford University Press.

Kymlicka, Will. 1998. *Finding Our Way: Rethinking Ethnocultural Relations in Canada*. Oxford: Oxford University Press.

Kymlicka, Will. 2000. "Political Theory and the Rights of Indigenous Peoples." In *Political Theory and the Rights of Indigenous Peoples*, edited by Duncan Ivison, Paul Patton, and Will Sanders, 216–36. Cambridge: Cambridge University Press.

Kymlicka, Will. 2001. *Politics in the Vernacular: Nationalism, Multiculturalism, and Citizenship*. Oxford: Oxford University Press.

Laborde, Cécile. 2003. "Toleration and Laïcité." In *The Culture of Toleration in Diverse Societies: Reasonable Tolerance*, edited by Catriona MacKinnon and Dario Castiglione, 161–78. Manchester: Manchester University Press.

Laborde, Cécile. 2008. *Critical Republicanism: The Hijab Controversy and Political Philosophy*. Oxford: Oxford University Press.

Laborde, Cécile. 2017. *Liberalism's Religion*. Cambridge, MA: Harvard University Press.

Laegaard, Sune. 2010. "Grand-Mosque' Projects in Copenhagen: Intersections of Respect, Tolerance and Intolerance in the Distribution of Public Space." *Politics in Central Europe* 6 (3): 60–80.

Laegaard, Sune. 2020. "Accommodating Toleration: On Balint's Classical Liberal Response to the Multiculturalism Challenge." *Critical Review of International Social and Political Philosophy* 23 (2): 211–17.

Lakhani, Hyder, and Stephen S. Fugita. 1993. "Reserve/Guard Retention: Moonlighting or Patriotism?" *Military Psychology* 5 (2): 113–25.

Larmore, Charles. 1987. *Patterns of Moral Complexity*. Cambridge: Cambridge University Press.

Lenard, Patti Tamara. 2008. "Trust Your Compatriots but Count Your Change: The Roles of Trust, Mistrust and Distrust in Democracy." *Political Studies* 56 (2): 312–32.

Lenard, Patti Tamara. 2012. *Trust, Democracy and Multicultural Challenges*. University Park: Pennsylvania State University Press.

Lenard, Patti Tamara. 2020. "Inclusive Identities: The Foundation of Trust in Multicultural Communities." In *Liberal Nationalism and Its Critics*, edited by Gina Gustavsson and David Miller, 155–71. Oxford: Oxford University Press.

Lenard, Patti Tamara, and Peter Balint. 2020. "What Is (the Wrong of) Cultural Appropriation?" *Ethnicities* 20 (2): 331–52.

Lenard, Patti Tamara, and David Miller. 2018. "Trust and National Identity." In *Oxford Handbook of Social and Political Trust*, edited by Eric Uslaner, 57–74. Oxford: Oxford University Press.

Levey, Geoffrey Brahm. 2001. "The Political Theories of Australian Multiculturalism." *University of New South Wales Law Journal* 24 (3): 869–81.

Levey, Geoffrey Brahm. 2019. "The Bristol School of Multiculturalism." *Ethnicities* 19 (1): 200–226. https://doi.org/10.1177/1468796818787413.

Levine-Rasky, Cynthia. 2014. "White Fear: Analyzing Public Objection to Toronto's Africentric School." *Race, Ethnicity and Education* 17 (2): 202–18. https://doi.org/10.1080/13613324.2012.725043.

Levy, Jacob. 1997. "Classifying Cultural Rights." In *Ethnicity and Group Rights*, edited by Will Kymlicka and Ian Shapiro, 22–68. New York: New York University Press.

Locke, John. 1689/1983. *A Letter Concerning Toleration*. Edited by James Tully. Indianapolis, IN: Hackett.

Maclure, Jocelyn. 2020. "The Merits and Limits of Conscience-Based Legal Exemptions." *Criminal Law and Philosophy*. https://doi.org/10.1007/s11572-020-09553-6.

Mahoney, Rhona. 1995. *Kidding Ourselves: Breadwinning, Babies, and Bargaining Power*. New York: Basic Books.

Mansbridge, Jane. 2003. "Rethinking Representation." *American Political Science Review* 97 (4): 515–28.

Margalit, Avishai, and Joseph Raz. 1990. "National Self-Determination." *Journal of Philosophy* 87 (9): 439–61.

Martin, Nick. 2011. "Muslim Families in Winnipeg Want Children Excused from Certain Classes." *National Post*, February 5, 2011. http://life.nationalpost.com/2011/02/05/muslim-families-in-winnipeg-want-children-excused-from-certain-classes/.

Martin, Nick. 2020. "Exemptions, Sincerity and Pastafarianism." *Journal of Applied Philosophy* 37 (2): 258–72. https://doi.org/10.1111/japp.12386.

Melton, Ada Pecos. 1995. "Indigenous Justice Systems and Tribal Society Indian Tribal Courts and Justice: A Symposium." *Judicature* 79 (3): 126–33.

Michalowski, Ines. 2011. "Required to Assimilate? The Content of Citizenship Tests in Five Countries." *Citizenship Studies* 15 (6–7): 749–68. https://doi.org/10.1080/13621025.2011.600116.

Miller, David. 1995. *On Nationality*. Oxford: Oxford University Press.

Miller, David. 2016. "Majorities and Minarets: Religious Freedom and Public Space." *British Journal of Political Science* 46 (2): 437–56. https://doi.org/10.1017/S000712341 4000131.

Minow, Martha. 1991. "Identities." *Yale Journal of Law and the Humanities* 3 (1): 97–130.

Modood, Tariq. 1998. "Anti-ssentialism, Multiculturalism and the 'Recognition' of Religious Groups." *Journal of Political Philosophy* 6 (4): 378–99.

Modood, Tariq. 2006. "The Liberal Dilemma: Integration or Vilification?" *International Migration* 44 (5): 4–7.

Modood, Tariq. 2007. *Multiculturalism: A Civic Idea*. Cambridge: Polity Press.

Moore, Margaret. 2006. "Identity Claims and Identity Politics: A Limited Defence." In *Identity, Self-Determination, and Secession*, edited by Ignor Primoratz and Aleksandor Pavković, 27–44. London: Ashgate.

Moore, Margaret. 2015. *A Political Theory of Territory*. New York: Oxford University Press.

Moran, Matthew. 2017. "Terrorism and the Banlieues: The Charlie Hebdo Attacks in Context." *Modern & Contemporary France* 25 (3): 315–32. https://doi.org/10.1080/09639 489.2017.1323199.

Moreau, Greg. 2020. "Police-Reported Hate Crime in Canada, 2018." Statistics Canada. https://www150.statcan.gc.ca/n1/ pub/85-002-x/2020001/article/00003-eng.htm.

Myers, David G. 2014. "Behaviours and Attitudes." In *Social Psychology*, edited by David G. Myers, 120–51. Sydney: McGraw Hill.

Myrberg, Gunnar. 2011. "Political Integration through Associational Affiliation? Immigrants and Native Swedes in Greater Stockholm." *Journal of Ethnic and Migration Studies* 37 (1): 99–115. https://doi.org/10.1080/13691 83X.2011.521366.

National Ethnic Press and Media Council of Canada. 2012. "About Us." *National Ethnic Press and Media Council of Canada* (blog), January 18, 2012. http://nationalethnicpress.com/ aboutus/.

New South Wales Parliament. 2000. *Community Relations Commission and Principles of Multiculturalism Act 2000*. Sydney: New South Wales Parliament.

New York Police Department. 2020. "Patrol Guide: Performance on Duty-Personal Appearance, Procedure No: 203-07." New York Police Department.

New Zealand Parliament. 2009. "Origins of the Maori Seats— New Zealand Parliament." May 2009. https://www.parliam ent.nz/en/pb/research-papers/document/00PLLawRP03 141/origins-of-the-m%C4%81ori-seats.

Nieguth, Tim. 1999. "Privilege or Recognition? The Myth of State Neutrality." *Critical Review of International Social and Political Philosophy* 2 (2): 112–31.

Nielsen, K. 1996. "Cultural Nationalism, Neither Ethnic nor Civic." *Philosophical Forum* 28 (1–2): 42–52.

Nimni, Ephraim. 2007. "National-Cultural Autonomy as an Alternative to Minority Territorial Nationalism." *Ethnopolitics* 6 (3): 345–64. https://doi.org/10.1080/174490 50701487363.

Norman, Wayne. 2006. *Negotiating Nationalism: Nation-Building, Federalism, and Secession in the Multinational State.* Oxford: Oxford University Press.

Norval, Aletta. 2009. "Democracy, Pluralization, and Voice." *Ethics & Global Politics* 2 (4): 297–320.

OECD. n.d. "Social Expenditure—Aggregated Data." Organisation for Economic Co-Operation and Development. https://stats. oecd.org/Index.aspx?DataSetCode=SOCX_AGG.

Oh, Inae. 2015. "Watch the First Black Woman Who Served in the US Senate Go Off on the Confederate Flag." *Mother Jones* (blog), June 23, 2015. https://www.motherjones.com/polit ics/2015/06/carol-moseley-braun-confederate-flag-video/.

Okin, Susan Moller. 1999. *Is Multiculturalism Bad for Women?* Princeton, NJ: Princeton University Press.

Ontario Ministry of Education. 2020. "Elementary School Profile: Africentric Alternative School." 2020. https://www. app.edu.gov.on.ca/eng/sift/schoolProfile.asp?SCH_NUM BER=344930&x=12&y=17.

ORA. 2020. "ORA—Organization for the Resolution of Agunot." ORA—Organization for the Resolution of Agunot. 2020. https://www.getora.org.

O'Sullivan, Dominic. 2006. "Needs, Rights, Nationhood, and the Politics of Indigeneity." *MAI Review* 1: 1–12.

Pande, Rohini. 2003. "Can Mandated Political Representation Increase Policy Influence for Disadvantaged Minorities? Theory and Evidence from India." *American Economic Review* 93 (4): 1132–51. https://doi.org/10.1257/00028280376 9206232.

Parekh, Bhikhu. 2002. *Rethinking Multiculturalism: Cultural Diversity and Political Theory*. Cambridge, MA: Cambridge University Press.

Parvin, Phil. 2020. "Diversity in an Anti-Immigration Era: Theories, Controversies, Principles." *Ethnicities* 20 (2): 251–64.

Patten, Alan. 2014. *Equal Recognition: The Moral Foundations of Minority Rights*. Princeton, NJ: Princeton University Press.

Patterson, Orlando. 1999. "Liberty against the Democratic State: On the Historical and Contemporary Sources of American Distrust." In *Democracy and Trust*, edited by Mark Warren, 151–207. Cambridge: Cambridge University Press.

Patton, Paul. 2016. "Philosophical Justifications for Indigenous Rights." In *Handbook of Indigenous Peoples' Rights*, edited by Corinne Lennox and Damien Short, 13–22. Oxford: Routledge.

Pederson, Anne, Iain Walker, and Mike Wise. 2005. "'Talk Does Not Cook Rice': Beyond Anti-Racism Rhetoric to Strategies for Social Action." *Australian Psychologist* 40 (1): 20–31.

Phillips, Anne. 1995. *The Politics of Presence*. Oxford: Oxford University Press.

Phillips, Anne. 1998. "Democracy and Representation: Or, Why Should It Matter Who Our Representatives Are?" In *Feminism and Politics*, edited by Anne Phillips, 224–40. Oxford: Oxford University Press.

Phillips, Anne. 2007. *Multiculturalism without Culture*. Princeton, NJ: Princeton University Press.

Pierik, Roland. 2012. "State Neutrality and the Limits of Religious Symbolism." In *The Lautsi Papers: Multidisciplinary Reflections on Religious Symbols in the Public Classroom*, edited by Joreon Temperman, 201–18. Leiden: Nijhoff.

Putnam, Robert D. 2007. "E Pluribus Unum: Diversity and Community in the Twenty-First Century: The 2006 Johan Skytte Prize Lecture." *Scandinavian Political Studies* 30 (2): 137–74.

Queen's University. 2020. "Home | Multiculturalism Policies in Contemporary Democracies." Accessed September 5, 2021. https://www.queensu.ca/mcp/.

Quillian, Lincoln, Anthony Heath, Devah Pager, Arnfinn H. Midtbøen, Fenella Fleischmann, and Ole Hexel. 2019. "Do Some Countries Discriminate More Than Others? Evidence from 97 Field Experiments of Racial Discrimination in Hiring." *Sociological Science* 6 (June): 467–96. https://doi.org/10.15195/v6.a18.

Quong, Jonathan. 2006. "Cultural Exemptions, Expensive Tastes, and Equal Opportunities." *Journal of Applied Philosophy* 23 (1): 53–71.

Ramadan, Tariq. 2010. *The Quest for Meaning: Developing a Philosophy of Pluralism.* London: Penguin Books.

Rawls, John. 1999. *A Theory of Justice.* Rev. ed. Cambridge, MA: Belknap Press.

Rawls, John. 2001. *Justice as Fairness: A Restatement.* Cambridge, MA: Belknap Press.

Rawls, John. 2005. *Political Liberalism.* Expanded ed. New York: Columbia University Press.

Raz, Joseph. 1994. "Multiculturalism: A Liberal Perspective." *Dissent* (Winter): 67–79.

Reeskens, Tim, and Marc Hooghe. 2010. "Beyond the Civic-Ethnic Dichotomy: Investigating the Structure of Citizenship Concepts across Thirty-Three Countries." *Nations and Nationalism* 16 (4): 579–97. https://doi.org/10.1111/j.1469-8129.2010.00446.x.

Richardson, Hannah. 2014. "'Radicalisation Risk' at Six Muslim Private Schools, Says Ofsted." *BBC News*, November 21, 2014. https://www.bbc.com/news/education-30129645.

Roscigno, Vincent J., Diana L. Karafin, and Griff Tester. 2009. "The Complexities and Processes of Racial Housing Discrimination." *Social Problems* 56 (1): 49–69.

Rothstein, Bo. 1998. *Just Institutions Matter: The Moral and Political Logic of the Universal Welfare State.* Cambridge: Cambridge University Press.

Rothstein, Bo, Marcus Samanni, and Jan Teorell. 2012. "Explaining the Welfare State: Power Resources vs. the Quality of Government." *European Political Science Review* 4 (1): 1–28.

Rothstein, Bo, and Eric M. Uslaner. 2005. "All for All: Equality, Corruption, and Social Trust." *World Politics* 58 (1): 41–72.

Rousseau, Jean-Jacques. 1762/1998. *The Social Contract.* London: Penguin Books.

Sabbagh, Daniel. 2014. "Groups and Affirmative Action." In *How Groups Matter: Challenges of Toleration in Pluralistic Societies*, edited by Gideon Calder, Magali Bessone, and Federico Zuolo, 109–22. New York: Routledge.

Sanders, Lynn. 1997. "Against Deliberation." *Political Theory* 25 (3): 347–76.

Scottish Government. 2019. "Scotland's Right to Choose: Putting Scotland's Future in Scotland's Hands." December 19, 2019. https://www.gov.scot/publications/scotlands-right-choose-putting-scotlands-future-scotlands-hands/pages/7/.

Seglow, Jonathan. 2020. "Respecting Multiculturalism? Respecting Religion?" *Critical Review of International Social and Political Philosophy* 23 (2): 218–23.

Shachar, Ayelet. 1998. "Group Identity and Women's Rights in Family Law: The Perils of Multicultural Accommodation." *Journal of Political Philosophy* 6 (3): 285–305.

Shachar, Ayelet. 1999. "The Paradox of Multicultural Vulnerability: Individual Rights, Identity Groups, and the State." In *Multicultural Questions*, edited by Christian Joppke and Steven Lukes, 87–111. Oxford: Oxford University Press.

Shachar, Ayelet. 2001. *Multicultural Jurisdictions: Cultural Differences and Women's Rights*. Cambridge: Cambridge University Press.

Shachar, Ayelet. 2008. "Privatizing Diversity: A Cautionary Tale from Religious Arbitration in Family Law." *Theoretical Inquiries in Law* 9 (2): 573–607. https://doi.org/10.2202/1565-3404.1198.

Shachar, Ayelet. 2009. *Multicultural Jurisdictions: Cultural Differences and Women's Rights*. Cambridge: Cambridge University Press.

Shah, Saeeda. 2012. "Muslim Schools in Secular Societies: Persistence or Resistance!" *British Journal of Religious Education* 34 (1): 51–65. https://doi.org/10.1080/01416200.2011.601897.

Shalit, Avner de-. 2018. *Cities and Immigration: Political and Moral Dilemmas in the New Era of Migration*. Oxford: Oxford University Press.

Shulman, Stephen. 2002. "Challenging the Civic/Ethnic and West/East Dichotomies in the Study of Nationalism." *Comparative Political Studies* 35 (5): 554–85. https://doi.org/10.1177/0010414002035005003.

Simmons, A. John. 2016. *Boundaries of Authority.* Oxford: Oxford University Press.

Sinno, Abdulkader H., and Eren Tatari. 2009. "Muslims in UK Institutions: Effective Representation or Tokenism?" In *Muslims in Western Politics*, edited by Abdulkader H. Sinno, 113–34. Bloomington: Indiana University Press.

Sniderman, Paul M., and Louk Hagendoorn. 2007. *When Ways of Life Collide.* Princeton, NJ: Princeton University Press.

Song, Sarah. 2005. "Majority Norms, Multiculturalism, and Gender Equality." *American Political Science Review* 99 (4): 473–89. https://doi.org/10.1017/S0003055405051828.

Song, Sarah. 2007. *Justice, Gender and the Politics of Multiculturalism.* Cambridge: Cambridge University Press.

Song, Sarah. 2009. "The Subject of Multiculturalism: Culture, Religion, Language, Ethnicity, Nationality, and Race?" In *New Waves in Political Philosophy*, edited by Boudewijn de Bruin and Christopher F. Zurn, 177–97. London: Palgrave Macmillan. https://doi.org/10.1057/9780230234994_10.

Soutphommasane, Tim. 2012. *The Virtuous Citizen: Patriotism in a Multicultural Society.* Cambridge: Cambridge University Press.

Spinner-Halev, Jeff. 1999. "Cultural Pluralism and Partial Citizenship." In *Multicultural Questions*, edited by Christian Joppke and Steven Lukes, 65–84. Oxford: Oxford University Press.

Stack, Liam. 2020. "Hasidic Funeral in Brooklyn Draws 2,500, Creating Crisis for Mayor de Blasio." *New York Times*, April 29, 2020. https://www.nytimes.com/2020/04/29/nyregion/coronavirus-jews-hasidic-de-blasio.html.

Steptoe, Andrew, Jane Wardle, Ray Fuller, Sigurlina Davidsdottir, Bettina Davou, and Joao Justo. 2002. "Seatbelt Use, Attitudes, and Changes in Legislation: An International Study." *American Journal of Preventive Medicine* 23 (4): 254–59.

Taylor, Charles. 1994. "The Politics of Recognition." In *Multiculturalism: Examining the Politics of Recognition*, edited by Amy Gutmann, 25–74. Princeton, NJ: Princeton University Press.

Thalia, Anthony, and Will Crawford. 2013. "Northern Territory Indigenous Community Sentencing Mechanisms: An Order for Substantive Equality." *Australian Indigenous Law Review* 17 (2): 79–99.

Thomas, Paul. 2007. "Moving on from 'Anti-Racism'? Understandings of 'Community Cohesion' Held by Youth Workers." *Journal of Social Policy* 36 (3): 435–55.

Tillie, Jean. 2004. "Social Capital of Organisations and Their Members: Explaining the Political Integration of Immigrants in Amsterdam." *Journal of Ethnic and Migration Studies* 30 (3): 529–41.

Tucker, James Thomas, and Rodolfo Espino. 2006. "Governmental Effectiveness and Efficiency: The Minority Language Assistance Provisions of the VRA." *Texas Journal on Civil Liberties & Civil Rights* 12 (2): 163–232.

Tully, James. 1995. *Strange Multiplicity: Constitutionalism in the Age of Diversity*. Cambridge: Cambridge University Press.

Uberoi, Varun, and Tariq Modood, eds. 2015. *Multiculturalism Rethought: Interpretations, Dilemmas and New Directions*. Edinburgh: Edinburgh University Press. https://edinb urghuniversitypress.com/book-multiculturalism-rethou ght.html.

Uslaner, Eric M. 2002. *The Moral Foundations of Trust*. Cambridge: Cambridge University Press.

Verba, Sidney, Kay Lehman Schlozman, and Henry E. Brady. 1995. *Voice and Equality: Civic Volunteerism in American Politics*. Cambridge, MA: Harvard University Press.

Vertovec, Steven, and Susanne Wessendorf, eds. 2010. *The Multicultural Backlash: European Discourses, Policies, Practices*. London: Routledge.

Vitikainen, Annamari. 2015. *The Limits of Liberal Multiculturalism: Towards an Individuated Approach to Cultural Diversity*. Springer.

Vitikainen, Annamari. 2020. "Indigenous Citizenship, Shared Fate, and Non-Ideal Circumstances." *Citizenship Studies* 25 (1): 1–19. https://doi.org/10.1080/13621 025.2020.1837738.

Waldron, Jeremy. 1992. "Minority Cultures and the Cosmopolitan Alternative." *University of Michigan Journal of Law Reform* 25: 751–93.

Wall, Steven. 2010. "Neutralism for Perfectionists: The Case of Restricted State Neutrality." *Ethics* 120 (2): 232–56.

Walzer, Michael. 1997. *On Toleration.* New Haven: Yale University Press.

Weber, Eugen. 1977. *Peasants into Frenchmen.* London: Chatto & Windus.

Weinberg, Leonard, and Eliot Assoudeh. 2018. "Political Violence and the Radical Right." In *The Oxford Handbook of the Radical Right*, edited by Jens Rydgren, 412–32. Oxford: Oxford University Press. https://doi.org/10.1093/oxfordhb/978019 0274559.013.21.

Weinstock, Daniel. 1999. "Building Trust in Divided Societies." *Journal of Political Philosophy* 7 (3): 287–307.

Wells, David. 2019. "What Military Regulations Say about Beards and Facial Hair." *Forbes Net*, November 10, 2019. https://www.forces.net/uniform/what-military-regulations-say-about-beards-and-facial-hair.

White, Stephen, Neil Nevitte, André Blais, Elisabeth Gidengil, and Patrick Fournier. 2008. "The Political Resocialization of Immigrants: Resistance or Lifelong Learning?" *Political Research Quarterly* 61 (2): 268–81. https://doi.org/10.1177/ 1065912908314713.

Williams, Melissa. 1998. *Voice, Trust and Memory: Marginalized Groups and the Failings of Liberal Representation.* Princeton, NJ: Princeton University Press.

Wolf, Patrick J., Stephen Macedo, David J. Ferrero, and Charles Venegoni. 2004. *Educating Citizens: International Perspectives on Civic Values and School Choice.* Washington, DC: Brooking Institution Press.

Woodruff, Todd, Ryan Kelty, and David R. Segal. 2006. "Propensity to Serve and Motivation among American Combat Soldiers." *Armed Forces and Society* 32 (3): 353–66.

Woods, Kerri. 2014. *Human Rights: Issues in Political Theory.* Basingstoke: Palgrave Macmillan.

Yack, Bernard. 1996. "The Myth of the Civic Nation." *Critical Review* 10 (2): 193–211.

Young, Iris Marion. 1989. *Justice and the Politics of Difference.* Princeton, NJ: Princeton University Press.

Young, Iris Marion. 2004. "Two Concepts of Self-Determination." In *Ethnicity, Nationalism and Minority Rights*, edited by Stephen May, Tariq Modood, and Judith Squires, 176–95. Cambridge: Cambridge University Press.

Zellentin, Alexa. 2012. *Liberal Neutrality: Treating Citizens as Free and Equal.* Berlin: De Gruyter.

Zuolo, Federico. 2014. "Beyond Groups? Types of Sharing and Normative Treatment." In *How Groups Matter: Challenges of Toleration in Pluralistic Societies*, edited by Gideon Calder, Magali Bessone, and Federico Zuolo, 199–218. New York: Routledge.

INDEX

For the benefit of digital users, indexed terms that span two pages (e.g., 52–53) may, on occasion, appear on only one of those pages.